RUNNING WITH THE
FIRM

To Angie ... Love from your boys

RUNNING WITH THE FIRM

My Double Life as an Undercover Hooligan

JAMES BANNON

EBURY
PRESS

5 7 9 10 8 6

This edition published 2014
First published in 2013 by Ebury Press, an imprint of Ebury Publishing
A Random House Group company

The Random House Group Limited Reg. No. 954009

Addresses for companies within the Random House Group can be found at
www.randomhouse.co.uk

A CIP catalogue record for this book is available from the British Library

The Random House Group Limited supports the Forest Stewardship Council® (FSC®),
the leading international forest-certification organisation. Our books carrying the
FSC label are printed on FSC®-certified paper. FSC is the only forest-certification
scheme supported by the leading environmental organisations, including Greenpeace. Our
paper procurement policy can be found at www.randomhouse.co.uk/environment

Designed and set by seagulls.net

Printed and bound by CPI Group (UK) Ltd, Croydon, CR0 4YY

ISBN 9780091951528

To buy books by your favourite authors and register for offers visit
www.randomhouse.co.uk

AUTHOR'S NOTE

In 1994 I wrote the original story to the feature film *I.D.* The film was about my experiences while working as an undercover police officer infiltrating Millwall football hooligans. Over time the film has gained a cult status and was subsequently digitally remastered and rereleased in May 2012. Up till then I had no desire to revisit that chapter of my life, but its rerelease reignited the long-standing debate, as to whether the film was based on a true story. Given that the operation was now twenty-five years old it seemed as good a time as any to tell it how it really was.

For those of you who know *I.D.* you will recognise some parts of this book from the film but a large element of the operation remains untold, until now. This book is a true account of what happened over the two years of the operation. The highs and lows, the moments of violence, sadness and humour are all exactly as they happened.

CONTENTS

PROLOGUE

For two years of my life, I was known as Jim, Jim from Wandsworth. Me and my mate Chris were painters and decorators. We supported Millwall. We fought with Millwall. We ran with the firm. But we had a secret, one that if exposed would be life-threatening...

We were also undercover coppers.

England was notorious for its football hooligans during the 1980s and Millwall's firm was the most notorious. Officers like me and Chris were brought in to infiltrate these gangs; to befriend them; to gain their trust and to obtain evidence against them to get them arrested and sent away.

It was true that sometimes I found it difficult to look into the mirror. These guys had become mates, we had talked and laughed and shared the ups and downs that go with being a football supporter. And we had fought together, against other gangs and police alike. But then I'd remember the senseless, mindless violence – like the time I witnessed a Millwall fan stamp on an innocent bystander's head while his wife and daughters looked on, all because he was wearing a Crystal Palace pin. And then I'd remember why I was doing this.

Because the truth was, sometimes I forgot. Yes, there were many times when I was scared shitless, but the adrenalin and the buzz were amazing. Being an undercover policeman is a rush, and that rush can be addictive. But also being a Millwall fan was fun. There was camaraderie there, a sense of belonging that I hadn't found anywhere else. Yes, I was doing this for the good of the community, but I cannot put my hand on my heart and say that I didn't have a bloody good time doing it.

Part of being an undercover cop is knowing that you could be exposed at any time. Any slip-up, and they've got you. And we got close to being found out…

A few months into our operation, Chris receives a message from Dave, one of the Millwall supporters that we had befriended. Dave is a great guy, intelligent, knowledgeable about the game and always up for a laugh. Dave wants to meet up with us in Catford with his mates Stu and Mark. It's slightly unusual, but not worryingly so. We leave a message saying that we will meet him in the pub at midday.

When we get into the pub, the atmosphere hits us first. It's not like the Old Castle or The Puffin, which have become our locals and where we've been accepted as one of their own. There's definitely an unfriendly vibe to it. It's busy but I don't recognise anyone. We go to the bar and Chris gets the drinks in.

Then Dave, Stu and Mark and some guys that we have never met come out of the adjacent bar. I know instantly that something's up by the look on their faces. Dave is carrying a pool cue and Stu a bottle. I look straight at Dave. 'All right, mate?'

Dave stares at me long and hard. 'No. I fucking ain't.'

Fuck. I sense that we're in big trouble.

Chris comes over with the drinks. 'All right, Dave?' he asks.

Dave steps forward and shouts, 'No, I fucking ain't all right. Who the fuck are you two? Cos we're all struggling to work it out.'

I glance at Chris and see the blood drain out of his face.

I shake my head. 'What you going on about? You know who we are.'

Dave taps the pool cue down on the ground. 'Well, that's just it, Jim, if that is your fucking name, we don't know who you are. You turn up out of the fucking blue, wanna be our best mates.'

Chris is scared and I'm trying not to shit myself. We're now totally surrounded by Millwall hard men. Ten against two; it's not good odds. Fuck.

I try to act bewildered. 'Dave, what's your fucking problem?'

He raises the pool cue and points it first at me and then at Chris. 'You and him. That's the problem.'

This is not going well. What do we do? Do we turn and make a run for it? Admit who we are and hope that we can get out in one piece? Or should we front it out and take our chances?

Fronting it out seems to be the best option. I square up to Dave. 'All right, so what the fuck are you saying?'

This time Dave pokes me and then Chris with the pool cue. 'What I am saying, you cunt, is that *you* and *you*, are fucking *Old Bill*.'

I stand there, staring at them all, and then burst out laughing. 'Are you having a fucking laugh? Me, Old Bill? Are you fucking serious?'

If Dave has any doubts he may have got it wrong he doesn't show it. 'You don't see any of us laughing…That's exactly what I am saying: you and him are fucking Old Bill.'

I turn and look at Chris. How the fuck are we going to get out of this?

ONE
BEGINNINGS

I was born on a sweltering summer's day in August 1965 at Lambeth Hospital, south London. Mum was a housewife while Dad was a serving police officer with the Metropolitan Police Force in London. We moved a couple of times in my early years before settling in Belvedere, a small village on the outskirts of south London. We lived on a small estate with privately owned and housing association tenants and I spent my formative years there growing up.

It was a close-knit community and everyone looked out for each other. I had a ball growing up there but with a dad as a serving police officer it did not come without its issues. Initially I had to prove to the kids on the estate that it was my dad who was the policeman and not me. 'You going to go back and tell your old man what we've been up to?' they'd ask, after we'd been up to no good. At the age of eight I proved I could be trusted when we broke into the local Co-op and stole a box of Texans and five pounds in two-pence coins. Someone had seen us depart the scene and called the police, who came calling. We were all interviewed and no one caved in. From that day on my loyalty was never questioned again.

By the time I'd got myself into grammar school, my dad's job had become something of a secret. Even without the kids knowing what my dad did for a living, I was the odd one out. My classmates had all been privately educated and were way ahead of me academically. All of my mates from the estate who knew and trusted me had gone off to the local comprehensive, so keeping my old man's job quiet seemed the easiest thing to do. When other kids asked I used to avoid answering or just say that he worked in local government. I was pretty good at keeping secrets it seemed.

Halfway through my second term, however, my secret came out. I had been picked to play for the school rugby team. We were playing at home and my dad was working so he couldn't come and watch, or so I thought. We were ten minutes into the game when the referee awarded our side a scrum. As I crouched down to feed the ball into the forwards I heard the crackle of a radio in the distance. I stood there frozen to the spot hoping that the noise I could hear getting louder and louder was not what I thought it was. I turned around and instantly I saw what I was dreading. Coming across the school playing fields was my dad on a police motorbike. He rode the bike to the touchline with the police radio blaring out and then removed his helmet and stared at me. 'All right, son?'

Looking back on it now it was really nice of him to make the effort to come and watch me play but at eleven years of age and at a new school I could really have done without it. I was the talk of the school on the Monday and by the end of the school day my secret was out. I hated it there and I did everything I could to avoid going. Eventually the school lost patience with me and by the start of my second year I was expelled and looking for a new school. Thanks to the intervention of the family priest I was accepted into the local Catholic comprehensive.

I hated it with a passion and then spent the rest of my schooling years coming up with every excuse possible not to go. I remember once feigning a broken arm with a dummy cast for five months. All was going swimmingly until my biology teacher let it slip at a parents' evening of how proud she was of my continuing battle with my greenstick fracture. My parents were not as proud and I remember very well the conversation with my dad on his return. What I didn't realise then was that natural skill I had of pulling the wool over someone's eyes would become very handy in later life. But at the time, I was just in deep shit. I eventually escaped from education at fifteen and went on the hunt for a full-time job.

My plan had been to avoid the long arm of the law, as a career at least. But after an uninspiring first job as a clerical officer for the Ministry of Defence and a chance encounter with an old school friend who had become a police cadet, the police force suddenly sounded appealing. Plus I had no qualifications, but I did have a dad who could put a word in for me.

And so a thorough medical, fitness test and interview (during which I found myself becoming surprisingly determined) later, I was accepted into the Metropolitan Police Force as a cadet in January 1982.

It would be true to say that my friends, with whom I had grown up on our small estate, were a little confused to start with. I remember being driven to the local police station to pick up my acceptance letter by one of my mates in a car that didn't belong to him. In fact all of us had driven a number of cars that did not belong to us. I looked on it then as all part of growing up in south London and frankly where I came from it was almost an accepted phase. Cars were easy to steal and we never damaged or crashed them. We would drive around in them for a day or so and then either return them or park them up safely where they could be found. That said, it was breaking the law and once I had been accepted into the police cadets that phase of my life had to cease. I passed out of Cadet College in March 1984, then I went to Hendon for twenty weeks to carry out my training to become a police constable. To my surprise, I excelled in the environment both educationally and practically and achieved excellent grades, passing out in July 1984 with a Distinction, and was posted to Greenwich. I was now a fully fledged police constable and ready for anything. Or, so I thought.

I attended Greenwich Police Station in July 1984, young, eager and a little wet behind the ears. As a probationary police constable you are shadowed for your two-year probationary period by a much more experienced officer. I got lucky. My sergeant was an inspiration. Archie, as he insisted on being called, was no ordinary sergeant. He had spent most of his career working in the West End clubs.

Whereas other sergeants would go out and walk the beat with you for the first month or so, Archie didn't take that approach. On my first day on relief he sent me out on my own with the words, 'I don't care what you do, just don't fuck up.' Within an hour I was back, having made my first arrest. I had recognised somebody from an earlier briefing and as I approached him to have a word he started to run. I chased him for over five minutes through various buildings and estates until eventually I managed to rugby-tackle him to the ground. I became an instant hit, and Archie was impressed.

Within two weeks Archie had me posted to the area car (or rapid response vehicle) as a plain-clothes observer. This was all I could have hoped for. It was rare for a probationary officer to be posted to the area car let alone as the plain-clothed observer. In fact, it was practically unheard of and raised a few eyebrows among the more senior members of my relief. Archie saw something in me and I didn't let him down.

I quickly gained a reputation as a 'thief taker', an officer who makes more arrests than most, and gained the nickname 'Golden Bollocks' as I constantly found myself in situations that led to arrests and convictions of criminals. Before long, I had attracted the attention of the area crime squad. They were keen to meet with this new probationer.

TWO

YOU IN OR OUT?

Archie and I continued to work together. His experience, coupled with my enthusiasm, made for a good team and we had a reputation as a solid and reliable unit. We were given the responsibility of policing the notorious Ferrier Estate in Kidbrooke, south-east London, and asked to clean up the drug problem. Archie, along with Robert, another seasoned officer, announced their arrival on the estate at a residents' meeting. Archie vowed to clean up the estate to the gathered masses. I was given a flat into which I moved as a resident. The only people aware that I was a police officer were Archie and Robert. I was given a free rein and used my anonymity to gather evidence and pass it back to Archie to do with what he deemed fit.

It was during this time that I began to get a flavour for undercover work. I was gaining the trust of the residents although they found it a little strange that I rarely slept at the flat and it was sparsely furnished. It was on this operation that I did my first drugs buy. This was, however, an unmitigated disaster.

Archie had been approached by an officer from Scotland Yard's drugs squad. They needed to match the drugs that they believed were being sold from a pub on the estate to a much bigger supply that was being offered for sale in north London. If the drug matched the drugs from the north London haul it would complete the chain. I was put forward as the buyer, the drugs squad agreed, and the buy was sanctioned.

The drugs squad officers briefed me as to what I needed to do and they plotted up and watched as I entered the pub. I was to get a drink and try and get into conversation with the landlord and if possible steer the conversation around to who was the best person locally for me to score some Moroccan (a term used for cannabis). They would be waiting for me outside.

I walked towards the bar nervous but excited at the prospect of my first drugs buy, but as I got closer to the bar the landlord turned and looked at me. 'Forget it. I won't be serving you, so I suggest you spin back around and fuck off back out the door.'

I was gobsmacked. My first ever drugs buy and he had sussed me within five seconds of entering the pub.

'Why not?' I asked, pretending to be affronted.

'Look, I've had the Old Bill in here this morning about underage drinking and I'm sorry but unless you've got something to prove you're over eighteen, which I doubt, I can't serve you.'

He hadn't sussed me as Old Bill, worse than that, he thought I wasn't old enough to be served alcohol. Seeing as I had nothing on me to prove my age, apart from my warrant card, I turned around and left.

I returned back to the station for a debrief. The drugs squad found the whole episode hilarious and I have to admit that the dummy and nappies that found their way into my locker made me laugh out loud. But it had sown a seed. I had loved every minute of it and was congratulated for not breaking cover.

My next drugs buy went according to plan. The district drugs squad had requested for me to assist with a drugs buy in a pub in Eltham. The police were aware of the dealing that took place there but had up until then been unsuccessful to effect a buy from the known dealer. As I was unknown, they were confident that I would be able to carry out a buy. I entered the pub one Thursday evening and made my way over to the bar where I instantly recognised the dealer. I hung around for an hour playing pool and drinking and then turned to the guy that I had been playing pool with. 'I hear that I can score some gear here.'

He didn't even look up from his shot. 'Yeah. The guy in the corner, he's a mate of mine. Just tell him that Adam sent you over.'

I looked over at the dealer and, cue in hand, walked over to him. I went up next to him and stood sideways on. 'I'm a mate of Adam's and apparently you're the man for a bit of gear.'

He looked back at me and pulled a bag from out of his hooded top. 'How much?'

I couldn't believe my luck. I stared back at him. 'I'll take it all if the price is right.'

He smiled. 'Sorry, fella, but I have regular clients. You can have a quarter and be happy with that.'

I nodded in agreement. 'Cool. Here you go,' I said and handed over the marked notes and went back and carried on playing pool with Adam.

After about twenty minutes I made my way to the entrance to the pub and walked outside. I put my two arms into the air to make out that I was stretching, which was the prearranged signal for the district crime squad, and as I went back into the pub they followed in behind me. The dealer was arrested and as I was introduced as an officer he turned to face me: 'Fuck, I never would've sussed you as Old Bill, never.'

I thanked him for the compliment and went home a happy man.

I was eighteen months into my probation when the detective inspector who ran the area crime squad approached me. Archie and I had by this time been working on the estate for six months with some good results. We had cleaned up the drugs problem, and had made numerous arrests with my anonymity still intact.

The area crime squad had, with Archie's approval, been given permission to offer me a place on their squad even though I was still a probationary officer. I was afforded special dispensation from the area commander and I waved goodbye to Archie and took up my posting.

I completed my probationary period attached to the area crime squad and during this time attracted the attention of the area drugs squad, who were keen to have me on board. I was offered an interview – or board, as we call it in the force – but the Friday before I was due to attend it was cancelled.

I was given no explanation for the cancellation until I received a phone call and was told to attend a meeting at Scotland Yard. A meeting that would change my life.

I attended New Scotland Yard on 3 March 1987 and walked into a room to find a deputy assistant commissioner, a commander and a chief superintendent from Lewisham sat around a large table with a number of files at one end.

They apologised for the short notice of the meeting and for the cancellation of my area drugs squad board. They were very complimentary of my career to date and said that I should consider the opportunity that they may present to me very seriously.

They were very vague to start with and asked lots of personal and prying questions about my long-term friendships and where I had grown up. After two hours of interview, which felt more like an interrogation, I was told that I would hear from them in due course. I was completely at odds as to why they had brought me in. Archie and I tried to find out what they were recruiting for but it appeared that this closely guarded secret was going to remain just that, a secret.

I was again called to Scotland Yard on 6 March 1987 for a further meeting, and it was there that they showed their hand.

They were looking for undercover officers to work on a specialised unit. Its goal was to arrest and obtain criminal convictions on known football hooligans by means of a covert operation.

I instantly knew this was for me. From my first drugs buy I had clambered to do more covert work. The adrenalin rush could not be matched. I knew a little bit about football hooliganism, having witnessed it at the games I'd been to growing up and having attended matches when in uniform.

The senior officers informed me that there had been a growing wave of criticism around violence in and around football grounds and it had now moved on from a policing issue to a political one.

We were to be given every available resource and assistance in our endeavour and it was assumed that the operation would last for a maximum of six months. There were, however, some pressing issues. There were currently similar operations at an area level but they were coming to a natural conclusion and this operation was to be conducted from Scotland Yard with full specialist operations support. The budget and decision-making would be conducted at the highest level. It was essential that the other undercover units at Millwall, West Ham and Chelsea were unaware of our involvement. It all seemed a bit cloak and dagger to me but if that's the way they wanted it played, who was I to argue?

I was sent away from the meeting with one question: are you in or out? If you're in, ring this number within the next twenty-four hours and report to Brockley Police Station on 30 March 1987 where you will be introduced to the other members of your team. If it is not for you then we will understand, and your decision will in no way prejudice your future career.

I left the meeting and made my way over to Archie's. He had heard some rumours about the new 'Ghost Squads', as they had been nicknamed, but even for the police force it appeared to have been kept very secretive. We spoke well into the evening about the advantages and disadvantages of accepting the offer but I knew my answer the minute I had walked out of the meeting.

I was in.

THREE
KICK-OFF

The day I was supposed to report to Brockley Police Station – 30 March – came and went. I never got there as I had to be at court, so I arrived on Wednesday 1 April. April Fool's Day. How ironic that I should meet the sergeant that was to be my partner as well as head up the squad on that day. I walked into the office at 9 a.m. and waited for him to arrive.

At a little after ten o'clock he appeared. He introduced himself as Chris and suggested that we go for a coffee and get to know one another. At first sight I remember thinking that he certainly didn't look like your run-of-the-mill police officer. He was too short for starters, five foot seven tops, and wore big Joe 90 spectacles. That aside, he seemed nice enough, and we wandered off to the cafe.

As we entered the cafe, I noticed a group of guys sitting over at a table who were obviously Old Bill. Chris instantly walked over to them and shook the hand of one of the guys sitting at the table. I went to the counter, bought the drinks and parked myself over on a table away from Chris and the others.

Chris shouted out, 'Jim, come and meet the guys.'

I stared back at him and raised a hand to gesture that I was happy where I was. I was a little surprised, as it had been impressed on me that we were to disassociate ourselves from other police officers and yet here we were sitting in a cafe with a load of Old Bill.

Chris eventually came back over and sat down. He stared at me and shook his head. 'Why didn't you come over? It's a bit rude, ain't it, to ignore them like that? D'ya know who they are?'

I shook my head. 'No. But by the looks of them I would say that they are Old Bill, and if it's all right with you – given what we are about to embark on – I would rather not associate with them.'

He started to laugh. 'Well, seeing that they are all members of the old covert team and we're sharing an office with them, that may prove a little difficult.'

I sat there open-mouthed. 'But I was told that we were to be kept a big secret and that no one, not even our family, was to know about the operation.'

Chris laughed again. 'You have a lot to learn.'

He was right; I did have a lot to learn.

Chris was in his early thirties and had joined the Metropolitan Police just short of his twentieth birthday. He had risen up the ladder quickly and was a detective constable within five years. He had recently passed his sergeant exam, which had resulted in him being posted to P District. Because of his CID background and recent promotion he looked like an ideal candidate to head up the squad.

We spent the next couple of days getting to know each other. I had just started dating a police officer called Dawn, so I chatted about her while Chris told me about his life. We had yet to be joined by the other two members of our team. Chris had been told that senior management were struggling to find suitable candidates but that they had more interviews planned over the coming weeks. So for the foreseeable future it was to be Chris and me who would be starting the operation.

I was introduced to the old covert team who had run the 'Lion Tamers' operation and were basking in the glory of having arrested and charged eighteen of Millwall's finest for conspiracy to commit affray and various other misdemeanours. This trial resulted in prison sentences for most of the accused only for the verdicts to be quashed on appeal due to irregularities in the evidence. They seemed nice enough guys and Phil the sergeant knew his stuff.

Chris and I decided that we would attend our first game that weekend, which was to be Leeds away. I had taken it upon myself to gather as much information about Millwall and their notable achievements over the past twenty years, which on the football front were few and far between. The same could not be said about the club's fearsome reputation for football hooliganism, the most recent example at that time being Luton away in 1985. When I watched the television footage of the Luton away game, and saw the massive scale of the violence, it dawned on me what I had signed up to. Watching hooligans attacking police officers, knowing that I was about to enter that world with only a fellow officer that I had just met was fucking terrifying.

There were numerous photographs of known targets and some surveillance tapes but most of the information I gathered was during conversations with the old covert team. They were sketchy around the club's history and even vaguer about the notable hooligans that they had failed to arrest. I was lucky in that I was able to sit down with Guy, one of the uniform spotters, who was able to give me an extended history of Millwall as he had supported them from childhood. He'd also been responsible for policing at Millwall for the last ten years and knew every hooligan and supporter alike. He travelled to every home and away game with his team and his information early on was invaluable, as was his support throughout the operation. It was clear to me Chris had no interest in football. He said that he would leave that to me. On Friday 3 April 1987 we decided that it was time for us both to show our faces.

We left Brockley Police Station at 7 p.m. that evening and drove down to the Old Kent Road to familiarise ourselves with what was to become our home for the next two years.

We entered The Woodcutter, having been told by the old covert team that it was a 'heavy Millwall pub', and had a quick drink. We were the only ones there and it became clear very quickly that we were unlikely to gain anything of use there other than information about the next month's meat raffle. We downed our drinks and left. Guy had mentioned one of the more notorious hooligan pubs, the Old Castle, and I suggested that we should go there. Chris was a little reluctant at first but I impressed on him that as our job was to infiltrate hooligans we needed to frequent their pubs and get to know them, they were not going to come to us.

As we approached the pub, I noticed a large group of people standing outside and immediately recognised one of them as 'Tubby Tony', aptly named because he was Tubby and called Tony. He was a well-known Millwall hooligan and I had seen him on a number of surveillance tapes. He had been questioned after the Luton riots but not arrested due to lack of evidence.

We entered the Old Castle at just gone 8 p.m. The pub was packed and most of the people from my first glance were Millwall. Most of the recognisable targets that I had seen on surveillance tapes were there. I walked up to the bar and ordered a pint of lager for me and a half for Chris. I began to look around and clock the faces. The pub was polluted with Millwall. I swiftly downed my pint, more out of nerves than thirst, and asked Chris to get me another one while I went to the toilet the long way round so that I could take in who was there. As I came out of the toilet I saw that the guys that I had clocked outside as we had entered the pub had surrounded Chris. Tubby Tony was looking on as Chris was being interrogated.

I rushed over and walked into the middle of the crowd. 'Oi, what's the fucking problem here?'

One of the guys stepped forward. 'This has got fuck all to do with you. We're talking to him.' And with that he shoved his finger into Chris's face. 'So answer my question. What the fuck were you staring at?'

I could not believe what I was hearing. No one *ever* stares at anyone in a pub on their first visit regardless of who they are, hooligans or not, it's just common sense.

I butted in. 'Sorry, mate, he don't mean to stare, he's just a bit fucking blind. I mean, take a look at them fucking glasses. Wouldn't you fucking have to stare if you were wearing them?'

They all looked at Chris and they started to laugh. 'Mate, you have got a fucking point there. They are a bit fucking thick. Sorry, mate.'

It looked like we had got away with it until Chris opened his mouth. 'Yeah, well, count yourself fucking lucky cos we're Millwall and we don't take any shit.'

I couldn't believe what I was hearing. The first night out in a notorious Millwall pub with him staring at everyone and then he announces that they had all better watch out as he's fucking Millwall. It then turned proper ugly and they all started to throw questions at him. 'Oh, you're Millwall, are you? Who's our keeper then?'

I interrupted, 'Brian Horne.'

I was told again to shut up. They continued to fire questions at him, which I continued to answer on his behalf until he sealed our fate. One of the crowd asks who we sold to Wimbledon. I again jumped in with John Fashanu and the chap turned and told me to shut the fuck up or he would shut me up. He could see Chris's fear and threw a comforting arm around him.

'Fashanu, yeah,' Chris nodded in agreement. 'Yeah, and I for one am glad he's gone, he was fucking lazy.'

Why he offered that up is beyond me, maybe fear, but I stood there waiting to die.

The guy then pulls him closer and announces to the rest, 'I'm with him, he was lazy. What we need is a young black striker like Ian Wright, unlike Fashanu, that lazy white cunt.'

Chris looks on and walks straight into the trap. 'Yeah, you're right, we need a young black striker.'

Frankly, by that time I wanted to hit him. Anybody who did not know that Fashanu was black and pure class shouldn't have been there. The punches then rained down on the both of us, resulting in the bouncers and Tubby Tony steaming in and breaking it up. We were kicked out of the pub and barred. I looked at Chris in disbelief. I remember just staring at him as we drove back to the station with blood pouring from his nose. 'How the fuck are you going to do this job? You drink half pints, stare at people, and then embarrass the fuck out of yourself and me by announcing that one of their best players in recent times, John Fashanu, is fucking white.'

He just looked ahead as we drove into the station. There was no apology, no reaction, no nothing. It seemed to me that the operation was over before it had started. As I started to walk away I suddenly had my arm thrust up my back and I was wrestled to the ground by two guys in plain clothes. I shouted at them to 'Get the fuck off me' to be told that I was under arrest for assaulting a police officer. It transpired that they had been carrying out an observation on the pub and had witnessed the whole thing. One of them recognised Chris and had assumed that I had been arrested. They were then informed by Chris that I was his partner and not his prisoner and had saved him from a proper kicking. They apologised and were very complimentary about the fact that I didn't look or behave like Old Bill.

Chris went into the station and we were both seen by the district surgeon, who treated our various cuts and bruises and Chris's broken nose. We retreated to the local pub where Chris and I had a proper heart to heart. He apologised for his lack of knowledge. He would research the team and from now on take a back seat where the targets were concerned. I looked the part, which had been borne out that evening with my being arrested at the station. We both decided that we would put tonight behind us and start out afresh tomorrow on the trip to Leeds away. I left the station that night with a renewed enthusiasm but with the knowledge that this was not going to be an easy ride.

FOUR

LEEDS AWAY

The next morning Chris and I met at the office as planned at 6 a.m. It was Saturday 4 April 1987 and we were both heading off on our first Millwall away game. The game in question was against the once mighty Leeds. By the mid-eighties they were no longer in their heyday, but they still had their hard-core hooligan element: 'The Leeds Service Crew'.

I had quickly learnt that all of the hard-core hooligan clubs had their own firms.

Chelsea: 'The Headhunters'.

West Ham: 'The Inter City Firm', aptly named as they used to travel to away games on the Inter City 125 rather than the less salubrious Football Special.

Arsenal: 'The Gooners'.

Portsmouth: 'The 657 Squad'. Again, their name was taken as a direct reference to transport, as the first train out of Portsmouth when their firm travelled away was the 6.57 a.m.

Birmingham: 'Zulus'.

But for me the award for the best-named firm goes to Hull City: 'The Silver Cod Squad'. Quality.

Anyways, we headed to King's Cross for the Football Special that was to take us on the four-hour trip to Leeds. We arrived at the station a good hour before the train was due to depart. There were already a number of Millwall fans milling about. It was only 8 a.m. and most, if not all of them, were on the liquid breakfast. Chris and I went over to the station restaurant and ordered a full English. I remember sitting there watching as more and more Millwall began to arrive at the station. It was difficult to miss them. They were all in fine voice and I heard for the first time Millwall's anthem 'No One Likes Us'.

Even at eight in the morning it was sung with gusto and passion.

I looked at Chris. It was obvious that he was not enjoying his experience of the operation so far and he was not slow to point that out. At least his heart was in the right place. I just wasn't sure he was cut out for this form of work. Covert policing, as we all learnt over the next two years, was something that you either had a sense for or not. It's not a skill that you can be taught. Yes you can run scenarios, discuss what to do should a situation present itself, but ultimately it will always come down to the individual officer and his ability to think on his feet, to take full advantage of a situation and – by far the most difficult of skills – know when to take a step back. It is definitely not for the faint-hearted. It takes a special officer to undertake covert police work. Some people say brave, others say stupid; I honestly believe that you have to be a little bit of both. But there is one rule that you can never lose sight of.

It is a job. The sole purpose for being there, whatever the situation or operation, is to obtain the evidence so that in the end you can arrest the bad guys. Plain and simple.

We finished up our breakfast and we then spied a group of Millwall coming up the stairs. It was Tubby Tony and his contingent from the fight at the pub the night before, singing 'No One Likes Us' at the top of their voices.

Chris turned to me. 'What the fuck are we gonna do?'

We had two options: either we fronted up or went home.

I turned back around and nodded to him. 'Come on.' I then started to walk towards them.

Tubby Tony saw me first and began to nudge the others. I walked up to Tubby Tony and put my hand out. 'Sorry about last night, fellas. No hard feelings.'

They all looked and stared at me. I turned to see that Chris had not come with me.

Tubby Tony looked me up and down. 'What was your name again?'

I stared right back at him. 'Jim. Jim from Wandsworth.' And I pointed over to Chris. 'And he's Chris.'

Tubby Tony took my hand and shook it. 'So you're Millwall. Why have I not seen you before?'

I looked back at him. 'Cos I've been away. I used to come with my granddad but I haven't been for a while.'

They all stared at me and then looked over to Chris. Tubby Tony nodded over. 'And him, what's his story?'

I looked over to Chris. 'Ah, don't mind him. He goes out with my sister. We work together as painters and decorators. He's all right, just a bit colour blind.'

And with that everyone laughed and I felt that we had been accepted. They couldn't have been friendlier. Apologies were given out on both sides and we made our way to the Football Special. Having never travelled on a Football Special before I was unsure what to expect. This one was made up of six carriages. They were without doubt the shittiest carriages that I had ever travelled on. They were dirty, smelly, with no opening windows as the catches were either broken or screwed shut. The toilets, of which there was only one that worked, had no running water from the sink and the flush worked intermittently. We pushed up to the front of the train and sat down with our new friends. I gave them the details of my cover story that Chris and I had compiled that week. It was a bit loose but at that time good enough.

I was Jim. A painter and decorator from Wandsworth where I lived with my wife and her parents. I had a small son who was a year old.

(Don't ask me why I invented a child, as to this day, I still couldn't say.) Chris was dating my wife's sister, although they had recently split up, and we worked together painting houses all over south London.

Chris wasn't comfortable but held up his end until about an hour into the journey when he 'fell asleep'. I talked the whole way up there and played cards, badly, getting as much information about our new targets as I could. I also drank. I was not used to drinking at that time of the day, and after three cans made my excuses. Most of the supporters on the train drank during the journey. That said, no one appeared drunk.

Four hours after we left King's Cross, the guard announced that we were soon to be arriving at Leeds Mainline Station. Everyone began to gather up their stuff. The mood began to change as we drew closer to the station. There were hushed conversations and as we pulled into the station the train erupted into song.

No one likes us
No one likes us
No one likes us
We don't care.
We are Millwall
Super Millwall
We are Millwall
From the Den.

This anthem was sung by all as we were ushered off the train and onto the platform. Due to the acoustics in the station, our chant doubled in volume. I had never experienced anything like it. Yes, I had been to football before but this was something else. I felt strangely proud and a little overwhelmed.

My feeling of euphoria was short-lived. The West Yorkshire Police had turned out in full force to greet us. They were all lined up and down the station. From the outset they were overly aggressive and started to push the Millwall supporters along the platform. I assumed that this was them signalling that they would take no shit. It backfired. We were five hundred strong and they totalled about fifty. No sooner had they started pushing us down the platform the mood changed. There then came a large surge from the back of the crowd and another chant followed.

Did the ripper
Did the ripper
Did the ripper fuck your mum?
Did the ripper fuck your mum?

As this was sung, all of the Millwall fans pointed at the police. It was obviously meant to provoke a reaction. It worked. No sooner had the chant started the police waded in with truncheons. One officer in particular was incensed and set about one of the Millwall. He very quickly became isolated within the crowd and they swallowed him up. He was punched and kicked to the ground unconscious. Eventually some of the Millwall supporters calmed the situation down and at the same time the police waded in to protect their colleague. I am not afraid to admit that I absolutely shit myself. The ferocity and speed of the attack was something I had never witnessed before. I was used to a bit of posturing and some dialogue and then maybe some windmill arms and kicks. Not here – this was calculated and instant. I was alongside Chris who I could see was as scared as me. I put my arm around him and pulled him close and whispered in his ear. 'Fuck me. Welcome to Millwall.'

He stared at me and raised his eyes to the heavens. 'I am too old for this shit,' and we both stared at each other and started to laugh, more out of fear than humour.

We were led out of the station and the chanting continued. 'Did the Ripper Fuck Your Mum' had been replaced with another repeat of 'No One Likes Us', sung with the same intensity. We were herded onto coaches and given a police escort to the ground. Not that it helped much. En-route the coaches were pelted from every vantage point. Bridges, side streets, passing cars. By the time we arrived at the ground every coach had suffered damage. There were windows smashed and dents down the sides of all of them.

We were then escorted from the bus to the ground. We entered the away end at Elland Road and it was already full of Millwall. I stood with Chris during the whole game and we watched on. The Millwall supporters sang throughout the entire game. The most memorable moment was when a rather large Leeds supporter, in a pink jumper, stood up to make his way up the terraces. He was spotted by one of the Millwall supporters who started singing 'Who's the fat cunt in the pink?' Within seconds the entire Millwall crowd were in full voice and pointing at the poor guy. The Leeds supporter ran down to the front of the pitch and began shouting and gesticulating. At this moment another Millwall fan started another chant and was quickly joined by the rest of us.

Who ate all the pies?
Who ate all the pies?
You fat bastard
You fat bastard
You ate all the pies.

He was then pelted with pies from the Millwall contingent closest to the away end. We were all pissing ourselves with laughter.

The banter continued throughout the game. During half-time hundreds of photocopied twenty-pound notes were handed around. I was a little confused until the start of the second half when the Millwall supporters began throwing the notes into the air with the chant 'We've got loads of money' and then raised the notes aloft and taunted the Leeds supporters with the chant:

Have you ever
Have you ever
Have you ever seen one of these?

Leeds gave as good as they got with their own chants and eventually won the game 2–0.

The game finished and we were left in the ground until all of the Leeds supporters had dispersed. We were escorted back to the coaches. The drive back to the station was uneventful and we were escorted off the coaches to the train. However, as we entered the station all of the Millwall, me included, broke into a last rendition of 'No One Likes Us' as a parting gesture. As we did so I began to see people exiting a stationary train opposite the Football Special that was to take us all back to London. There was a huge roar and a group of about a hundred Leeds supporters began to run across the tracks to get to us. They were not only coming across the tracks but also from the roof above. The police tried to hold the Millwall and Leeds supporters apart but were unsuccessful and a large fight started. I instinctively ran to the front and saw a large group of hard-core Millwall standing their ground. The violence was explosive and scary in its execution.

The fight lasted for a good two minutes, which trust me is a bloody long time, until the police regained some sense of order. Neither Chris nor I got involved but this was not from the want of trying on my part. It was very strange but I felt some sense of duty to step in and help.

What struck me most was that the ambush had been exceptionally well organised. They had obviously been there for some time waiting for us and the execution of their plan was well carried out. There were some arrests, mainly Leeds supporters, and a few cuts and bruises but nobody had been seriously hurt. We were eventually ushered onto the train and sent back to London. Both Chris and I slept on the way back. I was exhausted. We pulled back into London as it neared midnight and made our way back to the office to write up our evidence.

Our first away game as covert police officers had been eventful. We both agreed that we felt a little out of our depth. We wrote our evidence together and both agreed to include the 'overzealous' approach of the West Yorkshire police officers upon our arrival at the station, although it was probably justified given the chanting.

We looked back on our week. We had no targets, apart from those that we had got into a fight with. We had no useable evidence and a somewhat dubious opinion of another police force's behaviour.

I drove home, went to bed and slept all day Sunday not surfacing until Monday. It was a sign of things to come.

FIVE

CHARLIE

Chris and I were back in the office for Tuesday 7 April when we were introduced to the third member of the team, Charlie. He was in his early thirties and was a uniformed officer from west London. At the time his wife was six months pregnant with their first son. He was an exceptionally good driver, Advanced Class 1, was a fully qualified surveillance officer and was an authorised shot; although he was keen to point out that he hoped he would never have to use this skill during the operation. He was still to find out who his partner was to be, but he was a breath of fresh air. He had already done his homework regarding Millwall, and to this day, like me and his eventual partner, still supports them. He was likeable and approachable and was keen to get stuck in.

We spent the next couple of days getting to know each other. The more I spoke with Charlie the more I grew to like him. Chris had now also started to pay more attention to the history surrounding the club and we started to quiz each other on old teams, who was our greatest player, best manager. For the record Terry Hurlock gets my vote for Millwall's best player and Billy Gray for manager.

Chris and I went out again on the Friday night and fortunately, it was far less eventful than the week before. We then went to the Grimsby game on the Saturday and it was here that we had our first breakthrough. We entered the Old Castle pub in the Old Kent Road and tried very hard to blend in. It was full of Millwall and no one gave us a second look. We got speaking with a guy at the bar who told us that he knew all of Millwall's 'top boys' and that he was happy for us to stand with him during the game. This was all good news to us. We went to the game against Grimsby and stood with our newfound friend. He said hello to a few people that we had recognised from the Leeds away game. Millwall won 1–0 and we left in a buoyant mood. The bloke from the pub informed us that there was to be a pre-arranged fight at London Bridge. 'You up for it?'

This appeared to be too good to be true. We boarded a train from New Cross to London Bridge. It was packed with Millwall supporters and families travelling into London. Suddenly our new mate went over to a man who was sitting quietly with his wife and two daughters. Without warning he hit the man in the face and he fell to the ground. He then set about him, kicking him in the head and about the body, as his wife and kids looked on helpless. As a parting gesture he jumped up and down a number of times on his head. His wife and children started to scream as Chris and I looked on, helpless to intervene. He then turned and walked back over to us. A roar went up from further down the carriage and a section of the carriage began to chant. 'Millwall, Millwall…' followed by a rendition of 'No One Likes Us'.

Every part of me wanted to grab this guy and arrest him. Fuck the consequences. What we had just witnessed was sickening. I remember staring at him for what appeared to be ages going through in my head what I should do. I looked on and saw the man who had been assaulted being helped to his feet by his wife and his two young daughters. I looked at Chris. I looked at all the other people in the carriage. What the fuck do I do?

I stood up on my seat and raised my arms in the air triumphantly to the other Millwall supporters and at the top of my voice started to sing the 'No One Likes Us' anthem.

The guy joined in while Chris looked on open-mouthed. In the eyes of everyone on that train, I was a football hooligan. The man had been injured and it was a sickening display of violence but with our evidence he could be arrested at a later time and we could maintain our cover. Even so, the look from the injured man's daughters as we exited the train is one that remains with me to this day.

Upon arrival at London Bridge we went for a drink with our 'newfound friend' but after a short time it was obvious that the pre-arranged fight was not going to happen and I for one was keen by then to remove myself from his company.

It was not until we got back that Chris and I spoke about what had happened. We were sickened by what we had witnessed and wrote up our evidence in statement form so that we could pass it on to the investigating officer. We were unable to pursue the arrest/conviction of our target as the assault was never reported and consequently we had no details of the victim. It was a sign of things to come.

SIX

HULL DISASTER; IPSWICH TRIUMPH

I returned to the office on Tuesday 14 April having thought about nothing else other than the unprovoked assault on the train. It was on this day that we made probably our biggest mistake of the whole operation. We decided to attend the Millwall away game at Hull. We looked at the train times and travelled up on a normal service as no Football Special had been laid on by the club due to the small number of supporters anticipated.

On the train, we got talking to a couple of ardent Millwall fans who were very keen to find out who we were. We felt very exposed, and their questions became more and more probing.

When we arrived at Hull we made our excuses and went into town. I was all up for getting straight back on the train but Chris thought having come all that way we should show our faces. He was sure that lots of people would have travelled up by car. He was to be proven wrong. We entered the away end in which there were nineteen supporters and we were the new faces. Again we faced questions. Although none of the supporters that had travelled up that day were interested in carrying out any football violence, they were protective of their club and were keen to find out who we were.

The game finished and we made our way back for the train that was to take us back to London. We boarded the 22.50, which got us back into King's Cross at 06.50. There were even more questions. 'Why have we not seen you before?' 'When did you start coming?' 'You say you used to come with your granddad. Where did you stand?' Eventually the conversation got around to undercover police going to football matches to gather information and the recent arrests at Chelsea and Millwall earlier that season. We were told that most of the evidence had been made up and that the people that had been arrested, save one, were foot soldiers and not any of the 'top boys'. We were asked ever more probing questions and at this point it started to get very uncomfortable. It became obvious that everyone was on guard, not only football hooligans but genuine supporters too. More alarming were the rumours that the evidence had been made up or fabricated in some way. I was petrified that they were on to us.

Eventually everyone fell asleep, except for me. I sat on the train wide awake until we drew into King's Cross at seven o'clock. I went straight home to bed. It felt that the whole operation was unravelling before my eyes.

On Thursday I went back into the office and Chris and I decided that we would never enter a game again unless there were at least a hundred Millwall supporters present and that we would only travel by train when it was absolutely necessary. We also passed on the information to the old covert team about what the word on the street was concerning the fabricated evidence. They laughed it off.

The next few days were spent gathering information and on 18 April we went to the home game versus Brighton, determined to put the past week behind us. This was the lowest point for me on the whole operation. I spent the entire match looking over my shoulder, convinced that at any moment I was going to get recognised as Old Bill and beaten to a pulp. I was convinced by the end of the game that word was out as to who we were, and that at any moment, it was going to erupt into a free for all on the undercover Old Bill.

The game finished and Chris and I headed back to the office – we were in no mood to go out looking for targets. We sat in the office and drowned our sorrows. Neither of us were into drinking before we started the operation but that had changed. Over the first month of the operation I drank more than I had done for the previous year. Drinking was part of the culture and it also helped ease the fear.

The pressures of the job were already starting to take hold, and it wasn't going down well with my new girlfriend Dawn, who I was now living with. At first, I spoke with her endlessly about the operation and how we were progressing, but over time, it became more of a hindrance than a help. I eventually stopped communicating with her at all.

Chris and I met up on the Sunday and the Monday and tried to drink our way to a conclusion. Back in the office on Tuesday 21 April, we informed Charlie that we had decided that we were going to give it until the end of the month and if we still felt the same we would call it a day. He was a little bemused and tried to make us feel better but we were having none of it.

We decided to travel to the Ipswich away game that night and drive rather than risk the train again. We left mid-morning and were on the outskirts of the town when I saw some Millwall that I recognised from our surveillance tapes. I convinced Chris to pull over the car as I watched them enter a small wine bar. We parked the car and made our way to the entrance of the wine bar. It was early afternoon and already quite busy. We both took a large breath and walked in. Instantly someone came over who I also recognised from the surveillance tapes. He was smartly dressed and pulled no punches. 'Who the fuck are you?'

I stood there and stared at him. 'Sorry, you talking to me?'

He paused and looked us both up and down. 'Millwall?'

I was quick to respond. 'Yeah, you got a fucking problem with that?'

With that he started to laugh and put his arm around my shoulder. 'No, no problem, come in.'

He then led us over to the bar area where about twenty other Millwall supporters had congregated and told us to get a drink. We played pool and drank with our newfound friends. We weren't questioned as to who we were. We volunteered information before we were asked. We were Jim and Chris, the painters and decorators from Wandsworth. Within an hour the whole place had been taken over by Millwall.

Once again, I recognised people from our surveillance tapes. While it can help spot your target, it has its disadvantages too. The main one being that you know more about the person than you should know: their name, where they live, their previous convictions. So you have to be very careful not to appear too familiar, which sometimes is easier said than done. The positives are that you can steer the conversation around to stuff you are aware of. It is surprising the amount of information that people will give up on a first meeting. The easiest intro for me was to talk about previous criminal convictions, as most people who have them are only too keen to talk about them.

It was all going well until an argument broke out over the pool table. Within seconds the table was on its side and then two Millwall supporters jumped over the bar and raided the till. Chris and I watched on as the poor barmaid started to cry, saying that she would be held responsible for any monies missing and that it would come out of her wages. There was then a muffled conversation at the bar between five or six of the Millwall supporters. They agreed to hand her back the money in exchange for a few free drinks. I looked on as they made the two thieves hand back the stolen cash, which they did in return for a few free beers.

We then left the bar and travelled to the ground with the others. We managed to watch the whole game surrounded by people who had accepted us. It was a relief not having to spend the entire match looking over our shoulders. We left the match buoyed up and drove back to London with a newfound confidence. We had finally been accepted as Jim and Chris, the painters and decorators from Wandsworth.

SEVEN

GERRY AND THE SUMMER OF '87

Chris and I breathed a huge sigh of relief after the Ipswich game. We both felt that we had turned a corner. We had a renewed confidence in what we were trying to achieve. Charlie, however, was struggling. He was still battling on alone as the senior officers could not agree on the final member of the team and there was little Chris or I could do to help. We had taken up our position at home matches in the Cold Blow Lane end halfway up behind the goal but Charlie had elected to stand by the halfway line so even at games he was isolated from us.

The three of us spent the weeks leading up to the summer watching surveillance tapes and gathering as much information as we could. We were attending every game and even travelled down to Portsmouth on 2 May, even though Millwall fans had been banned by the FA and Hampshire Constabulary due to previous acts of disorder. We went out of curiosity and saw a few faces that we recognised from our surveillance tapes but with no reports of any incidents during or after the game we headed back to London.

We pulled into the Old Castle pub on the Old Kent Road. We had now taken to frequenting this pub, particularly on match days and weekends. The pub was heaving, as it was on most Saturday nights, and we bumped into Tubby Tony. He was quick to tell us that some Millwall were up for the Palace game on the Monday to show face with Portsmouth who were travelling up to play them. We were ecstatic. We finally had some useful intelligence and Tubby Tony had confided in us. We made our excuses and travelled back to the office.

I was currently doing a two-week surveillance course but phoned the instructor on the Sunday to make my excuses for my non-appearance on the Monday. We passed over our intelligence to the Football Intelligence Unit (FIU) at Scotland Yard, informing them that Millwall were looking to attend.

On the morning of the game Chris and I made our way over to Selhurst Park and found a pub close to the ground. I didn't see anyone from Millwall that I recognised until we entered the ground. I then saw a large contingent of them at the bottom of the Arthur Wait stand. As the game started suddenly about sixty Millwall supporters rose to their feet and started to sing the 'No One Likes Us' anthem. I got up and tried to make my way down to them but by that stage the police had intervened. No sooner had the police stepped in than another group rose in the Portsmouth end. By this time the Millwall fans in the Crystal Palace end were being escorted out.

In the Portsmouth end, it had well and truly kicked off and people were spilling onto the pitch. I saw Tubby Tony remonstrating with a police officer. He was about a hundred feet away from me and Chris. I saw a chance to get noticed. I ran into the aisle, arms aloft, and started to sing the Millwall anthem at the top of my voice.

No one likes us
No one likes us
No one likes us.

At this point all of the Millwall being led out of the ground let out a mighty roar and joined in as two police officers started to run up the aisle towards me.

We are Millwall
Super Millwall
We are Millwall
From the Den.

At this point the two police officers grabbed hold of me and escorted me down to the others. Tubby Tony was all smiles and I joined the rest as we were removed from the ground. Chris was nowhere to be seen. I had assumed that he would have got to his feet and joined in but maybe he had got caught up in the melee. We were constantly moved on by the Old Bill until it was finally agreed that we would all head back to the Old Castle for a celebratory drink.

I travelled back with Tubby Tony and his mates and enjoyed a few drinks with everyone. Chris showed up a couple of hours later. He told the others that he had been penned in and that he finally broke free as the game ended. After an hour or so Chris and I made our excuses and left the pub.

What followed then was our first of many disagreements. Chris was outraged that I had risked personal injury to us both by doing what I did. I pointed out that the police were only a hundred feet away. He was having none of it. According to him, I had left him alone with no back-up. He stated that if I ever pulled a stunt like that again I would be back in uniform.

I was incensed by his comments. He made the final point. He was the sergeant and I had to do what I was told or suffer the consequences. But, I thought he was wrong. I had in that split second got acceptance from Tubby Tony and his firm and had been invited back to drink with them. No one had been hurt and I had moved us up the ladder of acceptance.

I went home with a serious case of the arsehole and ignored Chris's calls until the next day when we met up to go to Sunderland at home.

We both apologised and went to the night game. For the first time a couple of people acknowledged us at the ground and it felt good to have some acceptance, however small.

I finished the surveillance course, during which Chris turned up to tell me that Charlie was finally going to get his partner, who was due to start while I was away on my advanced driving course. He also informed me that we had been given the go-ahead to continue with the operation. I was really pleased and Charlie, Chris and I went out and celebrated at a small pub in Kent, well away from those prying eyes in south London. I completed my driving course, and returned to the office on the Monday where I was to be introduced to Charlie's partner Gerry.

It wasn't the best of starts. As I walked in I noticed that the stuff on my desk had been moved to the desk in the corner and that Gerry had now taken up occupation. Cheeky fucker. So I removed his stuff and sat at *my* desk and waited for him to come in. When I heard them coming up the stairs I leant back in my chair and put my feet up on the desk. Gerry looked like no policeman that I had ever seen before. He was twenty-four years old, stockily built and very casually dressed in shorts and flip-flops. He had two earrings in his left ear, one in his right and a large tattoo of the winged horse Pegasus on his right upper arm. He also had shoulder-length permed hair. He had already carried out some undercover drug buys. The last thing you would take him for was Old Bill.

I stood up and held out my hand. He looked me up and down and then asked me why I was sitting at his desk. I informed him that it was my desk. He stared back at me, 'Not any more.'

I had two choices: if I made a stand I was an arse and if I gave up I was a walkover. I chose the arse route. 'Look, mate, this has been my desk from the start. You swan in mid-operation and decide that you're gonna sit here when it's my fucking desk. That's your desk over there in the corner.' Charlie and Chris observed us silently. Gerry just stood there and said nothing. I broke the silence again. 'You can't just take someone's desk without asking. It's my fucking desk.'

Eventually Gerry spoke. 'Fuck me, mate, it's only a desk. No worries, I'll sit over here.'

'Good.'

Charlie and Chris shook their heads. I now really had the arsehole. 'What's that fucking look for?' I pointed at Charlie. 'If you're so fucking concerned let him have your desk.'

Charlie started to laugh. 'Why would I do that? He doesn't want my desk, he wants yours.'

All three of them started to laugh. I pushed past Chris and walked out of the office. I returned an hour later and walked into the office and over to Gerry. 'Sorry, I'm a cunt. It's really nice to meet you.'

Gerry stood up and shook my hand. 'No worries, I'm the other cunt and it's good to meet you too.'

We spent the summer of 1987 getting to know each other really well. We all had a holiday in the sun and Chris took up windsurfing. He really got the bug and it helped with his appearance. He got the obligatory earring, had his hair highlighted, had permanent stubble, and replaced the Joe 90 specs with contacts. I had now grown my hair down to my shoulders and had both ears pierced. Charlie went unshaven every now and again and once he even grew his hair over his collar but it was short-lived. No earrings for him.

Summer was nearing its conclusion and the pre-season friendlies were nearly upon us. 'Come on you Millwall.'

EIGHT

THE PUFFIN

We were ready for our first full season as undercover football hooligans. The atmosphere in the office was one of huge excitement mixed in with trepidation and fear. We were still on the first floor at Brockley Police Station but there had been a lot of discussion about us being moved somewhere a little bit less conspicuous, as it did seem a little ludicrous to have us carrying out an operation of this nature from above a police station.

We were still no further ahead with documentation to assist us with back-up for our cover stories. Chris and I had some cards made up but were unable to put down an address or phone number. All that we were able to put on them was the name of our fictitious firm, 'Spectrum Decorating', a logo, and our made-up names, Jim Ford and Chris Walters. That was the full extent of our documentary cover. A bloody joke. We were expected to go out and convince some of south London's finest that we were who we said we were and the only thing to back it up was a Mickey Mouse business card with a picture of a paint pot with a brush in it. Even writing this now, it scares the shit out of me, the ineptness and initial lack of support was laughable.

However, over the summer we had all become experts on Millwall Football Club and could have all had it as a specialist subject on *Mastermind*, even Chris, who was still being ribbed for thinking that John Fashanu was white.

Chris and I looked at our options for the season ahead. We would continue to go behind the goal at the Cold Blow Lane end but we were still a long way off being fully accepted. We had not seen Tubby Tony since the last game of the season. As we had no point of contact, our only chance of seeing him was at the Old Castle but he had not been there since the season ended. It had also come to light that all of Millwall's top hooligans had taken to using a pub that had recently been taken over by a hardened Millwall supporter and one of south London's finest. Paul was well known locally and was very surveillance aware. He could spot Old Bill from a mile away. The pub had a reputation as a 'filth-free haven', and it was thought that all of the pre-arranged fights were openly arranged there. I convinced Chris that we had to go and take a look for ourselves. He was rather hesitant but agreed that we would pop in there a couple of weeks before the season started to check it out.

We entered The Puffin public house at 12.45 p.m. on Thursday 6 August 1987. We were wearing our work gear. I walked in with Chris at my heels and went up to the bar. I was served by the barmaid, who we were later to find out was Paul's wife. We bought a couple of pints and headed for the pool table. So far so good. The pub was deserted apart from an old couple who were sitting in the corner and Chris and I played pool for about an hour, had another drink and left. We decided to go back the next day at lunchtime. We entered the pub at around the same time and were served again by Paul's wife, who introduced herself as Tina. We told her our names and that we were from Wandsworth and left it at that. We played pool again and left after a couple of beers.

We were getting braver and decided to go again that evening as it was Millwall's first friendly match before the season started officially on Saturday 15 August. We turned up at the pub, which from the outside appeared quiet. As we opened the door the atmosphere hit us. The pub was full and as I made my way to the bar I recognised every single face from the surveillance tapes and photographs that we had up on the walls in our office. It was a who's who of Millwall's elite.

I got to the bar and saw Paul for the first time. He was a big man, stocky, with a huge presence.

Tina saw me coming to the bar and came over. 'Your usual?'

I stammered my reply. 'Err, yeah please.'

She stared at me. 'You all right?'

What I wanted to say was, 'No, actually, I'm shitting myself cos I have just seen your old man and if he susses me out as Old Bill I am fucking dead.' Instead I just nodded and said that I was fine.

She passed me my light and lager, I had taken to drinking that now, and asked where my mate was. I gestured over to where Chris was standing. He was standing bolt upright about twenty feet behind me, looking like I was feeling. Sick.

She then let out a laugh. 'Fucking hell, are you two okay? He looks like absolute shit.'

I managed to gather my thoughts. 'Yeah, yeah, we're fine, we've just had one of those days. Can I have a lager for him?'

She smiled and got Chris his drink. I paid and went over to where Chris was standing. He looked at me with his 'Let's get the fuck out of here' eyes.

For once I was not going to argue with him and we downed our drinks and left. We went to the friendly against Gillingham and took up our usual place behind the goal. A number of people said hello and we watched the game. Tubby Tony came and stood in front of us for the second half with the guys from Crystal Palace but apart from an 'All right' that was the highlight of the game.

We left the ground and made our way back to the car. It was Chris who announced that we should go to The Puffin for a nightcap. I agreed and we made our way there. There were now people standing outside drinking. Chris and I made our way to the bar and were again served by Tina. There was no dialogue this time, just a smile, and she presented me with our drinks without me having to ask. Chris and I took them outside and soaked up the atmosphere. We were outside The Puffin and no one was giving us a second look. We took our time to finish our drink and left.

I walked back to the car and punched the air. In the scheme of things it was such a small step but at that moment it felt huge.

We were in The Puffin every lunchtime the following week. We chatted to Tina, and on Wednesday 12 August we met Paul for the first time. We entered the pub as normal at 12.45 and Paul was serving behind the bar. As I approached him he looked me up and down. 'Nice to see you made an effort and dressed up.'

I shit myself. My first thought was, Fuck me, he's good. He can even tell that we've dressed up for the part.

He chuckled. 'Sorry, that's my sense of humour, get used to it.'

Chris, who was obviously thinking along the same lines as me, let out a ridiculous laugh and carried it on for far too long.

Paul stared at him. 'All right, it weren't that fucking funny. What you having?'

I instinctively replied, 'Err, the usual.'

Paul replied, 'Your usual. Well, who's the funny cunt? What is your usual?'

At this point Tina walked into the bar. It was a magical moment. She walked up and kissed him. 'Sorry I'm late, love, Steph's plane was late landing and the fucking traffic from Gatwick…' at which point she turned and looked at me. 'All right, babe? Is he looking after you?'

He looked at me and Chris and then at her. 'Do you know these two scruffy cunts?'

She started to laugh. 'Yeah, and that's no way to talk to your customers. Usual, boys?'

We both nodded. Paul disappeared back behind the bar. We stayed and played pool, had another drink and left. We were both ecstatic with how the afternoon had gone and as we returned to the office we were given some more good news. We had been offered some premises in Hither Green which were huge but empty and well away from prying eyes. They were to be made available to us by November so only a couple of months left at the police station and we were off to somewhere much more discreet.

We went back to The Puffin on the Friday, my birthday. The pub was unusually busy, which threw Chris and me a little when we entered. Paul was sitting at a table in the corner with four blokes talking loudly and having a good time. Tina came over and Chris told her that it was my birthday. She turned and then shouted over to Paul. 'Paul, it's Jim's birthday.'

He raised his arms up. 'So, what do you want me to do? Sing him Happy fucking Birthday?'

The four guys standing with him all let out a loud laugh and I felt like a proper mug.

Tina looked at me and smiled. 'Don't mind him, he's just showing off. He's all heart, really.'

She handed me and Chris our drinks. 'There you go.' And then shouted over to Paul, 'On the house, Happy Birthday.'

Paul looked over and started to laugh. Chris and I made our way over to the pool table and after another drink started to make our way out of the pub. As I started to walk past Paul he put his arm out and stopped me. 'We've got a local band here tonight. If you and your mate are about pop in, seeing as it's your birthday.'

I smiled back. 'Yeah, yeah we may just do that,' and we left.

We walked back to the car and drove back to the office. Both Chris and I were elated at having been asked back by Paul for the evening but this had created a bigger problem for me. I had promised Dawn that I would be back early and would not go out that evening. I rang her and tried to explain the enormity of Paul's invite. She failed to see its significance. What was more important: spending time with her on my birthday or with a bunch of hooligans down a pub in the Old Kent Road? She lost and was not best pleased.

We left the office at six o'clock and made our way down to The Puffin. I had taken to wearing dungarees as I wanted to try and wear something that made me stand out from the crowd, plus they were an easy reference point for the guys who worked the cameras, collating our surveillance evidence for us, at the home and away games. We walked into the pub, which was about a third full, and made our way to the bar. Tina came over and we saw Paul scowling at the end of the bar. I looked at her. 'Is he all right?'

She replied in a hushed tone. 'No, he has got the fucking raving arsehole. Somebody has stolen the new tables and chairs from out the front and he is not best pleased.'

You could tell that he was ready to explode. We got our drinks and made our way to the other side of the bar. As we did so I saw Paul staring out of the front window. He turned to the guy standing with him and pointed out the window. 'There's the pikey fuckers.'

With that he leapt over the bar and grabbed a large baseball bat from under the counter. He then marched out of the pub and started to walk across the road towards three travellers who were getting into a beaten-up old Transit. I instinctively followed him. As I got across the road, Paul was standing bat in hand and face-to-face with one of the travellers. 'Where's my fucking tables?' he asked.

The traveller turned and looked at Paul. 'You talking to me?'

Paul took a step forward. 'Who else would I be talking to? Where are my fucking tables?' This was now about to turn proper ugly.

It was now or never. I moved forward. 'Where's the fucking tables, you pikey cunt?'

Paul turned and looked at me. I had backed him up.

I could see the traveller weighing it up in his head. By this time people had started coming out of the pub and making their way over. The traveller took a step backwards. 'There in the van. Sorry about the mix-up. We thought you had thrown them out.'

He opened the back doors of the van to reveal the tables and chairs. At this point a police car pulled up and the officer in the front passenger seat wound his window down. 'There a problem here?'

I turned and responded, 'No, no problem, officer, we are just taking delivery of some new tables and chairs for the pub.'

He pointed at Paul. 'And the bat?'

'Oh, we needed that to help open the door of the van as the handle was stuck.'

It was clear that the police officer didn't believe a word of it. 'Okay. Have a nice evening.' He wound the window up as they drove off.

Paul turned to the three travellers. 'I suggest that you put that lot back over there where you took them from. Oh, and a word of advice, don't let me see you here again as the next time the only thing that this bat will be helping to open will be your fucking heads.'

Paul turned on his heels and made his way back to the pub. 'Come on, you lot, we have a birthday to celebrate.'

We all walked back into the pub and Paul made his way to behind the bar. It was then that I noticed a woman I hadn't seen before talking with Tina behind the bar. She was, simply put, beautiful. She was tanned, had dark brown eyes and had long dark hair spilling down her back. She looked to be in her mid-twenties and had a gorgeous figure.

Paul handed me a light and lager. 'Happy Birthday.'

I took the drink but my eyes were still transfixed on the girl. Paul grabbed hold of Steph and pulled her over. 'Have you met Steph? She's Tina's sister. Steph meet Jim; Jim meet Steph.'

I stood there unable to speak.

Steph broke the silence. 'Hello, I'm Steph. I hear it's your birthday.'

She knew it was my birthday so Tina and her must have been talking. I replied, 'Thanks. What did Tina tell you?'

She started to laugh. 'No, we weren't talking about you. I just heard Paul wishing you Happy Birthday.'

I felt like a complete fucking prick. 'Yeah, yeah, right, thanks. Can I get you a drink?'

She smiled. 'No, I'm all right, thanks.'

She then turned and made her way back to Tina.

Chris and I stayed in The Puffin for the whole evening. Paul came over and stood with us for a while and we talked about lots of stuff, but football wasn't mentioned at all. I was growing to really like him and his sister-in-law wasn't too bad either. Chris and I watched the band, and left the pub at about half past ten.

We went back to the office and met up with Charlie and Gerry. We all finished our paperwork and shared a birthday drink. Charlie asked me what I wanted for my birthday and Chris answered for me. Steph. He was not wrong.

NINE
DAVE, STU AND MARK

I arrived home at about 1 a.m. to the flat that I was sharing with Dawn in West Norwood. I made as little noise as possible so as not to disturb her. I needn't have bothered. She wasn't there. There was a note on the kitchen table telling me that she had gone to her friends for the weekend and that she would see me on Monday if I could spare the time in my busy schedule. I ripped up the note and threw it in the bin.

I lay in bed thinking about the success we had had that week. We had been accepted at The Puffin and more importantly I had forged a relationship with Paul. It was still early days but we were moving in the right direction. I needed some sleep as we had a big day ahead of us. It was our first away game of the season.

I met up with Chris at King's Cross to take the Football Special up to Middlesbrough. We were both knackered as it had been a heavy week but as we boarded the train the adrenalin soon put paid to any thoughts of sleeping. We pulled out of the station at 10.20 and sat ourselves down in the carriage furthest away from the toilets. As we sat down we were joined by three guys. They introduced themselves as Dave, Stu and Mark. They were all lifelong Millwall fans. Dave was twenty-two years old. He was receding, but had thick scruffy hair at the back and was lanky. He knew everyone and everyone knew him. Stu was the same age, while Mark was a little bit older. He was scruffy but very handy-looking. He did however have the same redeeming feature as his two friends; they all had a massive heart. In south London terminology they would all be described as 'top fellas'.

Dave, Stu and Mark were to become three of the most important people in our lives. None of them were hard-core hooligans. Yes they could have a row, and yes they would not run from a situation that presented itself, but they never once went looking for it. They accepted us for who we were, or at least the image that we portrayed, and one of my biggest regrets was to be that inevitably the friendship ended.

We chatted all the way up to Middlesbrough. Dave knew every hard-core hooligan by name and spoke about the reputation of Millwall. It was difficult to argue with some of his opinions around the media's representation of Millwall. He helped Chris and me to see that not all Millwall supporters were hooligans, although he had to agree that most were up for a row, given the chance, but he also pointed out that the Old Bill played their part in inflaming situations, rather than trying to diffuse them. His comments made us look at the situation from a different perspective rather than the one that we had initially focused on. Chris and I had now become adept at getting our cover story across. We would volunteer information on behalf of each other, therefore making it more fluid and believable. We then would steer the conversation back to football in the hope that we would glean information to satisfy our main objective.

During the train journey we were joined by another of their friends who began to talk openly about the recent arrests. Both Chris and I played ignorant and made out that we didn't know what they were talking about. Dave was quick to explain the whole scenario. The evidence that had been gathered was mainly made up and it would probably not even get to court.

The conversation was beginning to get a little too close for comfort and was worrying. Every time the recent arrests were mentioned there was reference to the evidence being false. Fortunately Chris and I were saved by the conductor announcing that we were soon to be pulling into Middlesbrough.

We managed to steer the conversation back to the forthcoming match and whether we had any chance of winning. Mark made a bold prediction that this was our year and that he could see us getting promotion to the then First Division. Dave pointed out that he had said that every season since he had known him. I held out my hand to Mark. 'Fifty quid we don't get promoted.'

He looked at me and smiled. 'I ain't got fifty quid so I won't take the bet but you watch.'

I felt a little sorry for him. 'Fuck it, I tell you what, if we get promoted I'll give you fifty quid anyway.'

Mark gave me one of his huge toothless grins. 'You're on.'

We all got up and made our way off of the train.

The greeting from the Cleveland police was a little less intimidating than the one we had witnessed upon our arrival into Leeds but our singing was no less intense or vocal. We made our way again to the ground by coach and we and the coaches arrived outside Middlesbrough's Ayresome Park unscathed.

This sadly was not to last. Once we entered the ground the attitude of the police officers in the Millwall section of the crowd could at best be described as hostile. They began wading into the crowd from the start. It created a tense and unnerving atmosphere. Millwall supporters were being dragged from the crowd for what appeared, on the face of it, to be completely arbitrary reasons. As the Millwall team came on to the pitch and made their way over to where we were all standing, the Middlesbrough supporters who were behind a large fence to the side of us started to pelt us with coins. This continued throughout the entire game. Whenever there was retaliation from one or a group of Millwall supporters the police instantly waded in and made arrests. I was appalled and shocked at the way the police officers in our section of the ground were behaving while the officers in the Middlesbrough end stood by as more and more coins and missiles came our way.

Millwall were 1–0 up at half-time, but the coins abated during the second half as the Middlesbrough team began to get a stranglehold on the game, eventually scoring fifteen minutes from full-time. There was a nervous final minutes as Millwall held on until the final whistle.

We were left in the ground until all of the Middlesbrough supporters had left. Chris had taken his programme out of his pocket and was frantically writing stuff down on the back. I stared at him as he put it back into his pocket. We made our way back to the coaches and were escorted back to the station without incident.

On the journey back we sat with Dave, Stu and Mark and spoke about the game. No one apart from me and Chris were surprised at the tactics used by the police. For them it was a normal day out supporting Millwall. We were asked if we were going to the Leyton Orient cup game on the Tuesday and we agreed to meet up at the Old Castle as Dave was not a fan of The Puffin due to (in his words) 'it being populated by mostly nutters'.

We arrived back in the office to a jubilant Gerry and Charlie. They had met up with some guys further down the train from us and had gleaned some information about the cup game with Leyton Orient. Apparently the Chelsea Headhunters were planning on a visit.

However the main topic of conversation that night centred around the tactics that had been employed by the police. It was becoming a worrying trend. First West Yorkshire and now Cleveland, carrying out their duty in a way that was totally unacceptable to all of us. During the discussion Chris pulled out his programme and started to write down on a statement sheet the numbers that he had written down on the back of his programme. 'I have the divisional numbers here of every one of those officers who overstepped the mark and I will be entering this programme as an original exhibit.'

I started to laugh. We had been recruited to infiltrate and collate evidence on suspected football hooligans. But our main evidence on that day was on the conduct and behaviour of the police officers that we were there to help. We all sat down and wrote out our statements on the day's events.

We reflected on our first full week as a team. We all agreed that we had made some great leaps forward but that we still had a very long way to go. I was pleased with how it was going on the work front but the atmosphere at home was becoming an issue. Instead of driving back to an empty flat I went to my mum and dad's for a bit of TLC.

TEN

PHONE CALLS
AND HIRE CARS

I went back to the office on the Tuesday having not returned to my flat. We were joined that day by our office manager Angie. She was to be responsible for looking after us for the next two years and getting all of the evidence, video and written, collated and kept in order. She was always there with a reassuring hand and was happy to talk things through with any of us. She was never shy in coming forward with her opinion and thoughts on any subject. She was also one of the very few police officers to be recognised for her bravery while in the line of duty and had been awarded the Queen's Gallantry Medal for apprehending a suspect who had stabbed and killed a fellow police officer. She was one of the nicest people that I have ever worked with and it was a sad day when I later learnt of her death from a brain haemorrhage two months into her retirement in 2007. She will be sadly missed.

We now had a full team but were still pissing in the wind with regards to any documentary cover apart from the previously mentioned business cards. Chris was constantly speaking with the detective inspector at the FIU, but so far we had not received any update as to when we were likely to see anything to back up our cover stories. We spent the rest of the day bringing Angie up to speed and liaising with the FIU regarding the intel that Charlie and Gerry had picked up regarding the possible visit from the Chelsea Headhunters. Extra police had been called in as a result of the information.

Just after five we walked into the Old Castle and saw Dave, Stu and Mark in the corner. Dave was talking with Tubby Tony and called Chris and me over. Dave greeted us with the same openness as the Saturday. Tubby Tony nodded a hello and made his way over to his mates. Dave was on really good form and asked how our day had gone. I remember making up some bullshit story about a house that we were decorating and not being able to get in because we had the wrong keys.

They asked us questions but it felt that they were only asking out of general interest rather than from any other motives and I was grateful that Chris and I had done so much ground work on our cover story.

We went to the match. Uniformed police were everywhere. Dave, Stu and Mark elected to come and stand with us. Lots of the supporters around us acknowledged us and the banter throughout the game was joyous.

At half-time Tubby Tony came down and let us know that Chelsea had bottled it and that the Headhunters were going to be a no-show for the pre-arranged fight at London Bridge after the match.

As Tubby Tony wandered off, Dave started to laugh, telling us that Tubby Tony would happily fight his own shadow. The game finished. Millwall had played well so we all made our way back to the Old Castle for a celebratory lager which turned into a session. We were finally all ushered out of the pub after a drunken supporter fell over a chair and wiped out a table of drinks.

I came into the office the next day hung over. We spent the day writing up our evidence and liaising with the FIU about the no-show of the Chelsea Headhunters, explaining that it was solid intelligence but that we were unable to force them to come. We then told them that we would be travelling to the next away game at Leicester via a hire car and asked them to sort one for us. They told us we could pick it up on the Friday morning before the match from a reputable hire company who they had dealt with in the past.

That afternoon, I went back to the flat and had a long conversation with Dawn. She was now getting concerned about my drinking and I remember apologising, even though I felt that I had nothing to apologise for, while she went on and on about my change in personality and excessive drinking. She had a point as I was now drinking more than I had ever done. I tried to explain. 'That's part of what they do. Drink.' But I agreed to pay closer attention to my alcohol intake.

I was settling down to watch some television when my home phone rang.

It was Chris. He had just had a very worrying phone call. When I heard this, loads of things started to go through my head. Had the squad been disbanded? Had we been found out? But nothing could have prepared me for what he then told me. He had answered the phone at home... to Dave.

'Dave?' I couldn't believe my ears. 'How the fuck has he got your home telephone number?'

There was a long pause and then Chris answered, 'I must have given it to him. I was pissed and can't remember.'

I started to laugh. 'You gave him your fucking home phone number? What else did you fucking tell him? That you're undercover Old Bill and that he had better watch out? For fuck's sake, Chris.'

Luckily, he had managed to collect his thoughts and told Dave that we would give them a lift to the Leicester game. They arranged to meet at Catford Railway Station at 8.30. Dave had told him that it would only be him and Stu. Chris made his excuses and said that we would see them both on Saturday. Chris was convinced that everyone would now be able to track him down and find out where he lived from his number.

After I finally stopped laughing I reassured him that we would contact the phone company tomorrow and get it changed.

Dawn had listened in on the conversation. 'Did I hear that right? Chris gave his number out to Millwall hooligans?'

I started to laugh as I answered, 'Yep.'

She was not happy: 'What is he playing at? This is getting beyond a joke and the sooner you can get yourself taken off the squad the better for us all.'

I jumped to his defence. 'It's fine. It will all be sorted tomorrow... and well it could have been worse. He could have given our number out.' I'd tried to lighten the mood but she'd failed to see the funny side of it. I could see from the look on her face that I was going to be spending another night on the sofa.

The next morning I left before she got up and went into the office to sort out the previous night's events with Chris. He was hugely embarrassed and bought us all breakfast by way of an apology for his 'moment of madness', as he liked to refer to it. We just took the piss. The phone number change was relatively easily rectified and by mid-morning Chris had a new number and no one was any the wiser. All it did was highlight the need for us to be given proper cover and the ability for our targets to be able to make contact. Chris, now, and with a little more vigour than before, pursued our need for better cover and began to make demands rather than requests. We continued to watch surveillance tapes, trying to identify known hooligans and where they stood and who they associated with. We watched ourselves entering the games and our – well, mainly my – behaviour on the terraces. Chris told me that I needed to restrain myself as the videos would eventually be part of the evidence for the criminal trial. I tried to explain that it was all part of my cover but Chris wasn't having it, and eventually I agreed to play it down.

We had received confirmation that the hire car would be ready for collection at 11 a.m. on the Friday morning. The car had been ordered under the name of Chris Walters and all of the paperwork had been sorted. All we had to do was turn up and collect it. We were a little concerned as to the location of the hire car company as it was just off the Old Kent Road and quite close to Millwall's ground, but we were reassured that all would be fine.

Chris and I got in early on the Friday and drove to the hire car company so that we could pick it up. As we entered the reception area I immediately recognised two targets. They were there like us to get a car to travel up to the Leicester game. We waited at the desk but nobody appeared. At this point another two guys, again who I recognised from our surveillance tapes, joined us in the queue. There were nods of acknowledgement but no conversation. Finally a middle-aged guy in a suit stepped from the office behind the desk. 'Sorry, chaps, bit of a fuck-up. Are any of you lot the Old Bill who need the car for Leicester tomorrow?'

I watched the blood drain from Chris's face.

I immediately answered back, 'What the fuck do the Old Bill want with a hire car?'

The guy in the suit shrugged his shoulders.

One of the guys from the queue turned to us all and said, 'Well, they're obviously going to the Millwall game tomorrow to spy on us.'

The guy behind the counter had now realised that he had fucked up and began to shuffle bits of paper around.

I stared at him. 'Is that right, you giving Old Bill cars to fucking spy on us?'

The guy looked at me and began to shake his head. 'No, no. I don't know. I just work here.'

The guy behind me butted in. 'What fucking car have they got?'

The guy at the counter became more and more flustered and started to rifle through the paperwork. He then pointed out of the window to a bright blue Ford Sierra Sapphire. 'That one.'

I turned to the others in the queue. 'Well, I'm fucked if I'm gonna hire a car from these cunts. They ain't having my fucking details to pass on to the Old Bill. Come on, Chris.' And we walked out.

We were followed by the others. We walked around the corner and made our way over to the car that I was driving at the time, a Citroën 2CV which I had christened Dolly. One of the guys from the queue walked up to us. 'Well at least we know what to look out for tomorrow. See you up there.' We laughed and got in the car and drove back to the station.

Neither of us could believe what had just happened. Chris thanked me for turning the situation around to our advantage but I had never seen him so annoyed. He made me drop him off at Lewisham Police Station as he was going in to have this out with the area commander. I dropped him off and made my way back to the office and recounted the story to the others. Both Charlie and Gerry found the whole thing hilarious but Angie was appalled.

Chris returned a couple of hours later with confirmation that a hire car had now been sorted with a nationally recognised firm and that the car would be dropped off for us. Chris pointed out that the guy at the car hire company was new and that it would not happen again. I told Chris that it definitely wouldn't happen again as in future we would either drive in our own cars and claim the mileage or sort our own hire cars and claim it back on expenses. We were all in agreement: that had been too close for comfort.

By way of an apology the FIU had managed to get us an upgraded car from Hertz and a spanking-new Ford Granada Scorpio turned up outside Brockley Police Station just before five. Charlie was very pissed off as Chris and I got into our 'weekend transport' and headed to The Puffin.

As we pulled up Steph was standing outside with Tina. We got out and said hello to them both.

I smiled at Steph. 'You all right?'

She smiled back 'Yeah, nice car.'

'It's not ours it's a hire car for the Leicester game tomorrow.'

Tina interrupted. 'Oh, Paul's going tomorrow. You should meet up with him. You can look after him for me.'

I laughed. 'Yeah, right. Like he needs fucking looking after.'

Steph then looked directly at me. 'He's the same as all of you. You all need looking after by someone. Who looks after you?'

This was now beginning to get flirty and I was enjoying it. 'My mum,' I said. As everyone laughed I walked into the pub and over to the bar.

It is strange to describe but I felt more at home in The Puffin than I did anywhere else. I got Chris and me a drink and we headed over to the pool table. There was no sign of Paul but there were a number of people that I recognised from the 'band night'. Chris was looking at me and smiling. I asked him what the fuck he was grinning at and he shook his head. 'You know what?'

I responded, 'No, I don't. Enlighten me.'

'You fucking fancy her, don't you?'

I snapped back. 'Of course I fancy her. Who the fuck wouldn't? But I'm happily married with a one-year-old son, if you remember.'

He leant in and put his arm around my shoulder. 'For what it's worth, I think she fancies you.'

I pulled away. As I did the main door opened and Paul entered with another guy slightly shorter but no less menacing in looks. It was his brother Ian. We knew who he was from our intelligence. Paul strode over to us both and introduced us. Paul announced that he was off out with Tina and Steph but that his brother would tell us about the meet tomorrow before the Leicester game and if we were up for it he would see us there.

I watched on as Tina and Steph followed Paul out of the pub. Ian gave us the details. There was to be a pre-arranged fight with the Leicester 'Baby Squad' in a pub car park away from the ground. We were told when and where to meet up.

We stayed in the pub for another hour, then drove back to the office and wrote up our evidence. Chris rang the FIU and passed over all of the information. Gerry and Charlie returned just before eleven. We told them about the pre-arranged fight and we were all elated. We were getting positive intelligence and justifying our role.

We all went home to get some sleep for the big day ahead.

ELEVEN

LEICESTER AWAY

On Saturday, Chris picked me up from my flat in the hire car and we headed off to Catford to pick up Dave and Stu. We didn't know what to expect. Would they be there? What were we to expect on the journey up? More questions about who we were?

We pulled into the station at Catford at 8.20 and there was no sign of them. 8.30 came and went. We looked at each other and as the digital display on the clock in the car changed to 8.40 a train pulled into the station. Chris pointed them out as they crossed the bridge. This was it. We were off to our first 'proper away game', knowing that we were going to be driving into a pre-arranged fight with the Leicester Baby Squad.

I got out and let Dave sit in the front and I sat behind Chris. We had both agreed that until we were 100 per cent comfortable with our targets if Chris was driving I would sit behind him, and vice versa. The reasoning behind this was simple: if our cover was compromised it would be much easier for our targets to attack whichever one of us was driving from behind rather than from the side, plus we could both get out of the car from the same side and back each other up should we ever need to.

Dave and Stu were in good spirits and we told them about meeting with Paul and his brother the night before and the pre-arranged fight with Leicester. They were both up for tagging along, but Dave was quick to point out that they didn't have a lot of choice seeing as Chris was driving. It dawned on me that we had two of our 'targets' in the car. We were driving them to a pre-arranged fight that we had told them about. Not a good move. The idea was that they took us, not us taking them. Yes, they were up for it, but it wasn't their idea. I hoped and prayed that Leicester would fail to appear.

We stopped for breakfast, which Dave insisted on buying, and Chris slipped off to make a phone call to report in to the FIU. We had agreed that we would when travelling away by car try and call in at least once on the way up and once on the way back to let them know that we were safe. Chris came back and out of earshot told me that he had called the FIU but that no one had bothered to answer. So much for the back-up.

We had made good time and as we began to hit the outskirts of Leicester we were well ahead of our schedule for the meeting at noon. We were nearly at the pub and I watched as the digital clock in the car changed to 11.53 and it was then that I began to get a weird sensation in my stomach. I had not had that feeling since school, when I had to have a fight with another pupil at break time in the playground. It reminded me all too vividly of what we were about to drive into.

We rounded the corner and all of us let out an audible gasp. I had never seen so many Old Bill concentrated in one area. They were everywhere. I told Chris to spin around and get the fuck out but it was too late. We were funnelled into the car park and ordered to get out of the car. As we got out I could see a number of Millwall's Bushwackers lined up against the wall and being searched. This was not good. It would be apparent to even the stupidest of hooligans that the police had been passed information regarding the pre-arranged fight. There would be absolutely no reason for them to be at this pub car park without that prior knowledge. I needed to do something so that the finger of blame was not likely to come our way.

All four of us had now been moved away from the car which was now being searched. I prayed to God that Chris hadn't left anything incriminating there and watched on as they continued to search the car. I looked about and surveyed my options. Should I make a scene and get myself arrested or look to a less radical form of action? As the officer searching me moved on to Chris I raised both my arms up and started to sing 'No One Likes Us'.

All the Millwall supporters joined in. I was grabbed by the police officer who had searched me and pushed against the wall and told to shut the fuck up. I tried to carry on singing but was then pushed to the ground and had my arm put up my back. I was hoisted to my feet and told that if I stepped out of line again or opened my fucking mouth it would be shut for me and I would be nicked.

I saw Paul and his brother being led out of the pub and he looked over and smiled. I nodded back to him and shook my head. We were kept in the car park until 2 p.m., at which point we were escorted to the ground. There were already whispers going around that the Old Bill had been tipped off and Chris and I were as vocal in our displeasure as everyone else.

When we entered the ground I saw Paul standing near the front of the pitch talking with people I recognised as being members of the Millwall Bushwackers. Millwall lost the game 1–0. We were again held in the ground until most, if not all, of the Leicester supporters had left and were then escorted from the ground.

The attitude of the Leicestershire officers at the ground was far more what I had expected than the overzealous approach we had experienced on our visits to Leeds and Middlesbrough. Sadly their jovial attitude towards the Millwall supporters was their downfall. The officers escorting us out of the ground were trying to be pleasant until suddenly about 150 hooligans, from what we were later to find out were the Leicester Baby Squad, ran around a corner and charged at the barrier that was being manned by only four police officers. As soon as the Millwall supporters saw Leicester charging towards them it was game on. The police escorting us were immediately swamped by the crowd and the four police officers who were attempting to stop the rival supporters getting at each other were no match for the 200 or so Millwall and the now retreating Leicester. I watched on as three of the four police officers instead of standing their ground as one, turned and ran, leaving their colleague to fend for himself. Sadly his bravery was no match for the ensuing mob and he was swallowed up. I watched on as he was punched and kicked to the ground. I ran past him and could see that he was in a huge amount of distress. He appeared to be limp and lifeless but I was in no position to afford him any help. I was swept up in the crowd and ran with Dave, Stu and Chris after the Leicester supporters. There were a few scuffles until eventually the police restored some sense of order.

It was alarming to watch how a situation had changed from banter to extreme violence. A small part of me began to understand Millwall's need to retaliate. None of this would have happened if the Leicester supporters hadn't charged at the barrier as we were being escorted from the ground and frankly the ones that did get caught by the advancing Millwall got what they deserved. This did not excuse the violence and serious assault that had been carried out on the police officer at the barrier but it may have been avoidable had his colleagues not run away and left him to face the mob on his own.

As we walked back down to where the officer still lay it was obvious to all that he had sustained a major injury. There were paramedics and police officers running back and forth to a waiting ambulance. The mood of the police had also understandably changed. They were quick to carry out arrests and all had their truncheons drawn ready to protect themselves should the need arise.

We eventually got back to the car and Chris drove us back to London. We talked about stopping off at the service station but all thought better of it and we eventually got back into south London for eight o'clock. I needed a drink but Dave and Stu were keen to get home.

We arranged to meet up with them for the Tuesday game at home to Birmingham. I tried to push Dave to meet us at The Puffin but he was having none of it so we agreed to a six o'clock meeting at the Old Castle. After we had dropped Dave and Stu at the station we headed for The Puffin. I was keen to show our face particularly given what had gone on earlier in the day. We pulled up outside The Puffin just before 9 p.m., parked up and walked in. It was absolutely heaving with people. There were new faces that I recognised as being part of the notorious Millwall firm, the Bushwackers. I made my way to the bar. I stood there until eventually I caught Steph's eye. She came over and smiled at me. 'I hear you lost.'

I smiled back at her. 'Yeah we did, in more ways than one. Can I have a light and lager, a lager for Chris and whatever you want.'

'No, I'm all right, I have got one thanks.' She then stared at me for what felt like an eternity until I broke the silence. 'What?'

She replied, 'Nothing, I was just staring. Sorry.'

'That's all right. Stare away. What do you see?'

She looked long and hard but before she could answer a huge arm came around my shoulder. It was Paul, who proceeded to give me a hug. 'What a fucking waste of time that was today.'

Paul then went on to explain that the word was out that the Leicester contingent had leaked the meeting to the Old Bill so as not to lose face when none of them turned up. Both Chris and I were happy to back that theory up as it stopped any speculation as to whether it was a grass or undercover Old Bill who were responsible for the leak.

At this point a guy came over. Marcus was one of the Millwall top boys and he had a fearsome reputation. Paul introduced me as Jim from Wandsworth and Marcus nodded in acknowledgement. At this point Paul turned to go. 'Birmingham Tuesday. Here for five-thirty?'

I nodded. 'Yeah, we'll be here,' and Paul wandered off with Marcus.

I turned to Chris and he gave me the look that meant it was time to go. As we started to make our way out of the pub somebody took hold of my hand. I turned around to see that it was Steph. 'We never finished our chat earlier. Are you off?'

Her hand was warm and I didn't want to let it go. 'Yeah, but I will be about on Tuesday before the Birmingham game. If you're around I might see you then.'

As I tried to take my hand away she resisted. She squeezed my hand and pulled me close to her, put her mouth to my ear and whispered, 'When are you going to ask me out?' She then slid her lips down and kissed me on the cheek.

I was completely thrown. No words would come out until eventually, 'Err, yeah. yeah. Let's talk Tuesday.'

She then turned and started to walk away, only to stop halfway and turn back: 'I'll be here. See you Tuesday.'

Chris grabbed hold of me and we made our way out of the pub. We got into the car and drove off. Chris pulled into a side street. 'Jesus, you lucky fuck, she has asked you out, ain't she? You are fucking in there.'

I wished that it was as simple as that. 'Fuck off, Chris, and take me home, will ya? This is the last thing I fucking need.'

'And she kissed you on the cheek. Come on, what did she say? Did she ask you out?'

'She didn't ask me out, all right? I just want to go home.'

Chris reversed the car back out onto the street and we headed for home. I remained silent until he got me back to my flat and he pulled up on the drive. 'You wait till I tell the others. In with Paul's sister-in-law.'

'Keep your fucking mouth shut, will ya? This has nothing to do with anyone else.'

I got out of the car and headed for my flat. Chris wound his window down and shouted as he drove off, 'I love you, Jim from Wandsworth.'

I couldn't help but laugh and I shouted after him, 'I love you too, Chris.'

I went into my flat and ran a bath. Thankfully, given the night I had just had, Dawn was working a night shift so I was on my own. I filled the bath as high as I dared and got into it. I lay there deep in thought. What the fuck was I going to do?

TWELVE

LEADING THE CHARGE

I woke up shivering in the bath. I got myself out and dried off. It was now 3 a.m. I had been asleep in the bath for two hours and I was shaking from the cold. I remembered what Steph had said to me as I left the pub. I made myself a hot drink and sat deep in thought.

I replayed the conversation with Steph over and over in my head. I was struggling in my head with how I was going to play it. She fancied Jim from Wandsworth. A painter and decorator and wannabee Millwall football hooligan. Would she still be wanting to go out for a drink if she knew that I was a Judas copper who was there to get information on her brother in-law so that he could be arrested and sent to prison? I tried to tell myself that she had only asked me out for a drink but I knew I was kidding myself. It wasn't the being asked out for a drink that scared me but where it would lead to. The feelings I had felt just holding her hand were ones that I had not experienced in a very long time. She was attractive, intelligent, fun, but the thing that got me the most was her smell. She just smelt, well, right. I could justify a relationship with her to myself. But the bigger question was: was it right or fair to do so? I sat staring out of the window until eventually tiredness overcame me and I fell asleep.

I woke back up just before 7 a.m. Dawn had not returned from her night shift and I was in no state to be having any kind of conversation with her so I left a note telling her that I had gone into work, got dressed and drove into the office. I sat and read through all the evidence that we had collated to date and then wrote up my statement from Saturday.

I spent the rest of Sunday and Monday deep in thought. Dawn tried her best to get to the bottom of what was troubling me but in the end gave up. I woke up late on the Tuesday morning and made my way to the office. Gerry looked at me as I walked in and started to laugh. 'Fucking hell, Jim, you look like I feel. You all right?'

Chris and Charlie looked up from their desks. Charlie was less subtle. 'So you gonna be having it off with the bird from the pub?'

I threw a look to Chris. 'What are you going on about?'

Charlie had a big grin on his face. 'Well, Chris was saying that you're in with that bird from the pub and that she was whispering in your ear. What she say?'

I winked at Charlie. 'She said that she thought Chris was a prick and that he has got a fucking big mouth.'

They all laughed, but it seemed that they all could tell that I was not in the mood to talk about it.

We spent the rest of the day collating all the evidence from the Leicester game. We discussed what had been done with the information that we had passed to the FIU and the potential harm that it could have done to our already sketchy backgrounds and cover. We agreed to carefully monitor any information that we passed across from now on. The way in which the Leicestershire Police had chosen to use the intelligence had been to saturate the area with extra police rather than have the units parked up close by so that if any disorder did occur they could react accordingly. We knew that we could not continually pass intelligence across if the only course of action was to flood the area with Old Bill.

We were contacted in the afternoon by the CID from Leicester who informed us that they had a picture of the Millwall supporter who had carried out the serious assault on the police officer at the barrier. We had already made enquiries as to his condition and had been told that he had sustained a heavy concussion and a broken jaw but that he was on the mend. He had been able, from handheld video evidence, to pick out the man who had assaulted him first and broken his jaw. Our focus then turned to the game against Birmingham that night. We had been informed by the FIU earlier in the day that Birmingham were bringing a fair amount of support, including a large number of their hooligan element, the Zulus. Chris thought that we should head for The Puffin for a quick drink before we met up with Dave, Stu and Mark. I – reluctantly for once – agreed. I had never been so nervous. The constant threat of danger or being recognised or accused of being Old Bill was nothing as to how I was feeling about how I would react when I saw Steph again.

At 5 p.m. we got into Dolly and headed for The Puffin. Once we were on our own I told Chris that I did not take kindly to him telling the others about Steph. He couldn't see the problem and said that we were a team and that we needed to share all our information with each other. I let him know that I would now adopt the same attitude and that when he did something that he didn't want broadcast to the others that it would now be fair game.

I pulled up outside of the pub and Chris and I entered The Puffin. It was already busy and Paul was serving behind the bar. There was no sign of Steph or Tina and I was a little relieved. I went to the bar and Paul came over. He told us that the Birmingham Zulus had put the word out that they were going to take over a Millwall pub and that he hoped for their sake that they didn't come here.

Paul got us our drinks and Chris asked him where Steph and Tina were. I threw him a look as Paul told us that he had sent them off to their mum's as he didn't want them about just in case Birmingham appeared unannounced.

We drank up and slipped out of the pub then headed for the Old Castle to meet up with our targets. We walked across the New Cross Road and were greeted outside by Dave, Stu and Mark. Dave had already got the drinks in and we started talking about the Leicester game. Mark apologised for not coming but said that Dave and Stu had told him all about the Old Bill outside the pub before the game and how I had nearly got nicked for singing. Chris chipped in with, 'Yeah, well, I'm not surprised. Have you heard Jim sing?'

I went to cuff him about the head, which made the group around us laugh. I turned away to avoid his glare and as I did so I saw a coach stop at a zebra crossing about a hundred yards up from the pub. It pulled off slowly and I carried on watching it as it pulled alongside the pub. There didn't appear to be anyone on the coach until just as it moved away a head popped up and looked out of the window. I was holding my pint glass and walked from the patio onto the pavement. As I got to the pavement I could see people beginning to appear in the side windows. I began to walk down the pavement and onto the road. I then saw four black guys appear in the back window of the coach and start to give me the V sign. I called to Chris and started to jog down the road after the coach. The traffic cleared and the coach started to move away. I could see more and more people appearing at the windows and give me the wanker sign. It was now obvious to me that the coach was carrying the Birmingham Zulus and that they were heading for The Puffin. I was now running to catch the coach up. As it neared The Puffin a car reversed out onto the road causing it to stop. It was then that I heard the huge roar from behind me. I turned around and realised that the whole pub was following me. There must have been more than a hundred people. I caught up with the coach and was immediately joined by the mob. At this point there was another large roar as I saw people begin to start piling out of The Puffin. I saw Paul's brother Ian throw a bottle at the coach window and the supporters on the bus started to duck down behind the side and back windows. The coach was then pelted with bottles, glasses, and at one point a large traffic cone smashed into the side door window. I watched on, caught up in the excitement. I saw Paul, Tubby Tony, a guy called Gary, Marcus and a large number of the Millwall Bushwackers trying to force open the door to the coach. There were no signs of any retaliation from the Birmingham Zulus until suddenly two black guys bravely appeared on the back seat of the coach and threw some bottles from the now smashed back window at the Millwall below.

Every window on the coach was now in and there was glass everywhere. Some of Millwall were trying to clamber up the side of the coach and get at Birmingham, and I ran over to where Paul was and tried to help force open the door. We could all hear the sirens coming and as they got louder more and more people ran over to the coach. Suddenly the coach started to rock and we could see that a large number of Millwall on the back corner had started to try and push the coach over. We left the door and joined in. Within seconds the coach was rocking violently from side to side as about a hundred Millwall worked in unison. The police turned up en masse just in time. I am certain that if they had been thirty seconds longer the coach would have been on its side. We ran back from the coach as the police waded in with their truncheons. I managed to duck out of the way as a truncheon skimmed over the top of my head.

We were now all on the pavement as somebody started up the anthem. I stood there with Paul and the others and sang 'No One Likes Us' for all I was worth. The police seemed happy to let us sing as long as we didn't stray from off the pavement. It was proper funny as the Birmingham Zulus popped up into view one by one, like meerkats. The police had now got the car removed that was blocking the coach, and as the coach was escorted away minus its windows with the Birmingham still on board we all raised our hands and waved them goodbye. They were to be escorted from the coaches further on down the road as the police erected a temporary cordon.

Paul grabbed hold of me and announced that drinks were on him and we all piled into The Puffin. I went straight up to the bar and was handed a light and lager. I was soon joined by Chris and the others. People who I recognised from the surveillance tapes started coming up to me and patting me on the back for leading the charge from the Old Castle. I had gained a reputation for myself from that incident and more and more people started to ask about us and who we were and it was a relief to finally get out of the pub and go to the ground.

We stood in our usual place and Tubby Tony came down and patted me on the back. 'Fucking quality, Jim. They fucking shit themselves.'

I was chuffed he had called me Jim and I was being singled out for praise. Our credibility had certainly moved us up a few rungs of the ladder.

In the match, Birmingham scored first and after the Leicester game we were all a bit on edge but we needn't have worried. We eventually won 3–1 and I left the ground as happy as when I entered. We all agreed to go for a drink and for once Dave was up for popping into The Puffin. As we rounded the corner and entered the pub some of the Bushwackers that I had spoken to earlier, Stan, Gary and some others, were standing outside talking to Marcus. As I walked past Marcus nodded at me and said hello. I nodded back and we went into the pub. It was rammed and after we got to the bar I saw Paul. He came over and bought us all a drink. He then gave me one of his stares. 'What the fuck were you doing leading a charge from the Old Castle?'

It went quiet around us and I stared back. 'Well I saw 'em and thought they were gonna ambush your pub.'

He smiled. 'Yeah, but what you doing leading a charge from the Old Castle? We not good enough for you in here?'

I breathed a sigh of relief. 'No, no, we were meeting Dave and the others there and—'

He leant over the bar and grabbed hold of me around the head and pulled me in to him. 'Well in future meet them here. This is your pub, not up there with those mugs.' He then put his arm around my shoulder. 'We fucking let them Zulu cunts have it today, son. You going to Bradford on Saturday?'

I decided to try and play it cool. 'I don't know. It's up to Chris.'

Paul turned to Chris. 'Well, Chris, we gonna see you there?'

Chris was chuffed. 'Yeah, yeah we'll be there.'

Paul smiled. 'Blinding. See you in the week and I'll let you know where we are all meeting.'

We nodded and Paul turned and left. Dave, Stu and Mark said that they weren't up for the Bradford game as they were planning to go to the Man City game away in a fortnight. I assured them that we would be definitely up for that and that we would see them at the Ipswich game the following Saturday. Dave, Stu and Mark then decided to leave and as Dave left he told Chris that he would call him in the week. Chris just nodded and they left. Chris and I stayed for another drink and then left and went back to the office.

It had been a good night for us, but Gerry and Charlie's night had not been as successful. Charlie had spotted someone that he had arrested before in the crowd standing in front of him, resulting in them both having to stand in a different section of the crowd than their targets. But they had got some good evidence. Apparently some geezer in dungarees and a hooded top had led a charge from the Old Castle and they had spent the last hour wondering who that might be. I explained that it wasn't a charge as such and that I was at first just curious as to where the coach was going and that it just went on from there. Both Gerry and Charlie could see the funny side of it; Chris was quick to back up my side of the story but pointed out that we would need to be careful how we presented our written evidence on that one.

At this point Charlie then turned and looked at me. 'Well, how was everything else?'

For a moment I had no idea what he was going on about and then the penny dropped. He was asking about Steph. I hadn't given her a moment's thought since leaving The Puffin to meet up with Dave, Stu and Mark. 'I don't know, she wasn't there. She had gone to her mum's.'

With that I got up and left. I got into Dolly and headed for home. It had been a good day. I had boosted our credibility and reputation by unwittingly leading the charge down the New Cross Road but I still had one burning question to sort.

What do I do about Steph?

THIRTEEN

MANCHESTER CITY COVERTS

We were all back in the office early the next day to write up our evidence from the night before. It was not easy trying to write down the reasoning behind leading a charge down the New Cross Road without it looking as if the charge and damage to the coach had been caused by me. I justified it in as much that I needed to be at the front to see what was going on but realised that under cross-examination when the evidence was submitted for trial I was going to be questioned at length as to whether my actions had caused the trouble. I stood firm in the belief that I had done the right thing and that I would worry about it when and if it was raised. Chris said that he would struggle to support my interpretation of events in court as he was convinced that they were a contributory factor to the damage to the coach. I pointed out that regardless of whether I led the charge or not the likely outcome would have been the same and I didn't see him complaining when Paul and everyone else were patting us on the back and buying us drinks.

The next couple of weeks were, to our dismay, relatively quiet. We had an uneventful away game to Bradford (this time by train) and we popped into The Puffin now and then, but Paul, Tina and Steph had disappeared to Spain and we saw few faces that we recognised. It had all gone strangely quiet.

So while we bided our time we concentrated on paperwork and tried to get some headway with our requests for cover, with only a brief interlude to help Leicester CID identify the suspect who had been responsible for the assault on the police officer.

Charlie and Gerry were struggling to get new information too and were becoming paranoid about the chance of being sussed as Old Bill. I tried to reassure them that it would get better but they were in that place where only a successful day or game was going to help. We all agreed to meet up at Gerry's house on the Sunday for a spot of lunch.

Dawn was keen to come to Gerry's so we set off late morning. When we arrived Charlie and Chris were already there as was Angie with her husband. Chris had a new girlfriend, Laura, but Charlie was on his own. Gerry had also invited Guy who had helped me collate Millwall's history at the start of the operation. We spent the afternoon putting the world to rights and drinking late into the evening. We were all having a great time.

Chris's girlfriend Laura seemed a nice enough girl. At one point she got us all on the floor and made us cross our legs while she lit some incense and got us all to breathe as one. We all struggled not to burst out laughing. Chris, bless him, was embracing the whole thing, although we all thought her hairy armpits were almost a step too far.

We were all drunk by the time we left apart from Dawn. She had been ready to go at five o'clock but I was having a good time and we didn't leave until gone eight. On the journey home she asked questions about whether I was drawn to have conversations with women.

I was quick to point out that none of my targets were women, but I did feel a pang of guilt regarding Steph. Even so, I wasn't happy with Dawn implying that I was unfaithful. For fuck's sake, Susan was Gerry's wife and Laura was Chris's girlfriend. It wasn't like I was trying to shag them over the Wendy house.

We pulled up at the traffic lights at the bottom of our hill and I got out of the car, announcing that I was going to the pub for a beer and to chat up anyone who was up for it. She didn't wait around and disappeared up the hill towards our flat. I went into the pub and drank on my own until the bell rang for last orders. I stumbled home and eventually got into the flat after five or six attempts with my front door key. As I entered the lounge I saw the duvet and pillow already laid out on the couch.

I woke up on the Monday, late, with a thumping hangover. Dawn had already left and I had the flat to myself for the day. I spent most of it in bed. Dawn came back later in the day and I apologised for storming out of the car and told her that I knew my behaviour was unacceptable. She was keen to point out that we were all drinking far too much and that it appeared that we were all on a death wish. I thought that was a little overdramatic but she had a point about the drinking. I told her that I would confine drinking to match days and that was it. I got off the sofa that night. I went into the office on the Tuesday refreshed and keen to get on with the job at hand.

In the middle of September, earlier than expected, we moved to our offices at Hither Green. On our last day in Brockley, while we packed up our stuff, Chris took a call from the Greater Manchester Police and was informed that they had their own covert team who were currently infiltrating Manchester City's hooligan element, the Guvnors, and that they were keen to meet up. Chris agreed to meet with them, hopefully before the Man City game on the 16 September.

We met up with Dave and Stu – Mark was working again – and went to the Ipswich game. We stood in our usual place behind the goal and after our 2–1 win headed back to The Puffin for an after-match drink. The pub was back to normal. It was packed and people were standing outside. I made my way to the bar and was served by an older guy but there was still no sign of Paul and the girls. We had a couple of beers and left, agreeing to meet with Dave and Stu for the Man City away game. We would be getting the train so would see them at Euston for 11 a.m. Dave mentioned to Chris that he had tried calling him but that his number was unobtainable and Chris managed to brush it off with an excuse about an ex-bird and having to change his number, which he couldn't remember off the top of his head. We went back to the office and both decided that our cover was now a priority and that if it wasn't sorted before the next game we would refuse to go to any more games until it was.

I went home for the weekend and went with Dawn to look at a house that she was thinking of buying in Catford as an investment. She wanted to buy it, do it up, and then sell it on. It was good value but it needed a lot of work. I said that most of the work apart from the roof was cosmetic. I could be there most of the time and Chris and I would have the perfect cover. She was reluctant at first but once I explained to her the financial benefits – I could do the refurbishment in work time with full permission as it added to our cover story – she agreed. I then told Chris my idea. He was up for it but said that he wasn't going to be spending much time there with me. Gerry was keen to help as it would back up his cover as a builder and he had worked as a painter and decorator while his application for the police was completed after school. We finally had some credible cover, albeit manufactured by ourselves, but it was a start.

The new offices in Hither Green were enormous and they were all for us. We had enough room to have an entire floor to ourselves and after a day's hard work we had the office sorted. Angie had her own sectioned-off area and we had a video room and a room for our 'Rogues gallery', where we put up all the pictures of our targets and their known associates. We had a huge commercial kitchen and a massive open-plan office that ran the whole of the second floor. Over the coming months, this room became our two-a-side football pitch – until one of us hit one of the fluorescent ceiling lights so hard it fell down and cut Chris's head open and he ended up in casualty.

We were still struggling with our cover but had some good news from the new FIU governor, a detective inspector who was called Robbie, and his sidekick Lawrence, the detective sergeant. Lawrence had been in charge of the recent West Ham covert team and headed up the arrests of members of the infamous ICF. He promised that he would make it his priority and that we would be sorted one way or the other before the month was out. Lawrence knew only too well what we were going through and that the lack of cover was totally unacceptable. He planned to speak with the specialist officers at SO10, the Metropolitan Police's specialist covert department. We were grateful to now have them on board as part of the team moving forward.

Chris and I went to The Puffin on the Monday evening and it was then that we learnt that Paul was due back later that night from Spain. Everyone was getting the 12.30 out of Euston on Tuesday and were meeting in The Carriage pub near the station.

The next day we were all in well before eight and we went for breakfast at the local cafe. It was such a relief to be away from Brockley and we all felt far more relaxed and that our needs were now being addressed. We had new offices and the promise of proper cover. Chris told us that he had spoken to the FIU first thing and had made them aware of the meeting at the pub but had been assured that there would be no overreaction this time round and that they would be dealing with the information in a more stand-off way.

Well, only time would tell, and Chris and I made our way to Euston and entered The Carriage just after 11 a.m. As I walked in I saw Paul holding court at the bar with his brother and his 'firm'. I was really pleased to see him and whereas before I had always been reluctant to make the first move, I bowled over to him. He seemed as pleased to see me as I was him. He gave me a huge hug and asked if I had been behaving myself while he had been away.

I smiled. 'Of course, but today may be a different matter.'

He shook his head. 'Fucking Mancs will be a no-show, they have no fucking arsehole, you mark my words, Jim. They are all fucking talk.'

I said that I would catch him later. I went to the bar and had a beer with Chris. We finished up and made our way to Euston. As we rounded the corner to the station we were greeted by a group of Old Bill. They were fucking everywhere. So much for the stand-off approach. They were stopping anyone buying tickets for Manchester who didn't have a legitimate reason for travel, which excluded going to watch the Millwall game. But all was not lost as they had kindly laid us on a Football Special at a special rate of £40 return. How nice of them.

Chris had the raving arsehole and he disappeared off to 'make a call'. As I was waiting for him I was joined by Dave, Stu and Mark, who had managed to get a day off work. We made our way to the temporary ticket booth that the station had erected for the sale of the Football Special tickets. I bought mine and Chris's, who eventually returned a little red in the face. Once out of earshot of the others he told me that he had rung FIU who had assured him that none of this was their doing and that it was the British Transport Police's idea of 'containment'. We got on the train, which for once had working toilets, and the journey to Manchester was actually quite relaxed. I told Dave that we may have a job in Catford coming up and that we could maybe see him and the others for breakfast or a beer after work. They were all up for that.

We got into Manchester and were escorted to the game in coaches with no incidents at all. The game was a complete wash-out and we lost 4–0. We were kept in the ground until most of the Man City fans had left and were escorted to our coaches and put back on the train home with no incidents. We travelled back on the train with Dave, Stu and Mark and slept most of the way back.

I bumped into Paul as we were getting off the train. 'Told you, Jim. Mancs all fucking mouth. See you in the week.'

I nodded and Chris and I made our excuses with the others and left. We were going to be travelling to Sheffield away on the Saturday alone. On the way back we decided that we would travel to Sheffield by car and would pay for it ourselves if we had to. I had had enough of trains to last me a lifetime. We got back to the office late and Charlie and Gerry eventually appeared an hour later. They had had a good day meeting up with their targets and getting invited back to a pub in Bermondsey for a few beers. They were elated that they had managed to seal a good bond with their targets on the journey up and back on the train. Their targets were not going to the Sheffield game so we all decided that we would travel up together.

On the Thursday we were again contacted by the Man City coverts and we confirmed that we would meet up with them after the game on the Saturday evening at a service station just outside of Sheffield. The FIU agreed to sort us out a hire car and another Granada Scorpio was delivered on the Friday night. After a speedy trip up north, we spoke with Angie who informed us that Millwall were not expecting any more than a hundred supporters to attend the game. We all decided to leave it until the last minute before we decided whether or not to enter the ground. We rang again at 2.50 from a call box just away from the ground and Angie confirmed the news that only forty supporters had shown up. We all agreed that it was pointless going to the match. We drove out of Sheffield and found a village pub that was serving late lunch and parked ourselves up in there and had a few beers. We watched the results show on the telly in the pub and it was good news: we had beaten Sheffield United 2–1. We had another round of drinks to celebrate and eventually left to meet the Manchester City covert team at the service station as arranged.

We were half an hour early. At exactly 7 p.m. two old Sierras and a beaten-up van drove into the car park and a group of guys got out and made their way into the service station. Chris had agreed to meet the head of their team outside the main entrance. He had been told that he would be easy to spot. They were, and did they look the part. They were head to toe in all the best clothing. The guy who was obviously in charge was wearing a long Aquascutum mac while the others were in Ellesse, Burberry and Stone Island. They were all wearing the latest retro trainers, apart from the guy in the mac who was in a really smart pair of suede desert boots.

Standing in the doorway, resplendent in his mac, was, as I was to come to appreciate, one of the most influential and significant people that I have had the pleasure of knowing and working with: Rory. He was the head of Greater Manchester's elite covert and undercover operations. He was at the top of his game, having worked in Ireland and America infiltrating and dealing with all manner of organised crime, and was responsible for a number of high-profile arrests and convictions of so-called 'untouchable criminals'. To meet him you would never know. He was unassuming and quiet although he had that air of authority.

He introduced himself to us as Rory and we made our way to the bar for a drink. He was quick to compliment Gerry and me on how we seemed to have embraced our roles and that we certainly looked the part. Chris asked him how we could help. He laughed and said that he didn't need any help but that as we were all in this together that he thought it would be sensible to meet up and compare strategies. He then talked us through what they were doing and what they were hoping to achieve.

The level of support that they were being afforded was mind-blowing compared with what we had been given so far. They all had full and documented cover stories with fake IDs, including passports and driving licences, to back it up. They had accommodation addresses and redirection on phones to assist with their contact with their targets. They had a flat and vehicles that were also registered in their false names. They had criminal records, the list went on. We had a fucking hire car that was probably hired under the name of the Metropolitan Police and a business card with nothing on it but our name and a picture of a paint pot and brush.

Far from laughing, Rory was incensed at our lack of cover and couldn't believe that we had managed to last as long as we had. We told him that we had been trying for the last six months to be taken seriously and that the cover was paramount to not only our safety but also our credibility with our targets moving forward. He assured us that he would take it upon himself to sort it out and that we would have everything that his team had in place within the next two weeks. If the Metropolitan Police didn't sort it, he assured us, he would do so himself. It was such a relief to have him on our side.

We finished up our drinks and went to the car park to check out their vehicles. They were another revelation. This was 1987 but the level of equipment in the cars and van were way ahead of their time. They had listening devices and the ability to tape all of their conversations inside and outside of the car to a range of about fifty metres. They had a secret compartment in the van where an officer could hide and listen and tape conversations, inside the van and outside it too. They had high-tech video surveillance and a high-speed camera on trial that could film people as they drove past them on the street at speeds of up to 50mph.

It was soul-destroying. Although it wasn't all bad; after all they may have the van but we had our secret weapon: Dolly, my Citroën 2CV. 'Hey, we could take the seats out of the back at any time should any of our targets decide that they needed them for an impromptu picnic.'

Everyone laughed but the situation that we found ourselves in was far from funny. We said our goodbyes to Rory and his team and got back into our hire car. We had the raging arsehole and it was all we talked about on the way back to London. We had been made to look like a bunch of mugs. Looking at the resources and money that was being thrown at the Manchester operation we began to question whether or not what we were doing was being taken seriously at all. As Rory had pointed out, Millwall had a far more fearsome reputation than Manchester, so on the strength of that it seemed logical that we should be afforded every resource.

We got back to the office, had a beer and decided on our next course of action. One thing we were all agreed on. If we didn't get what we wanted and quickly they could shove the operation up their arse.

FOURTEEN

CONVINCING COVER

When I came into the office on Monday, Chris had already written down a list of essential requests: false IDs, including driving licences and passports; a dedicated phone line for both teams with an answer phone; addresses for our businesses; bank accounts; our vehicles to be registered in our cover names; pagers so that we could have a point of contact with our targets; criminal records and the ability to hire cars or be provided with vehicles for away travel. That was our list. We all agreed that our requests seemed reasonable and that if we did not get a positive reaction we would look to the alternatives. We could not carry on the way we were and meeting with the Manchester covert team, although a little embarrassing, could only help our cause.

The next day, I came into the office much later than the others as I had taken Dawn to her solicitor's to sign the contract for the house in Catford. I entered the office around 10.30 and everyone was in a joyous mood. All of our demands were to be met and we would have all that we had requested by the Friday. We were now to report to the head of SO10, a guy named Bernard who we would meet on Friday, and he would ensure that our requests would be given priority.

It was obvious that we were only getting what we needed because Rory, a senior officer who was held in the highest of regard, had intervened on our behalf. But we weren't complaining. I was relieved that we had not had to threaten to leave or disband the squad if our demands were not met. I was having far too good a time to be contemplating that.

The FIU got in touch with us to say that they had intelligence that the Chelsea Headhunters were planning an ambush outside the ground at QPR tomorrow. We were a little taken aback. We told them that it was news to us but that if their source was reliable then they should take whatever action they thought necessary.

On Wednesday we spent much of the day in the office preparing our cover for our false documentation, including criminal records. Gerry gave himself a couple of arrests for burglary and car theft. Charlie was a little more sophisticated and had one for cheque fraud and a charge of theft. Chris decided on just the one charge for stealing a car. I went to town. I had a couple of charges as a juvenile, one for stealing a car and the other for assault. As an adult I had a charge for grievous bodily harm and another for assault on a police officer, for which I received a suspended sentence. These were all to be processed and we would have our CRO (Criminal Records Office) numbers by the following week. Once the false records were set up if we were ever stopped and asked for our names and date of births the police computer would list our fictitious criminal record, therefore backing the cover story about our previous convictions.

We all set off at about 4 p.m. for the QPR League Cup game and made our way over to west London. We had agreed to meet up with Dave, Stu and Mark at Sloane Square where we would have a beer and then make our way to the ground. We got to Sloane Square just before 5.30 and it was rammed with Millwall. Dave, Stu and Mark appeared and Dave announced that we should go over our way, Wandsworth, for a drink after the game. This was a potential fuck-up. We had always relied on the fact that we would drink in and around Millwall; it never occurred to us that our targets might want to venture out our way. I played it down and said let's see what's happening after the game and left that decision for later.

We got to Loftus Road, QPR's ground, and made it into the ground without any trouble. Just before half-time Tubby Tony made his way over. He pulled me aside. 'Chelsea are fucking here and it's gonna go off at half-time. Your lot with us?'

I nodded. 'What do you think? Where do you want us?'

Tony pointed down to the line of police that separated the QPR fans and Millwall. I went back to Chris and let him know what was on the cards. He disappeared off, announcing that he needed a piss. By the time he got back a large group of Millwall had already charged at the Old Bill and broken through. The ferocity of the charge shocked everyone around us and we surged down to the front. There were running battles between Millwall and the police as the QPR and Chelsea supporters had all retired to behind a second police line. The disorder lasted throughout the half-time break and the start of the second half was delayed until eventually the police regained control.

We then watched on as Millwall lost 2–1. As the game was ending, Tubby Tony came over and announced that everyone was heading for Shepherd's Bush as a bunch of Chelsea had stormed some Millwall on the way to the ground and he and the others were up for revenge. A group of about 150 of us headed for Shepherd's Bush. We arrived but there was no sign of any Chelsea. It was late and fortunately Dave, Stu and Mark decided against a trip back to Wandsworth. We let them leave and went to a local pub for a drink. It was absolutely full of QPR and Chris and I spent the entire time waiting to be sussed as Millwall but no one paid us any attention.

On our way back to Hither Green we both agreed that we had not thought the Wandsworth thing through properly. We needed to find a pub in Wandsworth and make it our local or change our cover story. We did both. We decided that Chris would announce that he was now living in Bromley and we would find a pub in Wandsworth and make it into a local. It would be a good back-up should we ever get the question asked again.

I drove into the office on the Friday excited about the meeting we were going to have with Bernard. Like Rory, he had an awesome reputation and had been working as a covert officer for as long as anyone could remember. He had started working the clubs in the West End and was one of the first police officers to specialise in covert operations. He was now responsible for the recruiting and training of all undercover officers and we were to be taken under his wing and given his full support and backing.

I was a little confused at first as I had been led to believe when we started the operation that it was to be led from Scotland Yard but as Chris explained it was all down to budgets and who paid. Our operation and its costs were being borne at area level and that meant that we were responsible to the area commander. The funding would remain at area level but we were now to be afforded all the specialist help and assistance that SO10 could provide. None of us were complaining too loudly. We didn't care who was responsible for the budget; all we wanted was some decent support and cover.

We were all in the office early. Chris had bowled up suited and booted while the rest of us looked like what we were employed to be: Millwall hooligans. Bernard arrived at the office with Robbie and Lawrence and introduced himself. He was a bear of a man and softly spoken. He talked us through what we were trying to achieve and apologised about the lack of support that we had received to date.

He handed us our driving licences and copies of our criminal records. We had log books for our cars and a dedicated number that we could call so that any further vehicles that we purchased could be dealt with in the same way. We were each given bank cards and a paying-in book and Gerry and I were also given a benefit book detailing that we were both receiving unemployment benefit. It was like Christmas. We were also to be given a pager for each team. Chris took ours and Gerry took the one for him and Charlie.

I smiled to myself as I looked at my new life splayed out in front of me on my desk. Jim Ford, the painter and decorator from Wandsworth, was now real and tangible; it was a strange feeling. Although I had been living with my new identity and cover story for nearly six months the sight of driving licences and criminal records made it all the more believable. I wanted to get out and among my targets and show off, sad but true.

I left the office with Gerry early evening and made my way over to Belvedere. There was a small van advertised in the local paper that looked as if it might suit me and Chris. Dolly was good for a laugh but she wasn't your average football hooligan's mode of transport. The van was perfect. It was a small Honda Acty, bright yellow in colour, with a large box on the back. Gerry and I took it for a test drive and we both agreed that it would fit the bill. It was a great addition to our cover and it would come in handy getting materials to the house in Catford, which Dawn was about to complete the purchase on.

My relationship with Chris was not without its challenges. His attitude over the coach incident with Birmingham had left a bit of a bad taste. It wasn't that he wasn't willing to support my version of events – he had a valid point about me leading the charge – it was more to do with the fact that he seemed willing to bask in our successes but not prepared to go the extra mile to get them.

It also didn't help that he was nominally in charge. There is an unwritten rule in undercover work that rank stays in the office and when you are on the ground you're equal. Chris was starting to exert his authority. In the office that was okay but I was beginning to feel that out on the ground he was trying to take charge and make decisions about what we could do.

The last straw finally came when we attended the Saturday game on 26 September 1987 against West Bromwich Albion. Chris had been in a foul mood all day on the Friday. Laura and he had split up. I had got into the office at ten o'clock the next day and Chris was already in. Gerry turned up at 10.30 and was soon followed in the door by Charlie. Chris then announced that both Gerry and Charlie were not to book on at ten, as was the norm for a Saturday home game, but that they were to show the time that they actually arrived. Gerry was quick to respond. 'Fuck off, Chris. Did you get out the wrong side of the bed?'

Chris jumped to his feet and shouted at the three of us: 'I am in fucking charge here and I have had enough of the three of you not giving me the respect that my rank deserves. From now on everything is to go through me. I am the sergeant here and I am not going to be left carrying the can for you lot.' It was a complete overreaction and took us all by surprise.

Charlie was quick to react: 'Chris, what's your fucking problem?'

Chris started to walk towards the door. 'You. All of you are my fucking problem. I have had enough and from now on what I say goes. Starting today. As of now when you book on I want to see the correct time on your time sheets not a time that suits you.' He stormed out of the office. We all looked at each other and started to laugh.

Charlie got up and walked over to his time sheet. 'Right. Eight o'clock start,' he said, before turning to Gerry. 'Shall I show you the same?'

Gerry nodded. The atmosphere was now tense and after about five minutes Chris returned to the office. He walked straight over to the time sheets. As he read what Charlie had written he erupted. 'Eight o'clock. Eight o'fucking clock. You both didn't show here until well after ten. This is exactly what I am talking about. This is a fraudulent act and unless you change it I will be taking it up with senior management.'

Charlie grabbed his coat and started to make his way to the door. 'I ain't changing nothing. If you have a problem with what I've written then I suggest you take it up with the guvnor.'

'I will,' Chris answered. 'And, I will note that I was here when you both swanned in at well after ten.'

Gerry was now also making his way out. 'If you wanna know, Chris, we met with our targets in Bermondsey at eight this morning for breakfast.'

'I don't believe you,' Chris interrupted.

Charlie spun around and marched up to confront him. Chris stood his ground, but it was touch and go as to what Charlie was going to do. He stared straight at Chris as he spoke: 'Fucking hell, you're out of order here. We had breakfast with our targets and we're off out now. And as for respecting your rank? In this line of work respect is earned. See you later, Jimbo.' With that, they both left. I sat looking at Chris, gobsmacked at his reaction but for once just kept my mouth shut. It was one of only two occasions I ever saw Charlie lose his rag.

We eventually left the office at about midday and made our way to The Puffin. We had no conversation whatsoever on the way and as I parked up the van he got out and made his way over to Dave, Stu and Mark, who were already outside. They had got us a drink, which Chris downed in one, and then he went off to get another one. He came back out with some more drinks and had finished his second pint while all of us were still halfway through our first. As he disappeared off to the bar for another round I shuffled in behind him. 'Chris, for fuck's sake, will you calm the fuck down?' He turned and stared back at me.

'Fuck off.' He pointed at Steph who was behind the bar. 'Why don't you go and chat to your bird?'

I grabbed hold of him and pulled him towards me and whispered into his ear, 'She ain't mine or anyone's bird and you had better wind your fucking neck in or else.'

He then pushed me away and shouted back, 'Or else what?'

It was loud enough for the people around us to hear and they all turned and looked. This was a bloody nightmare. Not only was I dealing with all the fear and anxieties that are always with you as a covert police officer I now had my partner behaving like an idiot – or so it seemed to me. I stared at him and eventually he made his way back out of the pub.

I made my way to the bar. Steph came over and I ordered us some more drinks and took them outside. Chris was well on his way to being pissed and Dave and Stu were finding the whole thing hysterical.

He eventually went and sat on the kerb on his own while I explained to Dave and the others that he had had a shit week. He had split up with his girlfriend and he was having a hard time accepting it. Mark went over and sat with him and I just had to hope that he didn't say something stupid. We finally left The Puffin and made our way to the ground earlier than normal.

As we entered the ground I tried desperately to get the eye of one of our uniform spotters, Guy, but he was busy dealing with other shit. My plan was to try and cause a bit of a scene and try and get them to arrest Chris for drunk and disorderly. I didn't care what, I just needed him removed from the situation. The opportunity didn't arise and we went into the game.

Thankfully, Chris couldn't drink any more alcohol now as we were in the ground, but he was a complete liability during the first half, shouting out random rants of abuse much to the amusement of those around us. At half-time Dave, Stu and Mark announced that they were going to move to the halfway line and watch the second half from there. I apologised for Chris but they said that they didn't have a problem with it and they might see us at The Puffin after the game. I was all for leaving but Chris was having none of it.

Fifteen minutes from time Chris saw Paul standing at the bottom of the steps talking with Marcus and Stan. He set off before I could grab him and stumbled down the steps to where Paul was standing. I watched on as he strode up to Paul and threw his arm around him. Paul turned and looked at Chris and then up at me and shouted, 'Jim, is he with you?' I made my way down to them and Chris was mumbling on about Steph and how much I fancied her. Chris then turned and raised his arms to the crowd and started to sing 'No One Likes Us' and the crowd joined in. He then stumbled back and fell onto Paul who caught him before he fell over.

Paul looked at me. 'I reckon it's time for him to go home, what d'ya think?'

'Yeah…yeah, sorry boys, he's had a shit week.'

I then grabbed hold of Chris and led him up the terraces. People were cheering as I finally managed to get him to the top of the stands. As I was leading him out of the ground we saw Guy and some other officers standing at one of the exits. Chris spotted them and before I could shut him up shouted out, 'All right, Mr Policeman. Did you enjoy the game?' I grabbed hold of him before he could do any more damage. He pushed me away. I swore at him and told him that the way he behaved today was a joke. As we got to the van, he told me to take him back to the office.

I stared back at him. 'That is about the most sensible thing you have said all fucking day,' I said, before pushing him into the van and driving off.

As we entered into the one-way system at New Cross, I turned and looked at him. 'What the fuck was all that about today? First you piss Charlie and Gerry off. Then you behave like a fucking dickhead in the pub.'

'I'm not listening,' he interrupted and put his fingers in his ears.

I grabbed hold of his arm and pulled it down. 'How fucking old are you? As if this isn't hard enough, I get partnered with someone who knows fuck all about football and then wants to pull rank when it suits him. You are a fucking liability.'

This appeared to strike a nerve. 'Me, a liability? You wanna take a look at yourself. You are more of a hooligan than all of them lot put together. Strutting about like you're some fucking top boy. I am the sergeant here and I am in charge and don't you forget it.'

I was now struggling to drive as I was so fucking angry and I stopped the van in the middle of the street. 'There you go again, pulling fucking rank. And as for strutting about, I am trying to do my fucking job.'

He then went all quiet. 'Yeah, well if I have my way, the three of you may have to look for something else.'

I was now being tooted at from the traffic that was now at a standstill behind the van. I set off. 'What the fuck do you mean by that?'

He looked out of the window and muttered something that I couldn't hear.

I grabbed hold of his arm. 'What did you say?'

He then spun around and shouted, 'If you grab hold of me again I will arrest you for assault.'

I stared at him. 'Why don't you just fuck off?'

I drove the van in silence back to the yard and as I pulled to a halt Charlie and Gerry were standing staring into Charlie's car window. I got out, followed by Chris. Gerry turned and looked and could instantly see that things were not good. 'All right, Jimbo?'

I shouted back, 'No, I fucking ain't all right.'

With that Chris pointed at me. 'That's it. I warned you. I have had all that I am going to tolerate from you. I will be speaking with senior management and I will have you back in a helmet by Monday.' He then stormed off into the office.

Charlie laughed. 'So what's up with Mr Happy?'

I told them about how he had behaved in the pub and then at the ground. I then noticed that Charlie had a cut hand and was holding a dust pan and brush. 'What the fuck you doing with that?'

Charlie replied, 'Sweeping up the glass from the window. Some fucker screwed my car and nicked the radio.'

I laughed. 'It looks like you have had much the same day as me. Shit.'

'Yep,' Gerry grinned. 'Only lasted to half-time as our targets failed to appear. What's he going on about having you back in a helmet?'

I shook my head. 'It's nothing, he's just got the arsehole. It's just another one of his threats.'

I was unaware that Chris had come back out and was shouting as he walked towards me: 'I don't make idle threats – as of now you are off the squad. I have just spoken with Robbie at the FIU. He has agreed with me that you are too involved and—'

Gerry interrupted. 'Chris, you had better not be serious. Jim is the best I have ever worked with. He was born to do this job.'

Chris responded. 'I am deadly serious and if you don't like it you are more than welcome to go with him.'

I was gobsmacked and Charlie and Gerry looked at me for a response. I shrugged my shoulders and walked towards Chris. 'That's fine by me.'

As I walked past him, all the rage of the day caught up with me. I hit him as hard as I have ever hit anyone before. My right fist connected with the bridge of his nose. I preferred to talk my way out of a situation, but Chris got what he deserved. He fell to the ground and it took every ounce of self-control that I had not to jump up and down on his head.

I walked into the toilets and stared at myself in the mirror. What the fuck had I just done? I had assaulted the sergeant in charge of my operation and had hit him. I was now properly in the shit. I punched the towel dispenser, knocking it off the wall, just as Gerry walked into the toilet. 'Fucking hell, Jim. You have proper messed him up. Not that he didn't deserve it.'

I looked at Gerry. 'How bad?'

Gerry puffed his cheeks and breathed out heavily. 'Well, Jimbo, on a scale of one to ten, I would say you are at about eleven.'

Fuck it. All that work. All the months and months of dedication and graft were to be for nothing. I looked at Gerry. 'Well, I had better go and face the music. What a fucking mess.'

Chris was nowhere to be seen but Charlie was hunched over the bonnet of his car and was laughing his head off. Gerry and I went over to him and asked what was so funny. He pointed towards the office. 'It's him, Chris. D'ya know what he said? Quality. He said that he was right about you. You are a fucking hooligan.'

I failed to see the funny side of it. We all behaved like dickheads sometimes but today was Chris's day. My head was spinning with the implications of what I had just done. I sat on the bonnet of Charlie's car while he and Gerry both rolled about laughing.

What the fuck was I going to do? Gerry disappeared back into the office and eventually reappeared with Chris in tow. He was no longer wearing his glasses that apparently I had broken when I hit him – he wasn't wearing his contacts that day. I stood up and walked over to him. He was a sorry sight.

I spoke first. 'Chris, I'm sorry. I was out of order.'

I then noticed that he had tears streaming down his face. He put his hand up to wipe them away. Through the tears he started to speak. 'Don't apologise. It was my fault. I behaved like a fucking prick all day. I got what I deserved.'

If I thought I was feeling like shit before, this took it to another level. I had my mate, partner and sergeant standing in the yard of our office, having been punched to the ground by me, crying and accepting responsibility for my actions. I put my arms around him and pulled him close to me. I had now also started to cry and the two of us stood there in the yard hugging each other and crying while Gerry and Charlie looked on.

We eventually made our way up to our office and sat down. We sat and drank into the early hours of Sunday morning. Chris explained to us all that he was struggling and that the split with Laura had been the last straw. He was envious of how easy I found it to be accepted by the hooligans. He agreed that he would never again use his rank as a reason as to why we should take a particular path unless it was outside of our covert duties, and to his credit he never did.

Gerry and Charlie talked about their lack of targets and how they wished that they had built up the kind of relationships that Chris and I had done. I explained that it had been a large amount of luck to start with but that from now on they could tag along with us. They were going to give the halfway line another couple of weeks but if they had no success then they would accept our offer.

We eventually left the office at two in the morning. I stumbled in the door and woke Dawn as I crashed about making toast. She got up and sat me down on the sofa.

She stared at me as she handed me my toast and a cup of tea. 'Good day?'

I took a bite of my toast. 'Don't ask.'

FIFTEEN

YOU'RE OLD BILL

The next day, Sunday, I slept well and went with Dawn to have a look at the house in Catford that she had bought. The roofers were due back in on the Monday. Dawn had been very careful not to let the roofers know what she did for a living. She told them that she had outside contractors in to do all the work – plumbers, electricians and painters and decorators – who were to be me and Gerry. The house was going to be a perfect opportunity to enhance our cover. We walked around and had a good look. All of the walls were going to need either stripping or re-plastering but it was a solid house. I reckoned that once the roofers had finished we could make a start on ripping out and I planned to start later that week.

Chris had some good news. He had given Dave the number of the pager and he had sent a message about meeting up prior to the Swindon game on Saturday. Chris had arranged to meet them at The Puffin for eleven. It seemed that there had been no harm done by his behaviour.

Strangely enough, the fight with Chris had cemented our relationship. He was now willing to listen to ideas. He embraced Charlie's ideas about a dedicated hire car. Charlie had decided to pass himself off as a driver/chauffeur for a high net-worth individual who only called on his services on an 'as and when' basis. He was employed full-time and well paid but he needed to be ready twenty-four hours a day to pick up his boss if he called. For that Charlie needed to be seen by his targets in a smart car. Charlie got approval, thanks to Chris's support, and was given access to the Ford Granada Scorpio on a phone call.

We returned to the office to find Chris had received a message from Dave. 'He wants to meet up in a pub in Catford for some reason. I haven't gone back to him because I wanted to check with you first.'

'Yeah, I don't see an issue with that,' I responded.

Chris rang him back and left a message telling him that we would see him on Saturday in the pub at midday in Catford.

At 11.45 we headed to the pub in Catford to meet with our targets. We hadn't been to this pub before and as we entered the atmosphere didn't exactly fill you with warmth. It was quite busy but I didn't recognise anyone. We went to the bar and Chris ordered the drinks for us and the others.

It was at this point that Dave, Stu and Mark and another group of guys that we had never met or seen before came out of the adjacent bar. I was instantly aware that something was up by the look on Dave and Stu's faces. Dave was carrying a pool cue and Stu a bottle. I looked straight at Dave and greeted him. 'All right mate. You all right?'

Dave stopped and stared at me long and hard. I now knew that we were in fucking big trouble. 'No, I fucking ain't.'

At this point Chris had come over and was standing next to me with the drinks. Chris looked at me and then at Dave. 'All right, Dave?' Dave took a pace forward and shouted, 'No, I fucking ain't all right. Who the fuck are you two? It's just that we're all struggling to work it out.'

I looked at Chris and watched the blood literally drain out of his face on the spot. I shook my head. 'What you going on about? You know who we are.'

Dave tapped the pool cue down on the ground. 'Well, that's just it, Jim, if that is your fucking name, we don't know who you are. You turn up out of the fucking blue, wanna be our best mates.'

Chris was now visibly worried and if the truth be known so was I. The others in the group now started to walk forward and within seconds we were totally surrounded. It was not good odds.

Ten against two. *Fuck.* I tried to go on the attack. 'Dave, what's your fucking problem?'

He then raised the pool cue and pointed it at me and then Chris. 'You and him are the problem.'

This was now not fucking good. We had a big decision to make. Do we turn and make a run for it? Admit to who we are and hope that we can get out in one piece or front it out and take our chances?

I stood for what seemed an eternity and then moved towards Dave. 'All right, so what the fuck are you saying?' Dave was not backing down; he poked me and then Chris with the pool cue. 'What I am saying, you cunt, is that *you* and *you* are fucking Old Bill.' It was now time to put up or shut up. I stood there staring at them all and then burst out laughing. 'Are you having a fucking laugh? Me, fucking Old Bill? Are you fucking serious?' If Dave had any doubts he might have got it wrong he didn't show it. 'You don't see any of us laughing. That's exactly what I am saying – that you and him are fucking Old Bill.'

I turned and looked at Chris and then back to Dave. 'Is this a fucking wind-up?'

Dave was now going red in the face. 'Who the fuck are you?'

'You fucking know who we are, you cunt. And you are now beginning to fucking piss me off.' I pointed at Dave. 'You're calling me Old Bill. Is that what you're saying?'

Dave and I were now eyeball to eyeball. He answered in a slow and deliberate tone, 'Yep, that's exactly what I'm saying.'

I pushed him back. 'Come on, then. You and me. Outside now. *Come on*, you balding cunt!'

Mark and the others held Dave back and Stu walked forward. 'So where were you Tuesday?'

I glared at Stu. 'What d'ya mean, where was I Tuesday?'

Dave then interrupted. 'Where the fuck were you Tuesday? We came to see you and no one knew who the fuck you were.'

I was now properly struggling to see where this was heading. 'Where was I Tuesday? What the fuck has that got to do with anything?'

Stu then walked up to me. 'We came to see you at the house in Glenfarg Road and when we got there no one knew who the fuck you were.'

I turned and looked at Chris and then back to Stu and Dave. 'What fucking house in Glenfarg Road?'

Dave tried to make another lunge. 'The fucking house you're meant to be doing up in Catford that Chris told us about on Saturday. He said you'd be there and when we came down no one knew who the fuck you were.'

I turned to Chris as it began to dawn on me what had happened. 'What fucking house in Catford?'

It was all Chris could do to say, 'The one we need to paint for Arthur. You know, the one in Catford.'

'Oh yeah…' I then turned back to Stu. 'What about it? We haven't been there.'

Stu looked on. 'Yeah, we know cos we went down there on Tuesday.'

'But we won't be there till next week cos they're stripping the roof,' I replied. 'What fucking use would we be inside painting with no fucking roof?'

At this point Mark intervened. 'See, Dave, I told ya. Jim and Chris weren't there cos of the roof, I said that, Jim, I said you weren't there cos of the roof.'

Dave pushed Mark aside. 'Mark, shut the fuck up.' He then pointed at me. 'But no one there knows who the fuck you are.'

I could sense that Dave was now beginning to question himself. 'I don't know them either. They're roofers, we've just got the job to do the painting. I don't know who fucking anyone is there.'

Dave was now buckling. 'But I still don't know who the fuck you are. For all I know you are both Old Bill. You turn up…'

At this point I ran forward to grab him and was stopped by Stu. 'I have had e-fucking-nough of this. Fucking come on, you cunt. You and me. Right fucking now.'

Dave was still being held by the others. Stu then turned to me. 'All right, Jim, calm down, mate. Chris, calm him down, will ya?'

At this point one of the guys standing alongside Dave stepped in. 'Dave, I ain't being funny, mate, but he proper don't come across as Old Bill to me. If he was he'd have fucking run by now.'

There was a brief pause and then Dave threw the pool cue to the ground. 'Fuck it, this is all fucked up.' He then turned to me. 'I'm sorry, Jim. I fucking overreacted. It's just two of my mates got nicked last time' – which was news to me and Chris – 'and when we went to the house and they didn't know you, I thought—' I didn't let him finish.

'Fuck off. I'm not fucking interested in any of that shit. You fucking accuse me of being Old Bill again and I will cut your fucking head off.'

Chris then stepped in. 'Whoa, whoa, fucking calm down, Jim, he's said sorry.'

I pushed Chris aside. 'I'm not interested in his fucking apology, fucking wanker. Me, Old Bill? Cunt.' I then walked outside and took in deep gulps of air. I was shaking out of fear and anger.

Stu and Mark came out and apologised for questioning me and Chris and said they were sorry it had come to this. Chris and Dave came out and Dave came up to me. He stood there on the pavement and stretched out his hand. 'Sorry, Jim. I was out of order.'

I looked at him and reached out and shook his hand. 'No worries. I'm sorry too.'

Dave then smiled. 'Just one thing though, I'm not a balding cunt. I may be receding, but I am *not* balding.'

Everyone laughed.

Stu had decided that we had had enough excitement in that pub and we walked along Catford Broadway to another one on the corner of the one-way system. I deliberately held back as we made our way to the door. I knew I was going to have to do something that would without question dispel any nagging doubts as to who we were.

We entered the pub and Dave and Stu made their way to the bar to buy the drinks. I went into the toilet and into the cubicle and sat down. I sat there for a couple of minutes gathering my thoughts, went to the sink and splashed my face with water and then went back out to the others at the bar. They were now all standing around a video arcade machine entitled Pot Black. The idea of the game was based around a game of snooker. You would answer a red question, which was relatively easy, and you would then choose a colour. The questions got harder depending on which colour you chose. Two points for a yellow question, three points for a green, etc, while black, the hardest question, scored you seven points. Mark was at the machine and Dave and Stu were shouting at him to answer. He answered the question and let out a roar as he got it right. It was Dave's turn next and he also answered correctly. They turned to me and Stu ushered me forward 'Come on, Jim, your turn. If you lose you buy the drinks.'

I walked forward and put my 50p in to start the game. I stared at the machine and it was at that moment that I made a decision that was to remain with me until the conclusion of the operation. The question came up: 'In what year did England win the World Cup?' It was followed by four possible answers. The others let out an audible groan as they read it but I just stood there and continued to stare at the machine. The clock began to run down and I still made no attempt to answer the question. Everyone was shouting at me. I stared blankly at the machine as the time ran out. I turned and faced everybody. 'Looks like the drinks are on me.'

They all looked at me a little confused and Chris was staring at me, completely oblivious to my intentions. I made my way to the bar and bought the drinks and came back. They were all still playing the game and I continued to stand and watch. It was my turn again and I walked forward and put in my 50p. I again stood there staring at the machine. The clock was ticking down and I still made no move to answer. They were all shouting at me again to answer. Dave was beside himself. 'Come on, Jim, answer the fucking question.' He then began to laugh as did the others. 'Jesus, what's your problem?'

I looked at them all. This was it. I turned back and started to hit the machine. I grabbed hold of it and pushed it onto its side. Everyone stood there open-mouthed. I then turned to Chris, who was staring at me with a complete look of bemusement on his face. I launched forward and grabbed hold of him. He wasn't expecting it and the shock was visible on his face. I pushed him against the bar. 'You've told 'em, haven't you? You cunt, you've told them even after you promised.'

Chris was now completely at odds as to where this was going. 'What the fuck are you going on about?'

I continued to push Chris against the bar and the others moved in and tried to separate us. I put my hand to Chris's throat and started to squeeze. He started to squirm and fight for breath. I was now shouting at the top of my voice. '*You cunt! You've told them, I fucking know you have.*'

Chris had absolutely no idea where this was going. Dave managed to prise my hand from Chris's throat and got between the two of us. He took hold of both my shoulders and stared at me as he spoke. 'Jim, fucking calm down, mate. Whatever you think he's said, I can assure you he ain't. What's your fucking problem?'

I then made an attempt to get back at Chris, but I was blocked by Mark and Stu. I pointed at Chris. 'Him, he's my fucking problem. He promised not to tell anyone. You fucking snide.'

Chris turned and pointed to everyone. 'I haven't told them anything.'

I had now played this out long enough and I turned and dropped to the floor. It was a little dramatic, to be fair, but I was playing my hand. We were at a pivotal moment in the operation. Everyone was completely confused. My eyes now started to fill with tears and as I got to my feet I turned to Chris. 'Why did you tell them? That was our secret. You promised me you would never tell.'

Dave walked towards me and put his arm around my shoulder. 'Look, Jim, I don't know what this is about, but honestly, Chris hasn't told us anything. Honest.'

I looked at them all and then to Chris. I now had tears streaming down my face. 'It's not my fault. I have tried, I have really tried. I just can't make the fucking words out. They're all just a fucking jumble of letters.'

Dave still had his arm around me. 'What you saying?' He then looked me straight in the eye. 'Can't you read?'

I shook my head. Mark then started to walk over. 'Jim, I ain't very good at reading either, mate.'

Chris finally got there and rushed towards me. 'Jim, I didn't tell 'em. I promise.'

I looked at the others and they all shook their heads. Stu was now alongside Dave. 'Jim, I promise, mate, Chris didn't say a word. Fucking hell, how do you get by?'

I pointed at Chris. 'He does it. He does all the reading and writing.'

I then turned and ran out of the pub. I walked to the corner and leant against the wall. I stood there for some time until eventually everybody came out of the pub.

Dave spoke first. 'Jim, it's not the end of the world, mate. I mean look at Stu here. He can't even tie shoelaces, which is why he always wears slip-ons.'

I laughed. Chris then came forward. 'Jim, I didn't tell 'em, mate. I promise.'

'I know. I know, I'm just, well, it doesn't matter.' I then looked around me. 'We're all mates here, right?'

Everyone nodded. Mark was now smiling. 'Too right, fucking best mates.' We all started to laugh and began to make our way across the road to our cars.

As we got to the pavement Stu started to laugh. We all stopped and looked at him. Dave was a little taken aback. 'Fucking hell, Stu, what's so fucking funny?'

Stu was now properly laughing and eventually got the words out. 'Fucking hell, that is funny.' We all looked on as he continued. 'I just got to thinking. There's us accusing Jim of being Old Bill… and he can't even read or fucking write!'

Everyone burst out laughing. Me included. The plan had worked.

SIXTEEN

HEAD VS HEART

I spent that weekend reliving the confrontation with Dave over and over in my head. What it had highlighted was that we were going to have to be far more alert as to what was said and to whom we said it. I met up with Chris on Monday to discuss exactly that and he apologised for letting slip about the house in Catford. We talked about the reading and writing revelation and the obvious implications, but I was confident that I could pull it off.

Chris was still impressed as to how I had managed to conjure up such a simple but effective level of cover. It was a stroke of genius, even if I do say so myself. My main objective had been to dispel any thoughts of me or Chris being Old Bill while at the same time not having a detrimental effect on anyone else, either physically or mentally. But it turned out to be much harder to make out that I couldn't read and write than I had expected, and on more than one occasion I wished I had found another more immediate way to dispel the Old Bill rumours than the illiteracy route.

We were all back in the office for Tuesday and Chris and I spent most of the day readying ourselves for the QPR game that night. We were due to meet up with Dave and the others at the Old Castle at 6 p.m. Chris and I nervously left the office just before six and I drove the van down and parked outside. Unbeknown to Chris I had gone to the local toyshop in Catford and had bought myself a present. I let him get out of the van and make his way over to Dave, Stu and Mark, who were standing outside the pub. I had decided to face the Old

Bill accusations head on. I walked across the road towards the others wearing my toyshop purchase: a plastic policeman's helmet and some toy handcuffs. It had the desired effect. Dave and the others absolutely pissed themselves as I strode up to them and stood before them on the pavement. Chris stood there open-mouthed as I, in my best *Dixon of Dock Green* voice, announced 'Evening, all'. It was a fucking mental thing to do but it was proper fucking funny. The hat was soon passed around, although Chris refused to wear it. It was eventually thrown into the road and as a large lorry drove over it the crowd outside the pub cheered.

We went to the game and popped into The Puffin for a nightcap. The pub was heaving and all the talk was about the Crystal Palace game on Saturday. I briefly saw Paul but only to say hello and said that I would see him on Friday night. We spent the rest of the week collating our cover and Gerry bought himself a new little van to use alongside his very old and tatty Mark1 Escort.

On the Friday evening Chris drove us down to The Puffin to show our faces. We wanted to glean some worthwhile information for the next day's away game to Crystal Palace. Paul was on great form and Chris and I spent all evening putting the world to rights. We were told that all of the Millwall were meeting up in The Granger at 1 p.m. but that no further plans had been made in order to keep the Old Bill guessing.

As we were about to leave Steph made her way over. She asked how I was and where we had been as we had not been about much. I said that we would be down more often as we had a house that we were redecorating in Catford. I so desperately wanted to grab hold of her and kiss her and it took every ounce of will-power for me not to do so. I knew that I could not drag her into this mess but it was becoming more and more difficult to resist the urge. I had been avoiding The Puffin. As much as it was our best source for information I was only too aware of where the situation with Steph could go and I was desperate to avoid complicating the operation any further.

I continued to stare at her until eventually she started to laugh. 'D'ya know what, Jim, I really can't work you out. Sometimes I think I know who you are and then other times, like now, you're a bloody mystery. Am I ever gonna get to the bottom of you?'

I smiled back. 'Sometimes I don't even know who I am.'

'I can well believe it,' she replied, and with that she put her arms around my shoulders and kissed me on the lips.

It took me totally by surprise. I reeled back and broke free.

She was a little taken aback by my response. 'All right, fucking hell, calm down. It was just a kiss. Anyone would think that you've never been kissed before. Jesus.'

I was now in a proper mess. I wanted to kiss her. Fuck me, if only she knew how much I wanted to kiss her, but this was now properly fucking me up in the head. I stood there like a complete fucking prick. I mumbled something along the lines of: 'Sorry, but I just can't fucking deal with this.' I left the pub.

I got out onto the pavement and took large gulps of air in an attempt to clear my head. I started to walk down the street. I could deal with the accusations of being Old Bill, the hooligans, the stress, even my apparent inability at not being able to read and write, but this was different. This was properly real. All of the other stuff could be packaged and parcelled up but this was different.

Chris eventually caught up with me and asked if I was all right.

But I was in no mood for a heart to heart. 'Do yourself a fucking favour, Chris, and fuck off and leave me alone.'

'Fucking hell, Jim, I'm your mate. We can sort this out together, you and me. Chris and Jim.'

Then I saw Steph walk out of the pub and start to walk towards us. This was turning into a fucking nightmare. I pushed him away and walked off. As I got to the corner I turned back to see Chris walking back to the pub with Steph.

I rounded the corner and walked over and sat down in a bus shelter. As I was sitting there a bus pulled up. I got on it and went onto the top deck; I walked to the front of the bus and sat down and stared out of the window. It was at this point that the tears started to flow. As much as I tried to control it, I was unable to do so. Here I was, super cop, undercover football hooligan, sitting on the top deck of a night bus on the road to nowhere crying my fucking eyes out. I continued to stare out of the window, sobbing, oblivious to everything around me. As the bus turned the corner I looked over and saw that it had taken me to the bottom of my nan and granddad's road. I got off the bus, crossed the road and walked up the hill to my grandparents'. My granddad answered the door, took one look at me and ushered me into the house. I had stopped crying but I must have looked like a real mess. He didn't ask me why I was there, he just got my nan to make me a cup of tea and told me to go to the toilet and freshen up. I sat with them both for about half an hour and then asked to use the phone and rang the office.

Chris answered on the first ring and was relieved to hear that I was all right. He arrived twenty minutes later. My granddad walked me to the door and put his arm around me. 'Boy, whatever it is you will sort it out. Me and your nan will always be here for you. Don't you ever forget that.'

I looked up at him. 'Yeah, I know. Don't worry, I will sort it one way or another.'

I got into the car with Chris and we drove off. I apologised for my behaviour and Chris told me that Steph was upset that she had offended me but he had reassured her that it was nothing to do with her and that I had always had a problem with showing my emotions. Frankly he wasn't a million miles from the truth, although the truth was getting more and more blurry by the day.

I thanked Chris for the lift when we got back to the office. Chris was keen to talk things through, but I told him that tonight was not the right time for a discussion and got into my van and drove home.

I parked up on the drive and walked into the flat and sat down on the sofa. I stared out of the window. I was in love with a woman who seemed to be in love with me. But she wasn't in love with me; she was in love with a character that I had created. The emotions and desires were fighting with my morals. Should I allow my desires to win, I could justify it to myself and others as it would elevate my cover and status to a new level. But was it right?

What a fucking mess.

SEVENTEEN

DAVE EVADES ARREST

I sat up all night pondering what to do. I was in love with Steph, and while having a relationship with the sister-in-law of one of Millwall's top boys would elevate my status, it wouldn't be fair to her. My friendship with Paul seemed solid, and although my relationship with Steph may help my cause, I didn't like to think about how it might affect her when the operation concluded. Yeah, my wishes would be satisfied – and I was without any doubt that the sex would have been amazing – but I knew it wouldn't be right to allow my desires to overrule my morality. Professionally or personally.

I drove into the office, parked up and went upstairs to join the others who had already arrived. When I walked in it was obvious that Chris had recounted the previous evening's events.

There were a few jokes but I was in no mood to get into a conversation about it. We left the office and made our way to The Granger for one o'clock. We arrived and entered the pub, which by now was packed with Millwall. The atmosphere was electric and everyone was in good voice.

It soon became apparent that we were not going to be able to leave the pub except en masse due to the large amounts of uniformed police officers that had started to arrive and take up position outside and across the road from the pub. It didn't seem to put anyone off and we stayed there until 2.30 at which point everyone decided to make their way to the ground. We walked 150 strong, flanked by Old Bill to the ground, and entered just before the match kicked off. The game passed off without incident, although Millwall had lost 1–0 it had been a good afternoon.

We were again left in the ground until most of the Crystal Palace supporters had left. As we came out of the ground and were starting to make our way back to the car a small group of Crystal Palace supporters came running from out of a side turning and started to throw bottles and rocks at us. The group that we were walking with then turned, and as one we ran towards them. The Palace supporters immediately turned around and ran back down the side street. We were stopped by Old Bill on horses and with dogs.

We all turned around and started to walk back towards the other Millwall supporters when one of them broke ranks and ran towards us. He launched himself towards Dave and punched him in the side of the head, accusing Dave of being a Palace fan. Dave took great exception to this and after a flurry of fists and kicks the guy was knocked to the ground. Within a matter of seconds a mounted police officer rode into the crowd and grabbed Dave by the shoulder and announced that he was arresting him for assault. I was a little taken aback by Dave's reaction. Instead of attempting to get away and or protest his innocence he accepted it and was by now being escorted by the mounted police officer towards a police van. Something inside of me flipped as I was incensed that Dave had been arrested for protecting himself. I ran towards him shouting out his name. As he turned and looked at me, I rugby-tackled him, which broke him free from the mounted police officer's grip and we both rolled to the floor. I hauled him to his feet. 'Run! Fucking run!'

At this we both sped off down the road. I was shouting at him as we were running to take his coat off and turn it inside out, so as to change his appearance. It was not until we had ducked into a small estate that I saw him. He had indeed turned his jacket inside out. Now, instead of a green bomber jacket, he was wearing a fluorescent orange one. His jacket had a high visibility lining and there he stood, hoping to blend into the crowd, dressed in orange. I quickly removed my hooded top and we swapped jackets. I turned it back to green and after about five minutes we slipped out of the flats and made our way back to Chris's car. The others were waiting for us. We quickly got into the car and drove off.

During the week, Gerry and I went to the house in Catford and managed over a couple of days to strip the house and prep it for redecoration. Dave appeared unannounced on the Friday, having been up most of the night, as we all had, dealing with the worst storm for over a hundred years. It had taken me two hours to fight my way into Catford. There were trees down everywhere and a lot of the country was at a standstill. It was great to see Dave – and a relief that the Old Bill accusations were well and truly behind us. I agreed for us to meet up with him and the others on Saturday at one o'clock, but, at my request, in the Old Castle and not The Puffin.

I was not ready to face Steph as the whole situation was still taking up most of my head time. Gerry was sympathetic to the obvious complications of becoming involved with Steph, but he was quick to point out that I was the one who ultimately had to make a decision. He could offer all the advice in the world but in the end it would have to be my call.

EIGHTEEN

RIVALS

The next Monday, Gerry and I went to the house in Catford and we spent the week redecorating. We stayed away from the Old Kent Road and as no one was up for the away game to Huddersfield we spent the weekend on the house.

Dave turned up on the Saturday morning as he was 'just passing' and Gerry – who Dave, Stu and Mark had come to accept by association – and I went with him for a quick beer in the local. We agreed to meet up at The Puffin before the game on Tuesday at home to Bournemouth. Gerry and I had made great in-roads into the redecoration and apart from a new kitchen and bathroom we were nearly there. We both had the Monday off and we were all into the office for the Tuesday.

We were all now becoming experts on the game; Angie made some good observations particularly about Sheringham's natural ability making up for his lack of pace. She brought in her radio as they were drawing the first round of the Simod Cup at midday and we were all keen to hear who we got. We all sat around the radio at just before twelve and waited to see who Millwall were to draw in the cup. The announcer called out the numbers and then announced the team. Halfway through the draw a ball was pulled out. 'Number 32: West Ham. Will play… number 22: Millwall.'

We all leapt to our feet and cheered and began to dance around the office. We could not have hoped for a better draw. For those of you not too up on your football rivalry this is as good/bad as it gets. West Ham despise Millwall and Millwall despise West Ham. The rivalry is well documented and stems from events eighty-three years ago, when hostility developed between two shipyards on either side of the Thames. To the north you had the workforce of the Royal Docks (the claret and blue of West Ham) and to the south, the Millwall, London and Surrey docks (the blue and white of Millwall). When the Millwall shipyard broke the 1926 dockers' strike, the anger across the river raised the tensions to boiling point. This wasn't helped when in 1976 a Millwall supporter, during a brawl with West Ham supporters, fell in front of a train in New Cross and was killed.

Robbie from the FIU was on the phone as soon as the draw was over, asking if we had heard it. No one at the FIU was happy about the draw – as violence between the teams' supporters was almost a given. We were to gain as much intelligence as possible and to attend a pre-briefing at Scotland Yard the following day. The match was not due to be played for a week but already it was at the top of the FIU list. We spent the rest of the afternoon talking about the West Ham game and at the end of the day, Chris and I headed down to The Puffin to meet with Dave and the others for six.

When we pulled up outside The Puffin people were already spilling out onto the pavement. We pushed our way to the bar. When Paul saw me he rushed over. 'You fucking heard. You heard.'

Paul was beside himself as was everyone else in the pub. The West Ham game was on everyone's lips. There was talk as to whether the Old Bill would postpone it and whether it would be an all-ticket game. The atmosphere was like nothing I had ever experienced before; clearly this was going to be our biggest test to date. We eventually left The Puffin with Dave and the others and went to the ground. The game was an anti-climax and Bournemouth won 2–1. No one seemed to care as all that anyone could talk about was the West Ham game in a week's time.

The game finished and we went back to The Puffin. It was the busiest I had ever seen it. There were people outside on the pavement and the queue to the bar was out the door. Chris offered to get the beers and I stood outside with Dave, Stu and Mark. Chris eventually appeared with bottles of Pils as they were out of glasses. As he came over Paul followed him. He had a light and lager in his hand and he passed it to me. 'There you go, Jim. Steph insisted that I bring this out to you.' He smiled and put his arm around me. 'You up for the West Ham game?'

'No, I thought I'd work that day... Of course I'm up for it. What's the plan?'

Paul pulled me aside. 'It's not finalised yet. I will let you know Friday night. So far it's here for breakfast at ten o'clock. But it's not open to everyone. Just you and Chris, all right?'

I was surprised that he had not offered it out to Dave and the others. 'Yep, understand, see you Friday.' As he started to move off, I shouted after him, 'Oh, and thank Steph for the drink.'

He waved his hand as he went back into the pub.

We stayed for about half an hour and then drove back to the office. All we could talk about was the atmosphere and the excitement. Charlie and Gerry had also had a good evening and they were going to meet up with their targets on the Friday to discuss their plan of attack.

We were all now fully aware that this was going to be the biggest game of the operation so far and the potential for disorder wasn't to be underestimated. Chris spoke with Robbie and Lawrence at the FIU and told them that we would be there for the pre-briefing tomorrow at 11 a.m. We were to be joined by both area commanders and most of the senior officers responsible for policing the West Ham–Millwall game.

I drove back to the flat and Dawn was waiting up. She had heard about the cup draw on the news and the press were already talking about the potential trouble between the opposing sets of supporters. She wanted reassurance that it would all be fine. I played it down as best I could but she knew that this was going to be no run in the park.

I woke up early and made my way into the office for the trip to Scotland Yard. Chris was already in and had shaved and was wearing a suit. I didn't have a suit that fitted any more so couldn't have worn one even if I had wanted to. Charlie and Gerry appeared, both minus their suits, and we left for Scotland Yard.

We arrived at the Yard and made our way to the front desk to sign in. Chris, Gerry and Charlie produced their warrant cards, which we had taken out of the safe in the office where they now resided, signed in and made their way to the lift. I then went up to the desk and produced my warrant card. The officer behind the desk looked at the card and then back at me.

I stared at him. 'Is there a problem, mate?'

He continued to stare at my card. 'Nope, no problem. You ain't coming in.'

'What?'

He pointed at my warrant card. 'This ain't you. This looks nothing like you. So you ain't coming in.'

I shouted over to the others. 'Can you fucking believe this? He won't let me in.'

The officer on the desk had now been joined by another couple of officers and the one in charge took hold of my warrant card and inspected it. 'Watch your language, son. I don't know who this is but it bears no resemblance whatsoever to you. I'm afraid that unless you can prove otherwise you are not coming in here today.'

At this point Chris, Gerry and Charlie were beside themselves with laughter. Chris came over to explain who I was but they were having none of it. The main officer then spoke again. 'Unless you can get somebody down from upstairs to prove who you are, you're not coming in.'

I stood there and started to laugh. This was unbelievable. I agreed that I looked nothing like the picture on my warrant card but I had three other police officers backing me up.

Chris explained I was his partner but the officers on the front desk weren't budging. Eventually I asked to use the phone and spoke with Bernard. He found the whole episode hilarious but agreed to come down and sign me in. He eventually appeared and went up to the officers on the front desk and explained who I was. They agreed to let me in but only as Bernard's visitor. They were flabbergasted that someone who looked like me could be a serving police officer. I was a little taken aback by their reaction but Bernard told me to take it as a huge compliment. In all the time that he had worked at Scotland Yard and for SO10, to his knowledge no covert police officer had ever been refused entry to Scotland Yard. Looking back on it now it was the highest of accolades.

The deputy assistant commissioner took the stage and introduced himself to everyone present. He went on about the rivalry between West Ham and Millwall and he then summoned Chris to the lectern to give everyone an update on the available intelligence. Chris was asked lots of questions about our role in the operation and at one point one of the senior officers suggested that we carried police radios so that we could pass up-to-date information back to the control room. It was at this point that Gerry and I stood up and introduced ourselves. We informed the senior officers present that we would not be carrying radios or calling in at arranged times to pass on any up-to-date information but that we would be on the ground trying to do our job and that the best they could all hope for was enough intelligence prior to the game to allow them a head start. They struggled to take this on board and began to question our role and what we were trying to achieve. Fortunately Chris and Lawrence explained that there were a number of avenues to explore re the policing of the match and that our involvement, although crucial, was not the only option open to them.

We made our way back to the office and discussed the bigger picture. We all agreed that the senior management, certainly those at the meeting today, were clueless as to our operation and the risks that we were taking. Robbie rang us and apologised to Chris about the lack of knowledge and respect for what we were doing. He assured us that he had made everyone fully aware of the risks we were taking on a daily basis and that we could rely on as much support as we were going to need on the day of the match. It fell on deaf ears. We would pass the intelligence that was necessary but I had no intention of passing anything over which could lead a trail back to me.

Chris and I left the office on the Friday just before six and made our way down to The Puffin to meet up with Paul. We had secured a hire car for the trip up to Aston Villa the next day and we drove it to the pub and parked up outside. We walked into The Puffin, which was much busier than normal, and Paul was behind the bar with Tina and Steph.

Paul showed us the T-shirts that he had had made up for the West Ham game. There was a picture of a rampant lion tearing the Hammers apart. Chris and I bought one each. Paul told us that everyone was going to the West Ham game and that most of the top boys would be in the pub on Tuesday morning. Paul had already heard from a reliable source that Old Bill were going to be everywhere, and not just in uniform, and that we were to be very careful who we spoke to on the way to, and in, the ground. I thanked him for his advice and after an hour or so Chris and I left and made our way back to the office.

Gerry and Charlie were already back as their targets had failed to appear and as Dave and the others were not coming with us to Aston Villa we all agreed to go together in the hire car. We met at the office the next day and Chris and I had both chosen to wear our new T-shirts. We made our way to the ground and parked up close by. We entered the ground and it was pleasing to see that the away support was swelling. We were a thousand strong and again all the talk was about West Ham. We were not the only ones to be wearing Paul's T-shirts and they were selling well. We left buoyant, having won 2–1, and made our way back to London.

We got back to the office relatively early and all sat down and went through the information that we had gathered. Charlie and Gerry had seen one of their targets at the game and they were going to meet him and the others at London Bridge at twelve o'clock on Tuesday. All we knew was that we were to be at The Puffin for 10 a.m. and we would take it from there. We were to be in the office for the Monday when the FIU were going to pass on to us the intelligence that had been gathered.

I went home and spent most of the Sunday in bed trying to catch up on some sleep. I had been struggling now for a couple of months to get any sustained periods of sleep. I would wake up constantly worrying about the operation or dream about being sussed out or, worse still, killed. The dreams were becoming more and more frequent and I had resorted to sleeping with the bedside table light on, much to Dawn's frustration. I found that it helped me remember where I was when I awoke from a particularly bad dream. Gerry had also confessed to having problems sleeping although Charlie freely admitted that he could sleep anywhere, something he put down to having a clear conscience.

I made my way into the office on the Monday and we spent all of it waiting for the FIU to ring with their latest intel. They rang us once at the end of the day to tell us that they had nothing new and that we were now very much on our own. We all decided to get home early and to be in the office for 8 a.m. the next day. I went home and got no sleep whatsoever. My mind was racing about the possibilities for the day ahead.

I was up at 6 a.m. and made my way into the office. Gerry was already there, as was Charlie, although there was no sign of Chris. The three of us went to the local cafe and each ordered a full English. Gerry joked that we should make the most of it as it could be our last. After breakfast we made our way back to the office. Chris was there, talking through the day with Angie. She said that she was worried for all of us and we promised her that we would be careful.

Chris and I waited until 9.30 and then went to The Puffin. We pulled up outside and I walked up to the door. I pushed it but it was locked. I knocked on the door and we waited. After a second knock the door was opened by Paul. He greeted us and invited us in. It was a who's who of Millwall's elite. I recognised everybody from our intelligence and video surveillance. Everyone was wearing Paul's T-shirt, including Tina and Steph, who were behind the bar serving drinks.

I went up to the bar and got myself and Chris a drink. The atmosphere in the pub was electric. The conversations were loud and animated and there was an undercurrent of anticipation. I finished my drink before Chris had even started his and ordered us another round. The door was now constantly opening as more and more Millwall flooded in.

I stood at the bar and Steph came over. She passed me my drink before I had a chance to order it. 'You looking forward to today?'

I nodded. 'Yeah, can't wait. If there's one thing I hate it's fucking West Ham.'

She laughed. 'Me too. But do me a favour, will you?'

I nodded. 'Yep, anything.'

She leant across the bar and put her hand on my cheek. 'Be careful.'

I took her hand and held on to it tightly. 'Don't you worry about me. I will be fine.' I held on to her hand and then raised my other hand to behind her neck; I pulled her head towards me and kissed her on the cheek. I looked at her as she smiled back.

At this point Paul slapped me on the back and I released her. 'Oi, you leave him alone, he needs to be properly focused for today.'

I stood at the bar talking with Paul, watching on as more and more Millwall entered the pub. Paul was in high spirits. The plan was to leave the pub at 1 p.m. and head for London Bridge, where we would make our way en masse to Liverpool Street and then on to Stratford, arriving there at about 3.30. We would then walk down the Romford Road to Upton Park. I threw Chris a look. The last thing I wanted was for him to call this in until at least a few more people had been told.

At this point Paul made his way over to another group who had just entered the pub and I was joined at the bar by a guy who I didn't recognise. He was wearing a black hooded top and a scarf covered half of his face. He asked if I was looking forward to today. He was sweating profusely and was wired. 'Yeah. You?' I replied.

He took his scarf off and placed it on the bar. 'Yeah. D'ya want a little helper for today?'

I nodded. 'Yeah, why, what you got?'

He then got off his stool. 'Not here, in the toilets.'

I followed him into the toilets. I don't know what I had expected to see but when I got into the toilet I was offered a lot more than I had bargained for. The guy pulled a gun from out of the front of his hooded top and I fucking shit myself. All sorts of things went through my head as the guy turned and pointed it at me. I honestly thought that it was all over. He turned the gun around and handed it to me.

I took hold of it and looked it over. 'Does it work?'

With that the guy grabbed the gun, backed away from me, cocked it and raised it into the air.

I shouted out, 'Not in here!' But it was too late and he pulled the trigger.

The gun went off with a flash and the sound was deafening. My ears felt like they had burst and I was finding it hard to hear.

He handed the gun back to me. 'Fifty quid and it's yours.'

I could hardly make out what he was saying. 'How much?'

'Fifty quid.'

I pulled fifty quid from out of my pocket. 'There you go.' and he handed me the gun.

I passed it back. 'Not today. Can I collect it in the week?'

He took the money and put the gun back into his hooded top. 'No worries, Paul knows me. I'll see you here eleven o'clock Thursday morning.' And with that, he rushed out of the toilets and back into the pub.

My ears were still ringing as I walked out of the toilets and back into the pub. Everyone was staring at me, and the pub was in complete silence. Chris, who was now grey, rushed over with Paul.

Paul spoke first. 'Jesus, what the fucking hell was that all about? We heard a gun go off, Andy comes running out and legs it out of the pub. I tell ya, Jim, we all thought he'd shot ya.'

I still had the gun shot ringing in my ears and was a little disorientated. 'D'ya know that fucking idiot? He just let one off in the fucking toilet.'

Paul started to laugh. 'I know, we heard it. It's Andy. He's a speed freak. Fucking hell, Jim, I really thought he'd shot you.'

I started to laugh, more out of relief than humour. 'Fucking hell. I need a drink.'

I went over with Chris to the bar. 'Fucking hell, Jim. Please don't do that again. What the fuck were you thinking?'

I put my arms around him and whispered into his ear. 'Thanks for rushing in and saving me.'

He reeled away. 'Yeah, right!' We both started to laugh.

Steph came over and put my drink on the bar. 'Jim, this one's on the house. Thanks for all the excitement.'

We stayed in the pub drinking until just before 1 p.m. when Paul made an announcement that it was time to head off. We made our way to London Bridge. We were joined at London Bridge by another hundred Millwall and by the time we got to Liverpool Street there were in excess of five hundred of us. Everyone was in high spirits and we boarded a train heading for Stratford. We had been joined by Dave, Stu and Mark, who had met up with us at London Bridge, and Gerry and Charlie and a couple of their targets. We made our way to Stratford and got off the train. There were no police to be seen anywhere and we started to march as one down the Romford Road. Everyone was in good voice and we were now walking down the centre of the road, causing the traffic to stop and look on. We could hear the police sirens in the distance and as they got louder so did we. As we rounded the Romford Road heading towards Upton Park, the police arrived. They flooded out of the vans and within minutes we were surrounded. I could see that we were going to get herded into a side street and held there until the police could get sufficient numbers in place to escort us to the ground.

I saw an opportunity and shouted out to those around me, 'Into the estate!' And with that a small group of us broke off and ran into the estate. We all went into a small supermarket and were able to buy some cans of lager. There were about thirty of us, including Chris, Gerry, Charlie, Dave, Stu and Mark. We stayed on the estate for a short while and then made our way back to the Romford Road. The police had now gone and we started walking down the middle of the road singing 'No One Likes Us'.

As we turned the corner I saw a van pull over onto the pavement and two guys got out and ran into a pub opposite. I then saw three men leaving a cafe on the corner. People were starting to come out from doorways and as we passed by a kebab shop I watched as a man came out carrying the biggest fucking knife I had ever seen then slid it beneath his coat. It was now obvious that it was about to come proper on top and the singing stopped. We then all could see vans starting to pull up in the road ahead and people coming out of the pub.

Suddenly one of the Millwall supporters threw his hands into the air. 'Come on, Millwall. Let's have it.'

With that, the guy who had come out of the kebab shop drew the knife out from under his coat. The Millwall guy who had called out then stopped and shouted, 'Come on, then. Stand, Millwall. Stand.' And with that a group of West Ham started to walk towards us.

People started to peel off from our group and within seconds there were only about fifteen of us left. I looked around. We were properly outnumbered and it would have been suicide to have stood there to await the inevitable kicking. At this point someone shouted out, 'Fucking run!' which is exactly what we did. I sprinted back onto the estate, Gerry, Dave, Stu and a couple of others were with me. As we ran into the estate and past a group of shops Gerry pointed at a shop on the corner. 'Hold the fucking chemist's!' We charged towards the chemist, burst in and ran to the back of the shop. Gerry grabbed two cans from the shelf and threw them over to me. He then picked up two for himself and we crouched down with our cans at the ready, waiting for the shop to be overrun. We were now all armed with aerosol cans of one sort or another until eventually the chemist poked his head around from behind the counter. 'I think whoever you are waiting for are not coming. Would you kindly give me back my hairspray and leave?'

We all looked at each other. It seemed he was right and we started to make our way out of the shop. As we neared the front of the shop the door swung open. We all rushed back to the rear of the shop and raised our cans in anticipation of the onslaught. We then watched on as two elderly women entered the chemist's. They stood in the doorway, staring in disbelief at seven grown men at the back of the shop, clutching cans of hairspray. We shuffled past them, returning the cans to the owner as we left.

We walked out onto the street and I turned to Gerry. 'Hold the fucking chemist's. Jesus.'

Gerry threw me a look. 'Well, I dunno know, it was in the heat of the moment.'

I started to laugh. 'And what the fuck was I s'posed to do with two cans of Silvikrin had West Ham steamed in? Offer 'em a fucking perm?'

We gingerly made our way back to the Romford Road. Fortunately for us we were now into rush hour. As we rounded the corner Chris and Mark ran over to us from the other side of the road. Chris had a cut to his head and Mark was pissing himself laughing. I had never seen him laugh so much. I stared at the cut on Chris's head. 'Fucking hell. What the fuck happened to you? Did you get done by West Ham?'

Mark laughed. 'Done by West Ham? He wishes. We ran and hopped onto a bus. And he…. he…' Mark was now pointing at Chris and struggling to talk through his laughter. 'He grabbed some old woman's shopping to…? What was it, Chris? Oh yeah, blend in. And she fucking hit him. She fucking did him with her umbrella. The bus driver then stopped the bus and the conductor threw us off. Done by West Ham, more like done by Old Ham.'

We all pissed ourselves at Chris's expense but he took it well and he did have a rather ugly cut above his right eye where the edge of the umbrella had caught it.

We made our way to the ground and slipped past a large group of West Ham who were standing on the corner surrounded by Old Bill. We made our way down to the away end and joined the rest of the Millwall supporters, who were now also surrounded by police officers, some on horseback and some on the ground in full riot gear holding shields. Paul came over and asked how we were. They had been escorted all the way to the ground by the Old Bill. He and some others had tried to peel off when they saw us leg it into the estate but had been stopped by the police. Then we saw a group of people come through the ranks of police and start to head towards us. I didn't recognise any of them. There were eight of them, two women and six guys. As they got closer I instantly realised who they were. They were plain-clothed police officers. They stuck out like sore thumbs dressed in their obligatory Barbour jackets and regulation comfortable shoes. What the fuck were they doing? Talk about a death wish.

As they got closer I could see that more and more of the Millwall were starting to stare at them. They got to within fifty feet when a roar went up. 'Fucking Old Bill!' And with that everyone charged at them. Gerry and I were close to the front and ran with the crowd. As we advanced, the eight crime-squad officers turned and started to run back towards the police line. As we got to the end of the road the uniformed officers turned back around, and now with the uniform officers standing behind them, stood there. There was loads of posturing and finger pointing but little else until suddenly one of the crime-squad officers rushed forward from out of the ranks, poked his truncheon at Gerry and hit him squarely in the bollocks. He went down like a sack of shit and was the focus of everyone's amusement, police and supporters alike. Done in the bollocks. Quality.

I helped him get to his feet. He was furious. Eventually Charlie and I dragged him back towards the entrance to the ground. His pride and his bollocks were bruised and he spent the rest of the game with the serious arsehole.

We were finally allowed into the ground at seven o'clock and we took up our position behind the goal. The atmosphere was the best I had experienced at any game of football I had ever been to. The singing and banter was legendary. Fights were breaking out all over the ground and just as one was being sorted another would start. I had never experienced anything like it. It was exciting, scary and aggressive, very aggressive. The team played their hearts out and at the final whistle Millwall had come out on top, 2–1. We were kept in the ground for half an hour after the match had finished and all of us sang at the top of our voices for the entire time. We were then escorted en masse to the station at East Ham and put on a train. Back home, we said our goodbyes to our targets and made our way back to the office.

We got there just before midnight and we all breathed a sigh of relief. Apart from a few arrests for public disorder the day had gone well, and, aside from Chris's cut and Gerry's bruised bollocks, we were all in one piece. Robbie rang and confirmed that the powers that be were pleased with the outcome of the day but Gerry was still going on about the intervention of the local crime squad. He was insistent that Chris should take it up with the FIU and lodge a formal complaint. He had a point. Had they got any closer and been swallowed up by the crowd I dread to think what would have happened. For certain the crime squad officers wouldn't have walked away unscathed.

We all agreed to meet back in the office at 11 a.m. the next day to write up our evidence. I was relieved to get into my van and drive home. I pulled into my drive, switched the engine off and sat there in the dark. I relived the whole day back through in my head. The atmosphere in The Puffin beforehand. The idiot in the toilet, shooting the gun. Marching as one down the Romford Road into what felt like a battle. Holding the chemist's with two cans of hairspray. And then the game. The atmosphere and the banter. It was a special day. A great day. One that I would never forget.

I had got off on the events of the day, and for a while I had forgotten who I was and why I was there. Was I Jim the hooligan or Jim the undercover cop? I pushed it to the back of my mind. But I was without a doubt enjoying myself.

Maybe a little too much.

NINETEEN

FLYING SQUAD

I was up early the next day as I was still full of adrenalin from the day before. I made my way into the office and Gerry was already there. He was still incensed over the crime squad's actions prior to the West Ham game. I suggested that he leave it as nothing would come of it. He insisted that I put it into my evidence. I stared at him, a little confused. This was so out of character for Gerry. Normally he would have seen the funny side of it but he was hell bent to make sure that this was dealt with. 'Fucking hell, mate. It was only a poke in the bollocks. And they could question why you were so close to the front.'

Gerry had got up from his desk. I then noticed that he was wearing shorts. 'Just a poke in the bollocks? D'ya call this just a poke in the bollocks?' He pulled his shorts and pants down. I walked over and bent down. I had never seen anything like it. His bollock was the size of a small orange and looked very painful. As I was crouching down inspecting it, the door to the office opened and Angie and Charlie walked in. Angie was the first to react. 'Morning. Everything all right?'

Gerry was now trying to pull his shorts and pants back up while Charlie and I burst out laughing. Gerry started to laugh. I could now understand Gerry's reaction and was surprised at how much damage the truncheon had appeared to have done. Gerry went to the doctor's and was given the all clear, although it took over a fortnight for the swelling to go and the crime-squad complaint was dropped.

Later that day we were contacted by SO8 – also known as the Flying Squad – who had been informed via SO10 that we were going back to

The Puffin on the Thursday to collect the gun. As a gun was involved we had no choice other than to accept their offer of back-up. It was agreed that Chris and I would be the only ones to enter the pub but that we would be under constant surveillance. They were also keen that we both wore wires for our protection and so that they could listen and tape our conversation in the pub for evidential purposes. I refused. I made the point that we were in and out of that pub on a regular basis and it was a bit late in the day to be offering us wires for our protection. Chris, however, agreed. I was a little surprised by this and told him that if I again went into the toilet with 'Andy' that he was to remain outside in the bar as I didn't want the entire Flying Squad listening in on my conversation. He agreed and it was all set up for the next day.

Back at home I again replayed the previous day's events in my head. The thought of having to get up and give evidence about people that I now classed as friends was beginning to weigh heavy on me. I picked up the phone and rang Chris, who admitted to having the same thoughts. I was fully aware that this was a job and that my role in it was to obtain the evidence to lead to a conviction of individuals who carried out unnecessary and at times unprovoked acts of violence. On paper that reads well but the reality is somewhat different. I now called my targets my friends and as friends we would all protect each other, even if it meant endangering ourselves. And not only did I count my targets as my friends but I was also enjoying that part of my life: the build-up to the game; the second guessing; the fear of getting sussed out; the march into battle; the charge down the Old Kent Road. And, if it was to happen, the fight. I was getting off on the whole experience and when down The Puffin or at a game I felt alive.

And I had fallen in love. That was still my biggest dilemma. I knew deep down in my heart that I couldn't pursue it. But what I would have given to have just got into my van and driven down to The Puffin and confessed everything to Steph. What did I have to lose? Well, apart from my head.

The next day I was up early and I popped into the house in Catford for 7am to meet with the plumber and kitchen installer. The plumber handed me an invoice and I handed it back to him, announcing that it was no good giving that to me as I was just the painter and couldn't read it anyways. I was keeping on top of pretending to be illiterate, although it was now more a hindrance than a help.

I was into the office for 7.30 and Chris was already there. He told me that we had a briefing with a detective inspector and a detective sergeant in Rotherhithe, where the Flying Squad were based at 8.30. We made our way over there and deliberately parked some distance from the police station. On this occasion no one on the front desk questioned who I was, however there were a few raised eyebrows as we were escorted down to the detective inspector's office.

The pre-briefing with the detective inspector and his D.S. was short and sweet. As we were going to buy a firearm it was deemed an armed operation, which meant that some of the Flying Squad officers would be carrying guns. The brief was simple: go in, get the gun, leave the pub and make our way back to the van. We would be arrested along with the guy selling it; all of us would then be taken to Rotherhithe to be interviewed and then released pending further enquiries, which would take as long as the operation lasted. If the target failed to appear on time we were to give him up to half an hour but no longer. In that situation, we would not be arrested but would come back to Rotherhithe for a debrief.

We both went up to the room where Chris was to have his wire fitted. He had a number of wires connected to a pack that was taped to his waist. The tape constantly had to be reaffixed as Chris was quite hairy and every time it was taken off he lost some hair. I had no sympathy; I was still a little aggrieved that he had agreed to wear it.

Once the wire was in place and tested we made our way to the squad briefing. The detective inspector briefed the whole team on the operation. The squad were great and really complimentary about what we were doing and I felt really proud at what we were trying to achieve.

Our plan was to get to The Puffin for just after 10.30 and wait for the doors to be opened at eleven and then wander in. We pulled up outside at just before 10.30 and sat and waited.

At about 10.45 I spied Steph and Tina making their way down the Old Kent Road, carrying some shopping. This was a perfect opportunity to get us into the pub early and we got out and walked towards them. They both seemed genuinely pleased to see us as we took the shopping off them and followed them into the pub. It was a very strange experience to know that someone was listening in on our conversation.

I carried the shopping to the bar and placed it down. Steph pointed to the back of the bar. 'Can you pop it through to the kitchen and put it on the table? It's up the stairs and on the right.'

I picked it back up and Chris and I went through the bar and up the stairs to the kitchen. It felt very odd to be upstairs. It had a real homely feel and you would never guess that you were above the bar in The Puffin.

Steph came up followed by Tina. Tina was the first to speak. 'Thanks for that, them stairs are a bastard. Beer?'

I looked at Steph as she took the kettle and turned it on. 'D'ya know what I fancy?'

And before I could finish Tina interjected, 'Easy, Jim. She is my sister, you know.'

I could feel myself going red in the face as I was only too aware that all of the Flying Squad were listening in.

I tried to defuse the situation 'No, no, not that…'

Steph glared at me. 'Oh thanks.'

This was now going from bad to worse. Chris just sat there with a stupid grin on his face, happy in the knowledge that he was relaying the whole thing to the squad outside.

'What I was trying to say was that I fancied a cup of tea.'

Both Steph and Tina started to laugh. 'We know, Jim,' Tina answered. 'But I gotta tell you: this playing hard to get is beginning to even piss me off. Are you ever gonna take my sister out for a drink?'

Shit. This was now a complete fucking disaster. If I said no I was a cunt. If I said yes I would have to go through with it. Fortunately Steph saved the day. 'Tina, leave him alone. All in good time, eh, J?'

This really threw me. Not because she had jumped in and saved me but because she called me J. Only my family and closest friends called me that. I threw her a look.

'What's that look for?' Steph asked. 'I tell you, you are fucking odd. I sometimes get you, but other times, like now, you are a fucking mystery.'

That was it. I was already on the fucking edge and with all the squad listening in my ego got the better of me. 'D'ya know what? Fuck the tea. I'll have a beer, and as for taking you out, name the day and I'll be there.'

I then turned to Chris. 'Come on, we have a gun to collect.' The girls stared at me and then at Chris. 'What, didn't you know we're here to get the gun off Andy?'

With that I got up from the table and made my way back downstairs. I sat by the bar and Chris appeared at the foot of the stairs. He went to talk and I put my finger to my lips. I had had enough of listened-in conversations and he came over to the bar and sat down next to me.

Tina appeared a couple of minutes later. 'I don't know what she fucking sees in you but she said to say that next Tuesday works for her.'

I nodded back. 'Fine, Tuesday it is.'

She then passed us our drinks and went back upstairs. We sat there waiting for Andy, who failed to appear. It was now obvious to us all that he was going to be a no-show and Chris and I made our excuses and left. We got into the van and drove back to Rotherhithe.

We pulled into the yard and went into the office. The detective inspector came in and thanked everyone for their assistance and Chris and I for our professionalism and wished us good luck with the rest of the operation.

There was one point made. No dialogue could be picked up once we had entered the pub but that wasn't a surprise to the technical guys. Their guess was that there was something on the premises that blocked the signal or that the building was lined in old asbestos sheeting.

I had got away with it. None of the conversation between Tina and Steph had been picked up. I followed Chris up and sat there with the same smile that he had etched across his face in the kitchen of The Puffin. He winced as they pulled the tape off and halfway through announced that he would never wear another wire. As we were leaving some of the Flying Squad rushed past us and out of the door. The last guy, a detective in his forties, turned and smiled at me. 'I know your old man. Bet he's really proud of what you're doing. Good luck.' I looked on as he disappeared out of the door. After the morning I had just had I was gonna need more than just good luck.

On the way back to the office Chris started to laugh. 'Well, Jim, looks like you have a date next Tuesday.'

I turned to him. 'Do you really think this is a good idea?'

Chris pondered the question. 'Actually, everything aside, I don't see that any harm can come of it, you're both consenting adults.'

I pulled the van over. 'But that's just it: we're not. She likes Jim the illiterate painter and decorator and Millwall hooligan from Wandsworth, not Jim the Judas cop who wants to send her brother-in-law to prison.'

Chris let out a sigh. 'When you put it like that, it does sort of take the romance out of it. I never thought of it like that. What the fuck are we gonna do?'

I started to laugh. 'Fucking hell, you've got some front. Since when has *we* come into it?'

Chris looked a little taken aback. 'It's always us now. Always. I might not be a natural but I will always have your back and you might not realise it, but I do my bit.'

I was now properly laughing. 'Do your bit? Like what?'

'Like today.'

I continued to laugh. 'Like today. You are kidding me. What the fuck did you do today to cover my arse?'

Chris started to smile. 'Think about it.'

I was now getting slightly angry. 'What the fuck does that mean?'

'The wire, think about the wire.'

I was now getting proper pissed off. 'What the fuck are you rattling on about?'

Chris sat there smiling. 'I turned it off.'

This took me by surprise. 'You what?'

He shrugged his shoulders. 'I turned the fucking thing off when we got in the pub. I asked the guy how to do it in case I needed to and he showed me. So when I saw Tina and Steph and we went upstairs I turned it off.'

I was absolutely gobsmacked. 'But why would you do that?'

He looked out of the window. 'Why do you think? To protect you. I didn't want you to have to say stuff that all of them could listen to, plus you were right. I should never have agreed to wear it in the first place.'

I now felt like shit. 'I'm sorry, fucking hell, why didn't you tell me?'

Chris laughed. 'Why didn't I tell you? Yeah, right. Oh, sorry Steph, can I just stop you there cos I need to let Jim know that I have turned the wire off and the Flying Squad, who are all outside by the way, can't now hear what he's saying.'

'Yeah, of course. Fuck. Thanks, Chris.'

He put his arm around my shoulder. 'No worries. Let's get back to the office.'

I nodded and pulled the car out from the kerb and we made our way back. We pulled into the yard and went upstairs to join the others. They were not surprised that Andy had failed to appear. Chris and I kept the Steph dilemma between the two of us and agreed to talk about it when we were alone later in the day.

Back in the office, we were called by the FIU who had received information that some Leeds supporters were looking to travel down on the Friday ahead of the game on Saturday and that they were going to be heading for the Old Kent Road. This was news to us but we thanked them for the heads-up.

Instead of going home, Chris and I went to dinner and talked through how we were feeling. The conversation quickly turned to Steph and how best we should deal with it. Chris had given it a lot of thought and we both agreed that we would just have to let it play out. Chris stated that wherever the situation took me with Steph I could expect his full support.

We finished our beers, I said goodnight and headed home. When I got there, the lights were still on and I made my way into the flat. Dawn rushed over and gave me a hug. I tried to respond but failed.

She pulled away. 'What is up with you, Jim? You used to be a laugh. It was fun. Now you are never here and when you are you may as well not be.'

'It's nothing,' I replied. 'It's work. It's just really busy. You know what it's like.'

She now started to raise her voice. 'No, I don't know what it's like. D'ya know why I don't know? Because you never fucking talk about it, that's why. I have no idea what you are doing from one day to the next. I've been at my parents for a whole week and you never called me once, not fucking once. I called you every time, and most of the time you weren't even fucking here, and when I did get to speak to you, you rushed me off the phone.' She then paused. 'Do you still love me? Well, do you?'

I was so not in the mood to be having this conversation but I answered back anyway. 'What sort of a question is that?'

She pounced on my response. 'A very simple question with a very simple answer. Do you love me? Yes or no.'

I didn't know what to say. The tears started to stream down her face and she screamed at me: '*Yes or fucking no? Answer the fucking question.*'

I still didn't respond. She ran towards me and slapped me. She then turned away. 'Are you having an affair?'

I am ashamed to say that I laughed. 'Am I having an affair? If only it was that fucking easy.'

I walked into the bedroom and she followed me in. 'Don't fucking laugh at me. You still haven't answered my question. Do you still love me?'

I sat down on the bed and looked up at her as I lied. 'Yes. Yes, of course, I do.'

'Well, fucking show it,' and with that walked out of the room.

I sat on the bed until eventually I got up and went back into the lounge. Dawn was sitting on the sofa in tears. I sat down next to her and put my arm around her. 'I'm really sorry.'

We just sat there, her crying and me staring out of the window, until eventually she fell asleep on my lap. After a while I woke her up and we both went to bed.

TWENTY
MILLWALL VS LEEDS

I was the first one in the office the next day and sat there on my own until Angie arrived. She made me one of her great cups of tea and then started to talk about Millwall being promoted and how great it would be for us as it would definitely extend the operation. I hadn't thought about the operation going on further than the season but Angie was right. Millwall were playing some good football and there was an outside chance that they might just do it.

At this point Gerry came in and the conversation quickly went on to the Leeds game the following day and the information received from the FIU about Leeds travelling down for the night before.

Chris and I decided to start in The Puffin and after a day in the office we made our way down at just after six. Paul was sitting at a table in the corner. He gestured for us to come and join him. He was in good spirits and he called over to Tina who was serving at the bar to bring us over some drinks.

We spoke about the West Ham game and he told us about a running battle after the game in the Mile End Road. None of this had filtered through to us. Apparently, there had also been a brawl outside a pub. All of this, to our knowledge, had gone unreported.

He then turned his thoughts to the Leeds game the next day. He told us that everyone was heading to London Bridge for one o'clock. He suggested that if we were up for it to be at The Puffin for eleven and we could all travel up together. Steph had now joined Tina at the bar. I caught her eye and made my way over.

Before I could say anything Steph spoke. 'Jim, I am going to have to cancel Tuesday as Tina and I are off to Spain tomorrow. Can we do something when I get back?'

'Yeah, no worries. How long you going for?'

'Two weeks and I can't wait.'

I turned to go back to Chris and Paul. 'See you when you get back.'

She smiled. 'Yep. You be good.'

I made my way back over to Chris and Paul and finished my drink. We agreed to see Paul at eleven and left. I told Chris about Steph cancelling and he could see that I was relieved but a little sad. 'Well, Jimbo, at least you can put it off for a couple of weeks.'

In the morning were both back in the office for eight and went for breakfast with Gerry and Charlie, which had now become a ritual before home games.

Chris called the FIU and asked if there had been any incidents after the West Ham game reported in the Mile End Road. There had been some reports and also some unsubstantiated information about an incident in one of the pubs. We confirmed that they were football related and that they were to be marked as such. Chris was vague with them about the London Bridge meet as we had learnt our lesson after Leicester and said that we would validate it when we had met with our targets.

We were now being very careful about what we passed across as the FIU's response always seemed to be to flood the area with Old Bill and thereby thwart any potential disorder. This in itself was fine but eventually it always raised the question as to how the Old Bill knew to be there.

We made our way down to The Puffin and met up with Dave, Stu and Mark. We travelled up together and were at London Bridge for just before one. We hung around until eventually a large number of police turned up and moved us on. We made our way back to the ground and watched the game. Leeds had brought a good crowd and were vocal with their support. Millwall played really well and we cruised to a 3–1 win. After the match we again travelled to London Bridge with Paul and the others but there were no signs of any Leeds and after about an hour we left and returned to the office. We wrote up our evidence for the day and I went home.

Dawn was working nights so I had the flat to myself. I spent the weekend quietly avoiding her. The next couple of weeks were pretty much the same and not much happened of any note. We didn't make the journey up to Stoke although we won 2–1 and the game against Hull on the 28th was similar, although Millwall won 2–0. We were still going to The Puffin and it was a much easier experience with Steph not being there. We met with Dave and the others for the Reading game on the Tuesday and Millwall won again, 3–0.

We were contacted by Rory as we were due to play Man City in a couple of weeks and we arranged to meet up with him and the Man City coverts as he wanted to catch up prior to the game. We decided to travel up to Manchester the next day and make a day of it.

We left early on the Wednesday morning and were into Manchester just after lunch. We arrived at Rory's offices on the outskirts of the city and he gave us a tour of their facility. It was similar in size to our offices but the level of equipment that was available to them was staggering. They had all sorts of specialised camera equipment and stuff on trial from the security services. It was like something out of a James Bond film. There were video recorders stacked five high. They had a dedicated team of two officers whose sole responsibility was to collate and log evidence. It was impressive stuff.

The Man City operation was going well and they already had a substantial amount of evidence but were going to let the operation run until at least the end of this season and maybe into the next before acting on it. We were unsure of our time frames but one thing we did know was that we still didn't have enough evidence to go to trial. We then watched a tape that they had recorded of an organised fight between Manchester City and United hooligans. The level of violence that we saw was way beyond anything I had ever witnessed. The video finished with a Manchester United hooligan on the floor unconscious with a Manchester City hooligan jumping up and down on his head. It remains the most violent thing I have ever seen. It put everything that we were trying to achieve in perspective.

Seeing Rory always focused the mind and this last trip had been no different. We returned to the office with renewed vigour, although a little jealous of all their equipment and back-up. We got back to the office early evening and Angie was still there. She was on her own working through the videos and collating all of the evidence. We decided not to tell her about the Man City set-up as she had been on it for twelve hours and was not even halfway through.

Millwall had a cup game against Leeds on the Tuesday and we spent most of the day liaising with the FIU. We had arranged to meet up with Dave and the others at The Puffin for 5.30. We pulled up outside and made our way over to the pub. It was a miserable night and we were both soaked as we entered the pub, which was heaving with Millwall. Dave and the others were already there and Dave told us that everyone was heading to Charing Cross after the game. Were we up for it? Of course we were, and after a couple of beers we headed for the game. Millwall played really well and we won the game easily 2–0.

In the stands, everyone around us seemed to know about the meet at Charing Cross. As we pulled into the station on the train we were met by a large crowd of Millwall. As we left the train there was a large roar from up in front of us. Everyone started to cheer and run forward.

I rushed to the front where I was confronted by a small line of police officers. Standing about fifty feet behind them were a large group of Leeds. The police were holding the line, just, but as we stood there more and more police arrived to bolster up the numbers.

I was then grabbed from behind and turned to see Paul. 'Come on.'

I grabbed Chris, Dave, Stu and Mark and we followed Paul through the Millwall and down a set of stairs at the back that led onto the Embankment. Marcus and some of the other Bushwackers were standing there. It went quiet as Marcus spoke. 'Right, we can come at 'em from the front of the station and get in behind them. Follow me. Come on, you Lions…'

With that we all began to run up a small road that led to the top of the railway station. We ran across the front and into the station behind where the Leeds hooligans were baiting the Millwall. It worked. There were about sixty of us and as we ran forward we steamed into the unsuspecting Leeds. They had nowhere to go and were now trapped with Millwall coming at them from behind and the police at the front blocking their exit.

I was now quite near the front and watched on as Paul, Marcus and the others piled in. The adrenalin rush was huge and all of my senses became heightened as I ran to the front, kicking out at people as they tried to run past me. I was hit on the side of the head and I instantly turned around and swung a punch. It landed on the jaw of the guy who had hit me and I followed it up with a kick that landed on his right thigh. He was much bigger than me and although he winced in pain he didn't go down. He then took another swing at me and I managed to duck as his fist flew past the top of my head. At this point another two Millwall charged into him and he was beaten to the ground. He was kicked a number of times, mainly in the torso, but the final kick landed with some force to the side of his head and it was obvious that it had knocked him out. It was brutal.

I then charged forward with the others as by this time the Leeds hooligans had broken through the police line only to be set upon by the other Millwall supporters who were in front of them. The police had their truncheons drawn and were indiscriminately lashing out at anyone who came near them. Leeds were hugely outnumbered and there were assaults taking place all over the station as they tried to run.

Eventually after about five minutes more police arrived and the fighting stopped. We were all herded to the front of the station and a large number of police surrounded us. We stood there singing and baiting the Leeds hooligans who had taken a proper beating. The atmosphere was now pure theatre and we were all singing 'No One Likes Us' at the top of our voices.

Suddenly there was another roar and we all turned and watched as a group of people spilled onto the concourse from the platform fighting. We all surged forward but the police held firm. I recognised a couple of the guys as Millwall and it was unfair odds as three of them set about someone who was obviously a Leeds supporter. Fortunately for him some police rushed over and after a struggle they were all handcuffed and led away.

Finally after about ten minutes of singing and continual baiting of the Leeds hooligans we were all escorted off the concourse and down the platform and put on a train back to London Bridge. Everyone was still high from adrenalin and all the talk was about Millwall having done the Leeds Service Crew. We pulled into New Cross and I ran up to Paul who was ahead of us. He turned and smiled. 'All right, Jim. I would say that we won that one hands down. Beer?'

I nodded back excitedly. 'Yep, see you in there.'

Chris headed off with me to The Puffin for a celebratory beer. He admitted that he had found the whole experience terrifying but that I, however, had appeared to really enjoy myself. He was right: I had, but the Leeds hooligans would have done exactly the same given the opportunity. Chris agreed but said that still didn't make it acceptable behaviour.

He was right but at that moment I was still living off the thrill. As we walked into the pub I raised my arms above my head and cheered. It was a great evening and Chris and I stayed in there, finally getting back to the office just after midnight. Gerry and Charlie were still there and had also had a good night. I was full of the fight at Charing Cross and how we had ambushed Leeds from behind. Chris cut me short and reminded me as to why we were there and that the behaviour was unacceptable in a civilised society and that somebody could have been seriously injured.

Once again, I knew he was right, but I drove home still on a high from the night's events.

The next morning I was in for ten and Chris was not far behind me. We wrote up our evidence and Chris read through my statement. He was not happy that I had got so close to the front but he resigned himself to the fact that this was part of what we had to do. The FIU called and confirmed that there had been ten arrests for disorder at Charing Cross but to their knowledge nobody had suffered any serious injury. That was good to hear as I kept thinking about the guy who had hit me and was then kicked unconscious.

We spent the rest of the week looking at video evidence and picking people out who were at the Charing Cross fight. On the Saturday we met up with Dave and the others at The Puffin before the Man City game. We had all heard that Millwall had drawn Arsenal away for the third round of the FA Cup. Result. Everyone was ecstatic about the draw. Arsenal away was going to be another fun day out.

Both Chris and I were surprised and touched when Dave, Stu and Mark gave us Christmas cards. It was now 12 December and Christmas hadn't really featured up until then. As I opened Dave's card he started to laugh. He had drawn a picture of me in dungarees standing next to what was obviously a picture of the others as he knew I wouldn't be able to read the names on it. We all had a good laugh at my expense and made our way to the ground.

There was a large police presence as always and the Man City fans were in a boisterous mood. As I looked I saw Rory and the others walking with a large group of other supporters who were obviously their targets. I pointed and shouted out, 'Manc wankers…' Rory saw that it was me. He pulled a can from out of his pocket and fired out a large blue stream of party string covering me and everyone around me. He then put his finger in the air and placed the can back in his pocket. I watched on as Guy, the spotter, went over and confiscated the can.

We lost the game 1–0. After a couple of drinks with Rory and his team, I went home to Dawn who was in high spirits as the house in Catford had sold. She was keen to put the money into another property and we spent most of Sunday and Monday looking at property together. Things were still not great between us but we seemed at that stage to have hit a happy compromise. I didn't talk about work and she didn't ask.

TWENTY-ONE

WE THREE KINGS

Back in the office on Tuesday all the talk was now about the Arsenal game in the FA Cup, Christmas and the forthcoming functions that we had been invited to as a team and were expected to attend. We had the local CID party on the Saturday evening.

The CID party was being held at a private club. It was well away from prying eyes. Our partners were also invited, and we arranged to meet at the venue for 7 p.m. for a drink before we sat down to eat.

Dawn had agreed to drive. We pulled into the car park alongside Gerry and Susan who had also just arrived. We all headed inside and made our way to the bar. Chris was sitting on a stool and we made our way over to him. As soon as I looked at him, I could tell that something was up.

'You all right?' I asked. He spun around on his stool and nearly fell off. Gerry grabbed hold of him and helped him to sit up.

'She ain't coming and before you ask, no, I don't wanna talk about it.' He was drinking lager with a scotch chaser, which I had never seen him do before. Gerry ordered some drinks and we sat down next to Chris. After his third scotch he got up and headed for the toilet. He was staggering and people were already beginning to notice as he disappeared into the ladies' toilet. There was a scream as he exited apologising and then he tripped and fell over.

Gerry and I pissed ourselves as we ran over to help him to his feet. We carried him into the toilet where he threw up. I had never seen anything like it. He could throw up for England. It was on the walls, all over the floor, in the urinal but he, apart from his shoes, had survived unscathed. Eventually we managed to get him to the sink. We ran the tap and splashed water on his face. We carried on splashing him with water and after about five minutes he started to get some colour back in his cheeks. His shoes were still caked in sick and then Gerry noticed a shoe-shine machine over in the corner. We helped him over and then held on to him as we stuck each foot under the machine. The brushes made short work of the sick and within seconds his shoes were returned to their former glory. A couple of members of staff then appeared with a bucket and mop and we left them to it as we escorted Chris over to our table.

Chris was now struggling to stay awake and Charlie suggested that he should go home and get some sleep. We called him a cab and ten minutes later he was gone. The rest of the night was pretty uneventful and Gerry, Charlie and I sat at the bar drinking, leaving the girls to chat at the table. We all left together at just after eleven and said that we would see each other on the Tuesday. Dawn drove back and I went to sleep.

I was back in the office for Tuesday and Charlie was already there. He had driven down Monday night and slept at the office to avoid the traffic and we chatted about the Saturday night and Chris. Chris was the last to appear and he apologised for Saturday, putting his vomiting down to a dodgy prawn sandwich at lunch.

We spent most of the Tuesday and Wednesday decorating the office with tinsel and fairy lights. We were all in the office early on Thursday as we had been invited to the FIU Christmas party which was being held at the Charing Cross club. We left the office at just before ten and made our way on the train into London.

We arrived at the club just after eleven and met with Lawrence and Robbie who had already been there an hour. We talked briefly about the forthcoming Arsenal game and Robbie told us that Arsenal had a covert team, which was news to us, but that they weren't very good.

However he thought that we should probably meet up with them after Christmas and that he would sort it.

We agreed and then started to drink and by one o'clock we were all well on the way to being pissed. We had a buffet lunch and then carried on drinking. At three Charlie announced that he was off home as he had a nativity play to attend in the evening. An hour later Gerry made his excuses, stating that he was off to Oxford Street to buy Susan some Christmas underwear. I stayed with Chris and the others until just after five and left. I was absolutely rotten and could hardly talk let alone walk. I managed to get to the train station and got on the first train I saw. I sat down and asked where the train was going. Lewisham. Great, I could get off there and walk to Hither Green. How I managed to stay awake and not be sick will forever be a mystery but I managed it.

The train pulled into Lewisham and I got off. I set off on my walk back to the office, wearing just my socks having given my shoes to a homeless guy. I was now really struggling and as I walked I would start to speed up until eventually I would be walking so fast that my feet couldn't keep up with my body and I would fall over. I must have looked a proper mess.

After about an hour I found myself outside our offices in Hither Green. My feet were now killing me. I pushed through the gate and went to the front door, which was locked. The office was in darkness except for the glow from the Christmas lights. I searched through my pockets for my office keys but couldn't find them. I needed to get into the office to get the keys to my van that were in my desk so that I could drive home. I was pissed and tired and now all I wanted to do was go home. There was no other option; I was going to have to break in.

I stepped back and ran at the door and charged into it with my shoulder. I smashed into the door and bounced back, falling into the yard. I got back up and this time decided that the better option would be to kick the door rather than to shoulder-charge it. I had forgotten that I was now not wearing any shoes. I pulled my foot back, aimed it at the lock and went for it. My foot smashed into the wood just below the lock, which was wet and my foot slipped upwards jamming my toes into the handle. I let out a massive scream as the pain shot through my toes and up into my brain. I was pissed, shoeless, locked out and in fucking agony. I was now rolling around on the dirt howling in pain and holding my now broken toes.

I had the proper fucking hump and in my pissed state limped over to my van. I could see a hammer in the footwell but both doors were locked. I then spied a brick down by the front wheel and picked it up and made my way back to the front door. I then spent ten minutes breaking through the wired security glass until eventually I had got through. I clambered through and then came to the next door. I turned the handle and fortunately it was open. I pushed the door. As I did so there was a couple of audible beeps and the alarm went off. In my pissed state I had forgotten all about the alarm. But this was not just any alarm. No, this was a central station alarm, which meant one thing, that in about three minutes this place was going to be crawling with Old Bill. I then did what any sensible, shoeless drunk would do: I legged it. I limped back over the broken security glass, cutting my feet in the process. I clambered back out into the yard over to the gate and staggered off down the road to the sanctuary of the Indian restaurant about a quarter of a mile from the office.

I burst in and sat down at the table. The waiter asked if I was all right. I told him that I was pissed and needed help to get home. He was great and called his brother who had a cab firm up the road. Within minutes his brother was there and they helped me into the cab and he drove off. As he rounded the corner to drive past our offices, there was Old Bill everywhere. Cars, vans, the lot. He drove past them as I slid down in the back. He drove me to my flat and I paid him. I buzzed the door and Dawn let me in. I got to the top of the stairs and she was waiting for me. She took one look at me and turned and walked back into the flat.

I woke up the next morning on the sofa, with my toes killing me and with the worst hangover I had ever had. Just breathing hurt. At just gone nine the phone rang. It was Charlie. I needed to get into the office as soon as possible as we had had a major breach of security. Somebody had tried to break into the office.

I walked into the yard to see a forensics team painstakingly sifting through the broken glass and fingerprinting the whole scene. I was let in through the door and made my way up to the office. I walked in and sat down. Gerry and Chris were still to arrive and Charlie was beside himself. He was really worried that our security had been breached and that we would definitely have to move after this. I just sat quietly and waited for the others to turn up. Within the hour everyone was in and all the talk was of the breach in security. I stood up from my desk and announced to everyone, 'Chaps, I have an announcement to make. Our security hasn't been breached, it was me.'

They stared back at me. Charlie was the first to respond. 'You? What do you mean, you?'

I bowed my head. 'I came back here fucking pissed and didn't have my van keys so I tried to break in. When I got to the second door the alarm went off and I legged it.'

Everyone sat there open-mouthed and then they started to laugh. Charlie shook his head. 'You cunt. Fucking hell, I thought we had been sussed. Shit. What are we gonna do? Who else knows?'

I sat looking at everyone. 'No one, just us and Dawn.'

Chris stood up. 'Right, we need to keep this to ourselves,' he said. 'If they find out this was you, you will be for the fucking high jump. Okay?'

I nodded. He was laughing but I could tell that he was not best pleased.

Later that day Chris received a call from Robbie and Lawrence from the FIU asking him if we had all made it home safely. 'Of course we're fine, we're Millwall', he said and wished them a Happy Christmas.

Christmas was soon upon us and after a couple of days getting the office right we all headed home for a few days off.

Dawn had made arrangements to go to her parents for the morning and then to my parents' for Christmas lunch. We would open our presents to each other before we left. I was happy to not have to make any decisions and went with it.

On Christmas morning, we sat down to eat breakfast and passed each other our Christmas presents. She opened up the presents that I had bought her. It was obvious that it was not what she was expecting. I had bought her an expensive jacket that didn't fit and some underwear. She took one look at the underwear and announced that it looked like something 'a barmaid would wear'. I laughed to myself at the irony of her comment, but it wasn't a great start to the day.

She gave me my presents, which were a selection of hooded tops and two new pairs of dungarees as my old ones were falling apart. She then handed me my final present only to inform me that this one she had bought for herself and that I was to give it to her. It was a small box and I stared at it, confused. 'What is it?'

She took it back off me and started to open it. 'Well, let's open it and find out.'

She then opened the box and took out a small diamond solitaire ring. I sat there, unable to comment as she thanked me and placed it on her engagement finger. She had apparently travelled with her father to see a friend of his in Hatton Garden and had seen this and couldn't resist it. The day had gone from bad to worse. She was ecstatic while I just sat there.

Finally I spoke. 'Do you not think we maybe should have had a discussion around this?'

She then looked back at me. 'What's there to discuss? It's only a ring.'

I decided not to make a scene. It was Christmas Day and it could wait. I knew deep down in my heart that the relationship was never going to last but frankly there is only so much shit that anyone could deal with at any one time. For me, given what was going on around me at the time, the relationship, or lack of it, was a low priority and I chose, selfishly, to not deal with it head-on at that time.

We left the house in the van and made our way over to Dawn's parents. She was quick to show off her ring to her mum, who admitted that she had already seen it, and to her sister who had recently arrived back from travelling. I pointed out that it wasn't an engagement ring and that Dawn had bought it but it fell on deaf ears. I just wanted to get out of there. Eventually we headed off.

As we pulled up outside my parents' house, I turned to her. 'Look, today isn't the day for a conversation about your or the ring's intentions and I would appreciate it if you would not wear it.'

She was out of the van before I could finish. She was barely in the front door before she was showing it off to my two sisters. I sat in the van contemplating what to do. She seemed happier than she had in ages, and I wanted her to be happy as she was a genuinely nice girl. I ran the various scenarios that were open to me through my head. I could come clean and announce that she had bought the ring herself and that I had no intentions of marrying her and that we were not engaged; I could smile and go along with it; or I could say nothing and deal with it later.

I chose the latter and got out of the van. All of my family were a little taken aback by my gift to Dawn. I had a candid conversation with my granddad, who said that I had done the right thing by keeping quiet but that I had to sort it out.

Finally we said our goodbyes and Dawn and I made our way back to the flat. When we got back home I made my way off to bed announcing that I needed to be in the office early tomorrow for the away game to West Brom.

I was in for 8 a.m. Charlie was already there having set off early from Padstow. Gerry was next to arrive and was wearing a jumper to rival all jumpers and one that you could only get away with at Christmas. It was red and white and had a massive fucking snowflake on the front of it. His mum had bought it for him and he strangely appeared to like it.

Charlie was his usual cutting self. 'Fucking hell, Gerry, are you wearing that for a fucking bet?'

Gerry stormed off with the hump, announcing that he was going to make the teas, as Charlie and I pissed ourselves.

Just after nine Chris arrived, apologising for being late. He had driven up from his parents' and announced that we had better set off to pick Dave and the others up as the traffic was shit. He then spied Gerry's jumper. 'Fucking hell, Gerry. What are you wearing?' Charlie and I again burst out laughing and in a moment of unprecedented rage Gerry took his jumper off, threw it on his desk and stormed off.

Chris and I decided to bid a hasty retreat and left. We drove to Catford in the hire car and picked up Dave and Stu. Mark had failed to appear. We arrived at the game in good time. The game was huge fun and Millwall won convincingly 4–1. We spent the last twenty minutes of the game doing the conga around the away end and the turnout was the best it had been all season, apart from the West Ham game.

We dropped Dave and Stu back at Catford. On the spur of the moment, Chris and I headed down to The Puffin for a quick one on the way home. When we got there, the pub was surprisingly busy. I didn't recognise many people, apart from Paul and Tina who were at the bar both wearing Santa hats. Paul wished us both Happy Christmas and gave us both a free drink. He told us that he had heard that Millwall had played well but that there had been some trouble at one of the services with Marcus and his crew with a bunch of Villa. It was news to us and we both stored it to the memory bank to deal with later.

Paul sat down with us for a short while. Nothing had as yet been decided about the Arsenal game, but someone had mentioned that if we were in the Clock End then they were up for nicking it. This had me and Chris laughing. The clock was fucking huge and wouldn't be an easy nick. We wondered about the chances of Millwall gaining promotion to the First Division and talk quickly turned to the thoughts of going to Anfield and Old Trafford. Paul went on about how the FA and the police would be shitting themselves at the thought of Millwall in the First Division and that the policing costs would be huge as Millwall would be taking a massive support away to most away games. I sat there and contemplated the thought of the First Division. It would be a dream come true, given that in our first season as undercover officers Millwall had finished mid-table. Would we be given the chance to extend the operation? It was a mouth-watering prospect, Millwall in the First Division. The chance to travel away as not only an undercover police officer but also now very much as a fan.

Paul headed back to the bar. I went to the bar to get Chris and me a drink and Steph, who I had not seen until then, came up and stood next to me. She was smiling as I turned to look at her. I smiled back. 'Happy Christmas.' I leant forward and kissed her on the cheek.

As I pulled away she pulled me back towards her and kissed me on the lips. 'Happy Christmas, J.'

She had again called me J.

I had to know. 'Why do you call me J when you know my name is Jim?'

She smiled. 'Why? Don't you like it?'

I sat down on the stool and she pushed herself against me and sat on my lap. 'No, no, it's not that. It's just that's what my mum and sisters call me and I was just wondering what made you think to call me that.'

Her hands were resting on my shoulders. She leant forward and whispered into my ear. 'That's what your mum said to call you.'

Instantly my head started to spin. How did she know my mum? Where had she met her? What the fuck had she said? I responded as calmly as I could, 'When did you meet my mum?'

She started to laugh. 'Fucking hell, Jim, you're easy to wind up. I was joking. I ain't ever met your mum.'

I tried to laugh it off. 'Oh right. It's just like when I met your mum and she told me that your real name was Ethel.'

She laughed.

Chris made his way over. 'Hi, Steph. Happy Christmas. Jimbo, we had better be going.'

Steph turned and looked at me. 'D'ya have to?'

I lifted her off my lap and stood up. 'Sorry, Ethel, but the boss has spoken. See you Monday?'

She stepped forward and again kissed me. Fuck, this was agony. I slowly pulled away. She carried on looking at me with her great smile and bloody perfect white teeth and beautiful shiny hair and answered, 'Yep, I'll be here, J. As always.' And she turned and walked away.

Chris looked at me and shook his head. 'Fucking hell, Jim. Look, I don't mind if you wanna stay.'

I shook my head. 'No, let's get the fuck out of here. I have had enough excitement for one day.'

Chris drove us back to the office. I told him about Dawn and the ring. He asked what I intended to do. I admitted that at the moment Dawn was usually the last thing on my mind and I only thought about her out of necessity rather than out of choice. But with Steph not a day went past without me thinking about her: her beauty, her personality, her obvious attraction to me and mine to her. We pulled back into the yard and went up to join the others.

The rest of the Christmas period was spent going to the home games against Sheffield and then Leicester which was the New Year's Day game. Chris and I went to The Puffin after both games but Paul and the girls were nowhere to be seen. We assumed that they must have headed off to Spain as no one seemed to know where they were. Millwall's promotion to the First Division now seemed to be fast becoming a real possibility rather than a dream. Mark would mention our bet every time I saw him but I continued to play it down.

The game against Arsenal was to be played in a week's time, on Saturday 9 January 1988, and like the West Ham game the FIU had been on the phone pretty much every day after the Christmas break. Robbie informed us that we were to meet the Arsenal covert team on the Monday before the game at their offices somewhere in north London and that we would again need to attend Scotland Yard for a briefing.

Arsenal versus Millwall. Highbury here we come.

TWENTY-TWO

ARSENAL IN THE CUP

Monday was the day we were to meet with the Arsenal coverts at their offices in Muswell Hill. We went to the yard behind the address that we had been given and knocked on the door. The sergeant who was running the team, a guy in his early thirties who looked like he had just walked off the set from an episode of *The Bill*, let us in. He was dressed in the obligatory crime squad Barbour jacket and comfortable shoes. He introduced himself and his partner, a Detective Constable Wick.

Once we had sat down, Chris launched into his usual speech about how we had found it hard to start with but that we were now firmly in with our targets. Thankfully, Charlie interrupted, 'Anyways, enough about us. What have you heard about Saturday?'

DC Wick told us that they would attend their local pubs and would talk to people at the game but as yet they had not been able to infiltrate Arsenal's hard-core element. We were all a little shocked. Their operation had been running for eighteen months and yet they were still struggling to gain acceptance. It became obvious that they had little idea of what they were doing when he said, 'Anyways, you and your lot had better watch out as the Gooners are gonna give Millwall a run for their money.'

We all burst out laughing. I was still laughing as I spoke: 'Sorry, this is Arsenal we're talking about, right?'

Both of them looked at me rather confused. 'Yeah…'

I looked at Gerry. 'Oh right, it's just that for a moment I thought we might have been playing West Ham or Chelsea. Our lot had better watch out. You are having a fucking laugh.' I looked at Chris. 'Our lot had better watch out? DC Wick? More like DC Dick.'

The sergeant stared directly at me. 'Sorry, who are you again? As you don't look like any policeman that I have ever met.'

Chris tried to save the day. 'I think what Jim is trying to say is that Millwall are looking to bring a large following on Saturday and that Arsenal are likely to get overrun if we don't act on all the evidence available to us.'

Gerry then joined in, 'Yep that's exactly what Jim was trying to say. And also that your lot are likely to get their fucking arses kicked if they are not careful.'

At that point DC Wick jumped to his feet. 'Let me tell you, Millwall can come here but at the end of the day it's your arseholes that are gonna be hanging out like an old red sock.'

We started to laugh. Charlie headed for the door. He opened it and gestured to Chris, Gerry and me to leave. 'Gentlemen, this has been a pleasure but I think that it is now time for us to depart and ready ourselves for Saturday with your good advice ringing in our ears.'

Back in the office, Angie informed us that Robbie had been on the phone and that Chris was to call him to discuss the meeting that we had just had with the Arsenal coverts. Chris took himself off to another office and we waited for him to come back. We recounted the story to Angie. She laughed and then reassured us that Chris would sort it out and with that he entered the room. It had been fine. Robbie also thought that they were a couple of mugs and that he would be surprised if they managed to survive until the end of the season. But Chris made it clear that he didn't want to be part of another meeting like the one we had just had. We agreed that we could have handled it better but we were all in agreement as to just what we thought of them.

Chris and I headed off to The Puffin at just after seven. The pub, apart from a couple of regulars, was empty although Tina was at the bar. She told us that they had all been to Spain for a few days. Paul joined us and was quick to tell us that he would have some more information about the Arsenal game later on in the week. He suggested that we pop back in on Wednesday for a beer and a catch-up. We said our goodbyes to Paul. As I made my way to leave, I turned back to Tina. 'Where's Steph?'

'She stayed in Spain, Jim. She met somebody out there. A really nice bloke with loads of money.'

A sick feeling started to course through my body. 'Oh. That's great news. I'm really happy for her.'

Tina nodded. 'Good. When I speak to her I will let her know.'

I struggled to reply: 'Yeah. Good. Do that. Thanks.'

Chris drove me back to the office where I got in my van and drove home.

I got to the flat, which was in darkness as Dawn was staying at her sister's for a couple of days. I went into the lounge, got a beer and sat down on the couch. Thoughts of Steph ran through my mind, thoughts of her with someone else. It was killing me. For a moment, I had the mad idea that I should fly to Spain, find Steph and lay all my cards on the table. Instead I went to the fridge to get another beer, and then another and another until eventually I fell asleep.

We met up with Paul on Wednesday as arranged. The plan was again to meet at The Puffin for ten, as per West Ham, but to leave at twelve and make our way to Euston and on to Arsenal via Seven Sisters. Paul didn't mention Steph and I didn't ask, much as I wanted to.

On the Saturday, we made our way to The Puffin. All the usual faces were there: Marcus, Stan, and a large contingent of the Millwall Bushwackers. Just before twelve Paul told us to drink up and we made our way to New Cross. At Euston there were Old Bill everywhere. They were stopping everybody at the tube entrances and questioning where they were heading. They were also stopping anyone who looked remotely like a football hooligan and searching them. Our group which had now swelled to well over a hundred were rounded up and escorted to Highbury. We didn't go quietly and sang 'No One Likes Us' at the top of our voices.

Upon arrival we were led around the back to the away end entrance. There were Millwall everywhere and the section that we had been escorted into became so full that the police had to remove the mobile barriers as it was now overcrowded. It was absolutely the correct decision to make. I am certain that people would have been crushed or seriously injured had the barriers remained in place. It did, however, result in sporadic confrontations between Millwall and Arsenal supporters, but the police were quick to step in.

I was now with Chris and Paul and a small splinter group that I recognised from The Puffin but had never met. We walked around to the North Bank entrances and stood watching the Arsenal supporters enter the ground. It had been an all-ticket game for Millwall but the Arsenal supporters were able to turn up and pay on the day. There were about fifteen of us. Paul turned to us all. He had a glint in his eye as he spoke: 'Right boys, let's see what the Arsenal have got.' And, with that he marched over and joined the queue for the Arsenal end. We were going into the North Bank with a hardened group of Millwall's elite and it wasn't to watch the game from a better viewpoint. I made my way to the turnstile, paid my money and walked in. Once we were all through, we started to walk up the steps towards the North Bank. I was shitting myself. My senses were working overtime and my heart was beating so hard that I could see my chest rise and fall. I began to sweat and take deep breaths and my head started to pound from the extra adrenalin.

It was still half an hour before kick-off but the ground was nearly full to capacity. In the Millwall end, they were singing 'No One Likes Us'. The sound appeared to be amplified as we made our way into the middle of the crowd behind the goal. I looked up at the huge corrugated tin roof that covered the North Bank and drew in a large breath. Paul was standing in front of me, I was in the middle of the group and Chris was standing next to me. He looked like I felt. His face was white and he had beads of sweat across the top of his forehead.

I leant across to him. 'You all right?'

He shook his head.

I couldn't help myself, I laughed. 'Me too. Just stay fucking close.'

I checked out the guy next to me. He was dressed in a smart black jacket and jeans and was wearing a pair of the whitest trainers I had ever seen. 'You all right, son?' he asked.

I tried to raise a smile and nodded. 'Yeah. You?'

He opened his coat. He was holding a long stiletto knife with a blade about six inches in length. He closed his coat and put his other arm around my shoulder. 'Just stick with me and you'll be fine. Fucking Arsenal mugs.'

I turned to look at Chris to see if he had also seen the knife but he was gone. I glanced behind me and saw him making his way up the terraces towards the exit. He caught my eye and mouthed, 'Sorry.' He disappeared over the top of the terraces. If I could have I would have done the same. But I was stood with Paul so had no choice: stay and keep my cover, leave and lose it forever.

Paul looked back at me. 'You all right?'

'Yeah. Let's fucking have it.'

As if this was his cue, Paul raised his arms aloft and started to sing. 'No one likes us, No one likes us' and we all joined in.

It didn't take the crowd long to realise who we were. I could see people in the crowd staring at us, affronted that we had invaded their territory, and quickly they began to point and scream abuse at us. Suddenly someone burst through from the Arsenal ranks and ran towards us. He didn't get far. One of the guys next to Paul took a pace forward and punched him in the face. His nose exploded and blood splattered across his cheeks and chin. He staggered backwards onto the ground. He was out before he hit the terrace and his head bounced off the concrete steps as he hit it. It was fucking horrendous.

Paul then turned and in full voice shouted to us. 'Come on, Millwall!' and charged headlong into the Arsenal supporters. I let out a roar and me and the others followed him. We surged through the Arsenal with our arms and legs kicking and punching out indiscriminately. I was hit and kicked a number of times as we made our way down the terraces. We spilled out onto the pitch. We were now being pelted with coins, pies, and hot drinks but no Arsenal ventured onto the pitch after us.

We were quickly surrounded by Old Bill. I was grabbed by a policeman, thrown to the ground and told that I was nicked. I was still singing and I was hit on the side of the head by a truncheon and told to shut the fuck up. I was then hauled to my feet. The officer who had arrested me pushed my arm up my back and started to lead me around the pitch. As we passed the seated area a number of Millwall jumped to their feet and started to sing the Millwall anthem.

I looked up at them and raised my free hand into the air, shouting as I did, 'Come on, you Lions!' I was immediately shoved in the back by the police officer who had arrested me and again told to shut the fuck up.

He headed towards the Millwall who were in the away end. As we got towards them the Millwall crowd went absolutely mental. He then tried to turn me around and as he did so he lessened his grip on my arm. I wrenched my arm free and ran towards the Millwall end. A police officer was running towards me but I easily skipped around him and dived into the crowd and began to crawl up the terraces. I got halfway up, dropped my dungarees and somebody handed me a grey scarf and a Millwall hat, which I put on.

People around me were patting me on the back and laughing. It was a great feeling. I had been into the North Bank and survived.

The rest of the game was played out with groups of police officers indiscriminately wading into the crowd with their truncheons drawn, grabbing hold of people and dragging them out. I couldn't see the logic behind any of it.

After the game, which we had lost 2-0, we were kept in the ground for over an hour before we were finally allowed to leave. As we left, we saw shops with their front windows smashed and cars on their roofs. Apparently, upwards of two thousand Millwall had failed to get tickets but had shown up anyway and made their displeasure clear at not being allowed into the ground.

I got back to New Cross and walked back to my van, which was parked a little way down from The Puffin. As I made my way up the New Cross Road I began to replay the day's events in my head. The North Bank incident had been as exhilarating as it had been terrifying. I was still buzzing from the experience. I got to the van and looked over to The Puffin. I knew I should go back to the office, but the draw of The Puffin was just too great. As I entered the pub, I was greeted with a large cheer and as I made my way to the bar people were slapping me on the back and laughing.

Steph was there. 'I hear from Paul that you all had a bit of fun at Arsenal. You all right?'

'Yeah. Couldn't be better. How are you?'

She passed me my drink. 'I can't complain, although it is nice to be back and see a friendly face.'

'It's nice to see you too. How's Spain?'

She started to laugh. 'If you mean, am I seeing the bloke that Tina told you about, I'm not. He wasn't for me. All money and no substance.'

I was elated and tried to keep a lid on it but failed. I leant forward and kissed her. As I pulled away Paul appeared behind the bar. 'Here he is, the top boy,' he said.

Steph moved aside as Paul leant over the bar and hugged me. 'What a fucking day, eh, Jimbo? Arsenal. I've shit 'em.'

Paul introduced me to the others from the North Bank. It was a blur of names as we spoke about the fight and spilling out onto the pitch. The Old Bill had decided not to charge anyone and they had all been kicked out of the ground during half-time. They had all come back here and didn't know what had happened to me until someone had said that I had got nicked, hit the Old Bill that had arrested me, dived into the crowd and got away. I stayed in The Puffin late into the night and just as I was contemplating leaving the door opened and Chris came in. He walked over to me and threw his arms around my shoulders and as he pulled me close he whispered into my ear: 'Thank fuck you are all right. I am really sorry.'

I looked at him and winked. 'No worries.' And, I meant it. He'd done what he thought was the best and most sensible thing to do in the circumstances. We both had a drink and then made our way to the door to leave. As we exited the pub I caught Steph's eye and winked. She smiled back and blew me a kiss. I opened the door and left.

Gerry and Charlie were still in the office when we got back. Gerry jumped to his feet as we entered. 'Fucking hell, Jimbo,' he said. 'Are we pleased to see you. Chris told us what happened.'

'Yeah? And what did he say?'

Chris walked over to me. 'I told them that we went into the North Bank with our targets and that I left my partner there to fend for himself.'

I threw my arm around his shoulder. 'Mate, it's not a problem.'

I talked them through what had gone on and they informed me that I was the talk of the terraces. 'Did you see the lunatic in the dungarees who was in the Arsenal end? Who the fuck was the geezer who legged it from the Old Bill into the crowd?' I had upped my credibility.

But there was a much bigger issue. I had enjoyed it. Really enjoyed it, and part of me was already looking forward to the next opportunity to present itself.

TWENTY-THREE
YOU'RE NICKED

I finally got home in the early hours of the Sunday morning and went to bed. I didn't surface until well into the afternoon, having slept straight through. Dawn had the money from the sale of the house in Catford sitting in her account waiting on the next purchase.

We went to my parents' on the Monday and they told us about a new development being built locally. Out of curiosity we went and had a look. After an hour of being walked around the site we liked what we saw so much that we put a deposit down on a four-bed detached house. My relationship with Dawn was not at its best, but the move would get me out of London and closer to my parents so the decision was easier than it should have been. It was a foolish and stupid decision to agree to buy the house and one that I would eventually regret but I went with it and that afternoon instructed the agent to sell my flat. I had an offer on it within days. Things were moving forward.

On Wednesday we met up at the Old Castle for the Simod Cup game against Norwich, which suited me as I was still unsure about what to do with my feelings for Steph. Chris and I walked in and people started coming up to me, congratulating me for the Arsenal game. My profile had gone through the roof, which was good in terms of my credibility, but was not without its problems. People were now showing more interest in me and were asking who I was and where I came from.

We left the pub earlier than normal and made our way to the match. We queued up and entered the ground. I needed the toilet and shouted to the others that I would see them in our usual place. As I left the toilet, I heard someone call out my name. I turned around and could not believe what I was seeing. Walking towards me was a police officer in full uniform. We had been at training school together. What the fuck was I going to do? I had a quick look round and no one appeared to have picked up on it. I stared at him, trying to force him to understand that this was really not the time or place for a catch-up. As he got within touching distance I turned and threw myself against the wall and raised my arms up above my head. He was thrown by my reaction but he was now close enough to me for me to talk without anyone overhearing. 'I am working, you cunt. Search me.'

A look of horror washed over his face as he realised what he had done. He started to pat me down. Guy, the uniform spotter, had seen what was going on and quickly made his way over to me. He moved the PC aside and started to search me with a little more purpose. He leant into me, 'Sorry, Jim. What do you want to happen?'

I responded. 'Nick me.'

I then pushed out at Guy and shouted out, 'Oi, oi, fuck off, will ya?'

Guy was then joined by Doug, one of our other spotters, who stepped in to help with the search. I was now shouting obscenities at them and as I looked up I saw Tubby Tony and Gary looking on. I then pushed Guy away and told him to fuck off.

He and Doug grabbed hold of me and spun me around, announcing that I was 'nicked'. I had attracted quite a crowd as I was escorted off to the temporary Portacabin that doubled up as a charging station on match days. I was led into the front desk and taken over to the holding cell. There was already somebody in there so I continued to shout abuse at Guy, who told me to shut up. I stayed in the temporary cell until half-time by which time I had now been joined by a number of other supporters who had been arrested. For the benefit of the other supporters who were in the cells with me I was charged and bailed to appear at Greenwich magistrates and then escorted from the ground.

I made my way back to the Old Castle where I sat and waited for the match to end. At about 9.45 Chris walked in with the others who came straight over to me and asked what the fuck had happened. Tubby Tony had told everybody that I had been nicked because of the fight at Arsenal and that it had taken three of them to restrain me.

After a couple of beers we all left. I explained to Chris what had happened and why I had to get myself arrested. He said that it had worked a treat and that everyone believed it was because of Arsenal. It couldn't have worked better had we planned it.

None of our targets were travelling to Birmingham for the game on 9th February. Chris had a family engagement so I travelled up there with Gerry and Charlie. There were pockets of disturbances during the game but the ground was heavily policed and any disorder was quickly and effectively dealt with. There wasn't much to write up, so me and Gerry went for a curry. As we chatted over our madras, we got to the subject of the women in our lives. Gerry spoke about Susan and how supportive she was and that he couldn't have been happier. He was doing a job that he loved and living with a woman he loved more. I was jealous of his relationship with his wife. She was understanding, attractive and obviously loved him. They made a great team and still do. Gerry went silent for a moment and then looked directly at me. 'Jim, I know it's none of my business, mate, and you can tell me to fuck off if you want, but what's the crack with Steph?'

I was a little taken aback but happy to answer his question: 'I don't know. Well, I do know, it's all a fucking mess. I find her attractive and really good fun to be with but I can't pursue it and it's fucking torturous…'

Gerry took a sip from his beer. 'And what about Dawn in all of this? D'ya not think you owe it to her with the new house and all that to try and make it work?'

This was now going into uncharted territory and I snapped back, 'What the fuck has this conversation got to do with Dawn?'

He looked back, a little shocked. 'Everything. This is as much about you as her. In fact, probably more so. She has made her choice and wants to be with you. The problem is that you're not sure. I don't know what's worse: the fact that you seem to be falling in love with Steph and can't do anything about it, or that you are having a relationship with somebody that loves you but you're not in love with her.'

I looked back at him and started to laugh. 'I know! I told you it was all fucked up.'

Gerry laughed too. 'Fucking hell, Jimbo, as if you ain't got enough to deal with? Fucking hell, what a mess. What's the answer? Cos I don't know.'

I was quick to answer back. 'Two more Cobras, please,' I said to the waiter.

Gerry laughed even harder. 'Fucking hell, this is turning out to be one hell of a ride.' After a couple more beers, we both headed for home. I got to the end of the road but instead of turning right I swung a left and drove towards The Puffin. What Gerry had said had been really playing on my mind. I was questioning everything about what he had just said and more. I had got off on the violence of the Arsenal game and I sucked up the notoriety that it had given me. I liked the people that I was infiltrating, in fact I liked them a lot, but it was all a fucking lie. I wasn't their mate Jim. I was a snide copper who was mapping out their downfall.

I pulled up outside The Puffin. It was now midnight and the pub was in darkness. There were a couple of lights on upstairs and I sat and stared up at them for an hour, thinking about the lies, the deceit, the excitement, the recognition, the notoriety, the buzz, the rushes of adrenalin, the pain.

Suddenly there was a knock on the window and the light from a torch filled the van. I looked up to see two police officers staring back at me. I wound down the window. They were my age and I recognised one of them from my time at Greenwich. He was the first to speak. 'Evening, sir. Can you tell me what you are doing sitting here in your van at this time of night?'

'Nothing, I was just thinking.'

He leant into the van. 'Have you been drinking?'

I started to laugh. 'Drinking. Yep, that's a large part of what I do, as is lying and using people to my advantage.'

He shone the torch back into the van and I could see his mind starting to race. 'Do I know you? You look familiar.'

I stared back. 'Nope, you don't know me. No one knows me. I don't even know my fucking self.'

Suddenly his radio burst into life with a call for urgent assistance from another officer. 'This is your lucky night,' he shouted out as they ran off. As they disappeared up the road, I started the van and pulled away from the kerb. As I headed for home I contemplated what he had said. If this was my lucky night than I certainly didn't want to be about for a shitty one.

I arrived home and went straight to bed. I knew that sitting up continually questioning what I was doing was not helping my state of mind. I woke early. Dawn was on a night shift and as I lay there I heard her come into the flat. It was nearly 7 a.m. I went into the kitchen and made her a drink. She was excited about the move to the country and I tried my best to appear happy about the fresh start as she had called it.

She asked me to wake her at two so that we could spend some time together. I left her to sleep and she eventually surfaced at just after four. She wanted to talk through furniture and curtains and carpets for the new house and I nodded in agreement as she took me through the various samples that she had acquired. They all looked fine to me and she folded over the various pages and was going to get some prices in the week. She made tea and at just after nine she left for work.

I sat there on the couch looking at all the sample books and magazines that she had collected. I picked one up and started to flick through it. It really made me laugh as I read about numerous couples and their quests for a better life, all from a refurbishment or new-build house. I wondered what the real truth was. The debt, the arguments over costs with the builder, the affair that Margaret had with the architect who designed her new barn that her husband knew nothing about. We all live a lie in one way or another, mine was just on a grander scale than most. I finished my beer and went to bed.

Dawn woke me as she came back from her night shift and I got up with a renewed vigour. I had a job to do and I was hell bent on doing it to the best of my ability and if that meant lying to a few people to justify the end result then so be it.

TWENTY-FOUR

US AND THEM

The solicitor called a few weeks later to say that they would be looking to exchange on the flat and the new house by the end of the week. I told Dawn the news about the flat and the exchange and she was beside herself with excitement. She was right: this was going to be a new start and I was going to do everything to make it work.

I had decided that I needed something a little more refined than the yellow van and I set about looking for a car as I would have a little money left over from the sale of the flat. I scoured the weekly car papers and finally found a BMW Baur convertible for sale in north London. The car was immaculate and after a little negotiating I drove back to the office. Charlie came down to the yard and went over it with a fine-tooth comb before giving it the seal of approval. We all jumped in it and I drove us out to the pub to celebrate. I came back to the news that the solicitor had called Dawn and she had left a message with Angie. The flat was now sold and the new house was ours. There was no going back now.

We were all in early on the Saturday. It was 19 March 1988, a day that I would never forget. We had taken to watching the football programme *Saint and Greavsie* before home games and I sat down with the others to watch the start as Angie went off to make the tea. The programme had just started when it was interrupted by a newsflash.

We watched on as an IRA funeral cortège made its way up what appeared to be a small suburban street. Suddenly a silver car rounded the corner and drove towards them. The car then stopped abruptly and reversed onto the pavement, trying to turn around and drive back from where it had come. A black taxi drove out of the funeral march and pulled in front of it, blocking its exit. The camera panned in as we watched the driver and passenger of the now trapped car frantically trying to get out. Within seconds the funeral goers started to attack the car. What had been a sad, sombre event only minutes earlier had now turned into an angry and violent scene with the mob venting their anger on the occupants of the car.

We all sat transfixed to the television when suddenly there appeared to be a gunshot. The shot had obviously come from the car as the mob all scattered. For a brief second you caught sight of the two occupants of the car. You could see that they were still looking around them for a possible escape route. The gunshot did not deter the crowd. Somebody ran forward and kicked at the passenger's door and then another and another. The camera continued to transmit the pictures as the two men were dragged out. They were kicked to the ground and were badly beaten. We watched on as they were hauled to their feet and dragged away from the scene.

We were to discover later that the two men who had been pulled from the car were in fact army intelligence officers working undercover (although this was later denied by the British Army). Their names were Corporals David Howes and Derek Wood. After being badly beaten, they had been driven to waste ground nearby, stripped to the waist and shot dead by the same people that were themselves attending a funeral march only ten minutes previously.

What scared me most was how quickly the funeral goers had turned into a violent mob. It really brought home to us all how quickly a situation could escalate out of control. What would happen to us if our cover was compromised and our true identity revealed?

I put myself in the shoes of the two soldiers who had just been killed. What would I have done? How would I have reacted to being surrounded and set upon, in my case, by a group of Millwall supporters who had sussed me out as being Old Bill? I wouldn't stand a fucking chance.

Although the funeral and the subsequent events were more severe than anything that we were likely to encounter, it was difficult to not draw a comparison. Two undercover officers, just like us, had been killed when it was discovered who they were. After watching the horrific events on the news, I wasn't hopping up and down with glee at the prospect of heading down to Millwall to meet up with my targets.

I took myself off and went out of the yard and walked around the block to clear my head. Was I overreacting? The realisation of what could happen with an incensed mob and what it could lead to weighed heavily on me. I was now seriously questioning if what we were doing was worth the risk. I was twenty-two years old and had my whole career ahead of me. I was enjoying it, maybe a bit too much, but I was trying to stay focused on the job in hand. There had been times on the operation to date that I had been scared, Arsenal, Leeds at London Bridge, West Ham away, but they were a pale comparison to how I was now feeling after having just witnessed two undercover soldiers being dragged from a car, beaten and killed. I was terrified.

As I turned the corner to make my way back to the office Chris pulled up alongside me. I got in. 'You all right?'

'No, not really. Fucking hell, Chris. Them poor fuckers. They didn't stand a fucking chance.'

And I started to cry, and I mean properly cry. Snot, tears, shaky voice, the fucking lot. I was sobbing. I felt such an affinity to the two soldiers that it overwhelmed me and by the end of it both Chris and I were in a proper mess.

After about ten minutes we both managed to pull ourselves together. We sat in the car in silence and then finally Chris spoke. 'What d'ya wanna do?'

I sat and stared out the window of the car. 'Fuck it. Let's go and watch some football.'

He looked back at me and smiled. 'Good idea.'

We drove down to the Old Castle and met with our targets. It was business as usual.

TWENTY-FIVE

BESIDE THE SEA

We attended the game against Huddersfield and after the sad events of earlier we were able to celebrate a 4–1 win. Dave and the others were on good form. There was a bit of conversation in the ground at half-time from the people around us about the death of the two undercover soldiers but it had been forgotten by the time the second half got underway.

After calling in at the office, I had had enough for one day and I headed for home. I turned on the news and sat and watched on as they played out the gruesome events of the funeral. It was now being reported that the soldiers had inadvertently taken a wrong turning, causing them to drive unexpectedly into the funeral procession. I listened on as commentator after commentator tried to explain the day's events. I turned it off, resigning myself to the fact that no explanation was going to bring the soldiers back.

We were at the new house on the Sunday and Monday measuring up for curtains and putting up mirrors in readiness for our big move in on the Friday. The flat was now all packed up and in boxes come the Tuesday morning and everyone had agreed to help with the move.

Millwall were not playing for a fortnight so we were all able to catch up on our paperwork and after the move I was able to spend a few uninterrupted days at the new house sorting stuff out. Dawn and I had met all of our close neighbours and fortunately the question of what we did for work had not been raised. She had agreed to travel to and from work in her civilian clothes so as not to attract attention to her leaving or coming home in uniform.

Millwall were playing well and currently second in the league. They had a few tough games coming up but if they kept their form they had a good chance of securing promotion. The FIU were worried about the potential for disorder if they did so, as Millwall would be playing against the likes of Manchester United and Liverpool. We were told that there was to be a meeting over the coming weeks to decide what was to happen with the operation but that we were to carry on as we were until we heard otherwise. It was ironic that our future had now become dependent on the Millwall players securing promotion.

On Saturday 6 April, Millwall were playing Leeds away, and I travelled up with Gerry and Charlie as Chris was on another windsurfing break. There were people now attending the games that I had not seen before, which presented problems to Angie and the uniform spotters. As more new faces appeared her days became longer and longer as she tried to catalogue and manage the evidence. She was now a font of knowledge and knew more about the hooligans and the small firms that hovered on the fringes of the main firm the Bushwackers than all of us and the spotters put together.

Our trip to Leeds saw us follow five thousand supporters – five times as many as our last trip. We thought it was really going to kick off, but a police road block made sure that encounters between us and the Leeds Service Crew were thwarted. But for once no one seemed to care and after a nervy game we eventually came out on top 2–1. We were lying second in the table and promotion was now ours to lose.

On Tuesday, Millwall were playing at home to Plymouth. Chris was back in the office, and we headed down to The Puffin for a pre-match drink. The pub was as busy as ever and it took us over twenty minutes to get served. Dave and the others joined us outside and we went to the game. Mark was still mentioning the bet at every opportunity, but I continued to tell him that it wasn't over till it was over. The crowd was the biggest I had seen and we won an easy match 3–2. We were now top of the division with four matches left to play.

We decided to go to the Old Castle as there was more room and smaller queues. Everyone was now talking about promotion and the away game to Bournemouth was a must-go-to game for everyone. It was to be played on the Tuesday evening of the following week and we agreed to meet up with Dave and the others on the Tuesday in Bournemouth. Chris and I had decided to go down on the Monday and stay over for the game the next day as we had heard that lots of Millwall were doing the same. We left the others in the pub and made our way back to the office. All was looking good. Millwall were top and we were all having success with our targets but we were still to hear officially about continuing our operation into the next season.

We spent the days leading up to the Bournemouth game attending meetings with the FIU and senior officers discussing the operation. We were now being subjected to scrutiny on a weekly basis. This was in no small part due to the cases against West Ham, Chelsea and Millwall where the validity of some of the evidence was being brought into question. Our evidence was now being looked at in much greater detail and we now had to submit our statements via our liaison officer Toby to the FIU. They would in turn forward them on to the senior officers with their comments. We were not concerned. We had nothing to hide.

Chris and I got a hire car for the Bournemouth game and made our way down to the coast. After a quiet night in the hotel bar, we went down for breakfast at 9.30. We finished up, paid and made our way into the town centre. The town was teeming with Millwall who were entering into the spirit of the day with lots of kiss me quick hats and cheesy sunglasses. We walked around for an hour or so taking in the atmosphere and stumbled across a small wine bar. It was relatively quiet with a few businessmen at the bar having meetings or an early lunch. We had a couple of beers each sitting in the corner by the window so that we could watch what was going on outside.

After half an hour, we suddenly heard a huge roar. Up the road we could see a group of about thirty Millwall walking down the centre of the precinct. They all had their arms held aloft and then started to sing 'No One Likes Us'. All of the shoppers looked on as they continued to walk down towards us. They got to the entrance of the wine bar and walked in. I was sitting with my back to the bar so I pulled my chair around to get a better view. I didn't recognise any of them. I decided to go to the bar and get a drink. I went up and stood behind three guys and waited to be served. They were amiable and polite to the bar staff and got their beers and moved aside so that I could get to the bar.

As I ordered one of them tapped me on the shoulder. 'You down for the game?'

'Yeah. You?'

I took my beers and turned to go as one of them walked in front of me. 'Who's our goalkeeper?'

I couldn't fucking believe it. I was being questioned as to whether I was Millwall by some cunt who I hadn't seen at any game or on any surveillance tape. I stopped and stared back at him. 'You what?'

'You heard. Who's our goalkeeper?'

I could see Chris staring over.

'Brian Horne and Paul Sansome. Wanna know any of the other player's names?'

He laughed. 'No, no mate, sorry. It's just we have all learnt to be fucking careful and I didn't recognise you, that's all. Can I get you a beer?'

'No, it's all right, mate. I've just got one.'

They then moved aside and I made my way back to Chris. After I told Chris what had gone on he was up for finishing his beer and moving on. As we sat there more and more Millwall started to enter the bar. The guy that had confronted me at the bar came over with two beers and put them on the table. 'No hard feelings, mate. Sorry about the interrogation.'

I took the beer. 'Thanks. Why you so nervous?'

He gestured to me over to the corner. 'A couple of my mates got nicked by undercover Old Bill at Chelsea and they were told that there's some in at Millwall so we've sort of stayed away.'

'Oh right. But the Old Bill have already nicked a load.'

He nodded. 'Yeah, but apparently they are still in.'

This was making my arse twitch. 'Still in? Fuck. You mean that Old Bill are still in at Millwall? Undercover?'

'Yeah, some copper who drinks with my mates told 'em.'

This was not good news. 'Fuck, thanks for the heads-up. Fucking hell, I wouldn't want to be one of them if they get found out.'

'Nah. Nor me. Fucking hell, could you imagine?'

I smiled. 'I wouldn't mind being there if they found 'em. Cunts.'

Suddenly there was a commotion at the front door. Chris was now standing opposite a guy at the door. I watched on helplessly as the guy leant back and head-butted Chris on the bridge of his nose. Chris staggered backwards and fell out of the bar, crashing into a sunglasses stand, sending them scattering onto the pavement. He was followed out by the guy who had head-butted him.

I got to the door and Chris was now lying on the floor. The guy then kicked him in the chest. I launched myself at him, knocking him to the ground. I then ran and aimed a kick at his head. Somebody grabbed hold of me before the kick landed and pulled me aside. I turned around to retaliate only to see that it was Tubby Tony. By now everyone had come out of the bar.

Chris had chosen to wear his glasses that day rather than his contacts. I had to laugh. He had a cut on the bridge of his nose and was still wearing his glasses although they were now bent and a bit skew-whiff.

I made my way over to Chris. 'What the fuck was all that about?'

He looked back at me. 'I dunno. One minute I was standing there, the next minute that cunt head-butted me.'

By this time the guy who had assaulted Chris was on his feet and was being restrained by a couple of his mates as he shouted over, 'He was fucking staring at me, the four-eyed cunt.'

Tony grabbed me as I yelled back at him, 'He fucking stares at everyone, you cunt. He's fucking blind, that's why he wears glasses.'

The guy then carried on. 'And I ain't seen him before, who the fuck is he? You can't be too careful nowadays.'

I tried to wrestle free from Tony. 'He's with me, you cunt.'

'He's with you? Who the fuck are you, I don't know you either.'

This was getting awkward. But then one of the guys holding back the bloke who had assaulted Chris stared at me. 'Fuck. You're the lunatic from Arsenal.' He turned to some of the others. 'He's the guy from Arsenal. Look, with the dungarees. He went in the North Bank with Stan.'

The guy who had hit Chris put his hands in the air. 'Shit. You're right. It's him. Fuck. I'm sorry, mate. It's just that he was staring. Fucking hell, sorry mate.'

He made his way over to Chris and apologised, and eventually came over to me. 'I'm sorry, mate. He just…'

'It's all right, it's forgotten. It was a mistake. Forget it.'

Tubby Tony then turned to Chris. 'Right, I'm glad that's all over with. Beer, Chris?'

Chris shook his head and walked off outside. The others had all come over to me and started to ask about Arsenal. I could see that Chris was not in a good place. 'Look, let me just go and sort him out, will ya?' I said and made my way over to Chris who was standing among the spilled sunglasses.

'You all right?' I asked.

'No. These people are fucking animals, Jim, and the sooner this thing fucking ends the happier I will be.'

I was not surprised by his response. 'Yeah, I know. Look, let's go and get something to eat and forget the whole thing.'

He shook his head. 'But we can't, we need to go back in and—'

I pulled him in close to me. 'Why? Fuck 'em. Come on.'

We found a quiet restaurant that appeared to be the only one not inhabited by Millwall. I again tried to make Chris understand that he needed to avoid eye contact with people unless he knew them. His nose was now quite swollen but it didn't appear broken.

It had been a shit start to the day but it could only get better. Dave left Chris a message on his pager and we met up with them at the beach where there were now a large number of Millwall playing a game of football. We decided to swerve the football and instead headed off to find a bar. Chris's nose was the talk of the day and although he said it had settled down it was now quite swollen and he was puffy around both eyes.

We had a few beers and then made it to the ground, getting there well in time for the kick-off. The atmosphere was electric and if Millwall won they would stay top of the Second Division with only three games left to play. The game was unbelievably tense. We got a penalty which was converted ten minutes into the game by Kevin O'Callaghan and then a wonder goal from the main man Terry Hurlock. Bournemouth then quickly pulled one back and the rest of the game was end to end until late into the second half Bournemouth were awarded a penalty.

The penalty was saved by Brian Horne and the place erupted. We held on, running out winners 2–1.

During the game Chris had seen the guy who had assaulted him and pointed him out to Dave and the others. By chance, Dave knew him from school and offered up his name. We were again kept in the ground for an eternity after the match but no one seemed to care.

Back at the office Chris dived straight into the intelligence documents to trace the guy who had hit him. I left him to it. Three more wins and we were guaranteed promotion, but would the operation get the go-ahead for another season? We were about to find out.

TWENTY-SIX

PROMOTION

In the office the following Monday all we could talk about now was promotion. The chances of being able to see Millwall in the First Division were fast becoming a reality.

We received a call from Robbie who let us know that he and Lawrence were coming down to see us the following day to talk some more about the previous and pending trials concerning West Ham, Chelsea and Millwall. I had passed on the intelligence about the police officer who had told some Millwall supporters that they were currently being 'looked at' and Chris and I were trying to piece together the group that we had met in the wine bar in Bournemouth.

Robbie and Lawrence didn't hold out much hope of ever finding the copper with the big mouth but they were keen to try so we continued to go through all of the tapes and picture evidence to try and identify as many as we could from the wine bar. We all went out as a team on the Monday for a drink in anticipation of what may happen tomorrow. I was confident that we would get another season but there were no guarantees as there had been a lot of speculation in the media recently about the other trials and the questionable evidence.

I went home to the new house, which now had carpets and curtains. Dawn was also keen to find out if the operation had been extended. She had made no secret of what she hoped would happen; that the operation would be concluded and I would be re-posted back to the crime squad. The thought of that didn't bear thinking about. I drove into the office the next day anxious about the outcome.

We all sat and waited for Robbie and Lawrence, who were arriving with our liaison officer Toby. When they arrived, Robbie was quick to let us know the score. 'Chaps, and of course Angie, I am pleased to tell you that your operation is to be extended into next season. This won't be dependent on whether Millwall are promoted but I would imagine that you are all hoping that they are. The FA and I, on the other hand, are hoping and praying that they don't.'

I was ecstatic. Millwall probably into the First Division and we all get to carry on. We were then taken through the evidence that we had to date. I featured a lot. An awful lot, when it came down to the evidence around disorder. I justified my need to be in and around the trouble, in order to gain acceptance, and that any violence or assaults that I had been party to, or might be involved in in the future, were to protect myself.

Lawrence opened up about the West Ham trial. He had been the officer in charge on the ground. He was upset at the lack of support that he was receiving from the senior officers. Away from the others, he complimented me on the evidence that I had achieved to date, but he said he was concerned that I was getting too involved and enjoying it more than I should. I pointed out to him that the purpose as I saw it of the operation was to gain evidence against football hooligans and that if it was going to be successful we were going to have to get our hands a little dirty. He nodded in agreement and threw an arm around my shoulder. 'I know,' he said and then we made our way back to the others.

After a few celebratory cans, I left the office and drove back home. Dawn was already there and I told her my news. She tried to be pleased for me but it didn't take long for the negative comments. In the end I took myself off to bed.

We spent the next couple of days getting used to the news that we would be continuing on with the operation. We continued to collate evidence and again our statements were scrutinised but this time by a specialist forensic team from the Yard. Chris was told that they needed all of the 'original statements' and not copies and we were only too pleased to oblige.

On the Saturday Chris and I headed down to meet with Dave and the others for the game at home to Stoke. When I got there, Dave handed me a beer and a small present.

I looked back at him a little confused. 'What's this for?'

Mark jumped in. 'It's for the baby. It's the third, ain't it? His birthday. I never forget a date.'

'Yeah, you're right, fucking hell I didn't think you'd remember. You didn't need to do that. Thanks.'

They all looked on smiling and Mark then gestured to the present, 'Well, you gonna open it?'

I now felt like fucking shit. 'Err, no, it's his so I'll let him do it.'

They all nodded and I turned and walked back to the car feeling like an absolute cunt and put it in the boot.

We made our way to the ground. There were now supporters everywhere. The ground was heaving by 2.30 and the singing had already started. We took up our usual position behind the goal and the game started. The first half was a real nervous affair and forty minutes in Kevin O'Callaghan made a break down the left and crossed to Teddy Sheringham. Ted had a great touch and a superb footballing brain but, and I am sure that he would admit it himself, he was not the quickest. The ball shot across the eighteen-yard box and the clearance was scuffed by one of the Stoke players.

We had a chance. The ball was rolling towards the touchline as Teddy ran towards it. If he got there and passed it, it would have been a certain goal as Tony Cascarino had taken up a great position in the penalty area. We all watched expectantly as Sheringham ran for the ball. He tried his best to get there but as he slid in an attempt to pass the ball back it rolled out of play. We all watched as Ted slid across the line and onto the small track that went around the outside of the pitch. The crowd let out a huge sigh. As Ted started to get to his feet there was a split second of silence.

Chris broke the silence with one of the most memorable lines ever. As Ted got to his feet and the goalkeeper placed the ball for the goal kick, Chris pointed down at him and shouted at the top of his voice, 'Sheringham, you're on drugs, and it ain't speed.'

The crowd erupted with laughter. Teddy had obviously heard it too. He looked up into the crowd, laughed, shook his head and made his way back onto the field. What a quality moment.

The second half started and Millwall were a different team. Whatever had been said at the break had worked. Five minutes into the second half Sheringham scored. He ran to the touchline and was engulfed by the team. As the others made their way back to the halfway line he ran to our end of the pitch and, looking up at us, did a quick run on the spot to show us his speed. What a class response. We absolutely pissed ourselves. It was no surprise to me that he went on to have such an illustrious career, even then it was obvious that he was a class act. The goal steadied the nerves and it was helped when we were awarded another penalty. We had now been awarded three penalties in the last three games. We scored and were now 2–0 up. There was no way that Millwall were going to let that slip and as the full-time whistle blew we had won.

As we left the ground I saw Paul who called me over. 'You coming for a beer?'

I nodded back. 'What do you think?' and with that everyone around us burst into 'We're going up… We're going up… Ei Aye Ade Oo, we're going up.'

The Puffin was already packed inside and out. It felt great to walk into the pub with Paul, and have the crowd move aside as we made our way to the bar. I got the drinks and went back outside to join the others.

We stayed all night and had a blast. Dave and the others had gone by eight but Chris and I were having a great time and later on Paul came over and joined us. He was on good form and looking forward to the Hull game. The results had gone in our favour and if we won we would be Second Division champions. I drank to that.

Steph had been flat out working all night. I went in to get my last beer.

'You all right, J?' she smiled as she got me our drinks.

I smiled back. 'Yeah. What a day.'

I reached out for the drinks and she took my hand. 'I'd really like to get to know you away from all this. Go out one night, just you and me, no strings.'

I looked back at her. Millwall were a game away from being promoted. We had another season, I really liked her, and it was just a drink. I smiled back at her, keeping hold of her hand. 'Yeah, I'd really like that too.'

At which point Paul shouted from the door. 'Jim, come and have a fucking look at this twat out here.'

I went to leave but turned back and kissed her on the lips. 'There's something to be getting on with.'

She laughed and I went back outside. Paul and the others were pissing themselves laughing. There was an old guy dressed in a Millwall flag and not much else walking down the middle of the road chanting 'Millwall' at the top of his voice. Cars had slowed to a crawl behind him and as they tried to pass him he would lash out. Suddenly a police van approached from behind with its blue lights on. With much jeering from us, he was nicked, put in the van and driven off.

I drove home and struggled to stay awake. I was in the BMW and I had the roof down. When I got home and pulled into the drive I tried to put the roof back on. Not a good idea when you are properly pissed.

Dawn opened the window and aired her displeasure: 'Leave it alone and come in the house.'

I was leaning against the door, trying to unlock it, when it suddenly opened. I fell into the hallway, crashing into the table and falling to the floor. I picked myself up, mumbled an apology and crawled up the stairs to bed.

The next day, I apologised for my drunken behaviour and tried to explain that we were celebrating the extension to the operation and the likelihood of promotion. It fell on deaf ears. So much for the new start.

On Bank Holiday Monday we travelled up to Hull for hopefully the win that would give us the Second Division title. The atmosphere as you could imagine was charged and again Millwall had turned out in force. No one was interested in any trouble. Everyone was behaving themselves and at three o'clock the game started. The atmosphere was like that of a carnival. Every Millwall pass was cheered and every Hull pass booed and then eleven minutes into the game Millwall were awarded another penalty. Four in four. Kevin O'Callaghan stepped up and slotted it home and we were 1–0 up and it stayed that way until the final whistle. Millwall had secured promotion to the First Division as champions and we were off to play with the big boys.

We drove back to London in high spirits and with the thoughts of next season running through our heads.

I was back in the office on the Tuesday and took in the present that Dave and the others had bought for my imaginary son. It was a small Millwall football, which I put up on the shelf in the office. I finally had to put it away in the cupboard as it made me feel like shit every time I looked at it.

We went to the final game of the season with Dave and the others and watched on as Millwall were well beaten by Blackburn 4–1. That night I presented Mark with a fifty-pound note to honour my bet. He then insisted that he bought everyone a drink and in one round his winnings had gone.

We finally ended up at The Puffin, which was rammed. There were people passing out drinks through the downstairs windows as the exits in and out were full of people. Chris had offered to get the drinks in and he eventually appeared twenty minutes later with a small crate of bottled beers. They were out of glasses and most of the beer on tap had been drunk. He had seen Tina who reckoned that within half an hour they would be drunk dry. We opened our beers and raised them in the air to celebrate our promotion to the First Division. I swigged mine and as I did so a Ford Granada pulled up slowly outside the pub. I couldn't believe it as I saw John Docherty, the Millwall manager, standing through the car's sunroof with the Second Division trophy held above his head. Everyone outside the pub went mad and instantly 'Johnny Docherty's blue-and-white army…Johnny Docherty's blue-and-white army' started up.

Who would have thought it at the start of the season? Operation extended, Millwall promoted, in with the top boys and surrounded by people that I genuinely had started to care about. First Division, here we come.

TWENTY-SEVEN

THE DAYS OF SUMMER

Now that Millwall had been promoted, the FA had made it very clear that they expected the police forces up and down the country to contain the disorder that Millwall would be bringing to the party. Already the demand for season tickets had outstripped supply – fortunately that was something that we didn't have to worry about as Guy had already sourced ours from the club – but still the main issue for all concerned with Millwall was how the fans were going to behave.

It got a little boring having to listen to the chinless senior officers bleating on about disorder and the huge risk of acts of violence to the genuine supporter. It was always Millwall they focused on, the Millwall hooligans, not West Ham or Chelsea who had as strong a hooligan element. The senior officers' concern was that Millwall had not been in the top division for upwards of forty years and their behaviour at that level had not been tested. They could only draw on comparisons from what they had witnessed from the matches at Luton in 1985 and the bigger games last season, West Ham and Arsenal in the cup. I tried to explain that they were cup games and that emotions run high, only for it to be pointed out to me that every game for Millwall in the coming season in the First Division would be a cup game: Manchester United, Liverpool, Arsenal, Tottenham. The only saving grace was that Chelsea had been relegated and that they wouldn't get to play each other. It became more and more evident that Millwall's promotion was something that the Metropolitan Police and the FA found an irritation and would much rather had not occurred.

All of the Millwall games for the whole season were to be classed by the FA and the police as 'Category A', which was sad for the club as the policing bill would be far more expensive. This had the knock-on effect of the club having less money available to them to pay better wages or attract new players as a large part of the budget had to go on policing costs. Our costs, incidentally, were covered by a different budget and were not passed on to the club. Fucking good job, as frankly our expenses claims would have meant the need to sell Sheringham or Cascarino to cover it. The other clubs hated it too as they were also having to pay more when they played Millwall and they argued that Millwall should contribute a greater amount to the policing costs as they were the club with the reputation and hardcore hooligan element.

The media were now really sinking their teeth into the collapse of the previous covert operations and subsequent trials. The Police Complaints Authority (PCA) was now involved due to a directive from the courts and a full investigation was underway on all three operations: Full-time, Own Goal and Dirty Den. The investigation would focus on the officers and the way in which they had obtained the evidence and their involvement and relationships with their targets.

It wasn't long before we were called to another meeting to discuss the operation. This time there were more direct questions about our statements. 'Why are there so many references and negative comments about the police? Is there a justification as to your actions? How can you remember the evidence when on your expenses claim you have spent over £200 on alcoholic beverages?' It began to feel like the Spanish Inquisition, but given what had occurred with the other trials collapsing and convictions being overturned it was understandable.

My main gripe was that our comments on some of the policing carried out at games, by not only the Metropolitan Police but also by other forces, was being overlooked. I tried to explain that, putting the football hooligans to one side, travelling supporters got a raw deal. Most football games at that time were policed by two separate groups of officers who would join forces to police the game. The first group were the officers who in the week drove a desk, and their only real contact with the public would be on a Saturday at a football match. The second group was the Tactical Support Group (TSG) but who were better known to us as the Thick and Stupid Group. The TSG were specifically employed to deal with crowds and or potential disorder and they loved nothing more than an excuse to run out of their van dressed in riot gear, carrying a baton and a large Perspex shield. Working on the ground, we were able to observe how the policing – or lack of it – consistently led to incident after incident that could have been avoidable had the police officers at the games been the officers that worked the streets on a day-to-day basis. Instead we got the inherently lazy and out of touch officers who drove a desk in the week and were there solely for the overtime, and officers from the Thick and Stupid Group who loved nothing more than a good tear up. This combination was a recipe for disaster and time after time we watched on as laziness combined with aggressive policing led to incidents that could easily have been avoided.

What compounded the issue were the senior officers in charge of policing the game. Most, if not all, would only have had experience of dealing with disorder in a training environment and did not have the experience to deal with a situation that could escalate to a much bigger issue if not dealt with instantly.

As a team, we spoke about this on numerous occasions. We had put forward the possibility of setting up a national team of officers who would police large events throughout the country, with an emphasis on cup games and local derbies that drew a large hooligan element. But we were told that this was a logistical and financial no-go. That attitude seemed blinkered to me.

I had the first week in June off on leave and spent most of it catching up with family. Things with Dawn were not great. At every turn she would moan about the operation and the effect it was having on me, her and our relationship. For me the start of the season couldn't come quick enough.

When I went back to work, Gerry and I decided that it was time to get fit, as we were both beginning to feel the results from the full English breakfasts, beers and Indians that we were now having on a far-too-frequent basis. We both put on our shorts and trainers and drove to the park in Hither Green to go for a run. What a fucking disaster. I ran 400 yards and I was puffing and gasping for air like a blowhard. When I turned to see Gerry he was hobbling behind me. He had managed about 100 yards before he had turned his ankle. We both looked at each other and made our way back to the car. We made a pact. We would come every day after work and run, walk, crawl or in Gerry's case hobble at least once around the park. We drove back to the office. We never went to the park again.

Chris had gone on holiday windsurfing for two weeks in Tenerife. Gerry, Charlie, Angie and I talked about the coming season. Gerry and Charlie were now well in with their targets and were drinking with them in a small local pub in Bermondsey two or three times a week. We talked about Chris's attitude to the operation. I wasn't sure how keen he was for it to continue but we all agreed that once the new season got underway hopefully he would go at it with a newfound enthusiasm. He had his moments but he was well liked by our targets and he had a good heart and I knew that he would back me up with the senior officers. He was always quick when in their company to step in and shower me with praise about my ability to think on my feet in times of great stress and my natural instinct for covert work.

I had driven past The Puffin a number of times but I knew that Paul was in Spain and that the pub would be undergoing some refurbishments/redecorations while he was away. Both Chris and I were a little relieved that he had not asked us to quote for the decorating work as neither of us would have lived up to that scrutiny.

We did arrange to meet up with Dave and the others for a summer drink. I took the yellow van and we drove it and parked up behind the London Dungeons. Just after seven Dave, Stu and Mark appeared. Dave had bandages on both his hands but he brushed it off.

When we got to the pub in Covent Garden, Dave was coughing quite a lot and was in obvious discomfort but he refused to talk about it. When he went to the toilet Stu told us what had gone on. Dave had been driving down the road when he noticed some smoke coming out of a top-floor window of a house. He had pulled his van over to investigate and as he did a woman left the house screaming that the house was on fire and that her baby was upstairs in the bedroom. Dave had grabbed a towel from his van, ran over to the outside tap, soaked the towel and put it around his head and face leaving a small gap so that he could see. Then, with no regard to his own safety, Dave ran through the front door and into the house. After about thirty seconds Dave appeared through the smoke carrying the baby. He had singed his lungs and his hands had been burnt on the door handle as he tried to open it first with one hand and then the other. He had then handed the baby over and got back in his van as he was late to deliver some flowers that he had promised he would get there before two.

Chris and I were not surprised that he would do that, nor that he fucked off so as to avoid all the fuss. We asked him about it when he came back but he just shrugged it off with a 'Well, it's what anyone would have done.' Sadly I was not so sure.

It was really good to see them and we talked about the forthcoming season and the games ahead at Old Trafford, Anfield and Highbury. We finally made our way back to London Bridge as they needed to catch their train back to Catford. We agreed to see them again sometime in August. On our way home Chris and I also agreed to pop into The Puffin over the next couple of days. It would be good to catch up with Paul and a little part of me was also looking forward to seeing Steph too.

TWENTY-EIGHT

WHAT A FUCKING MESS

The next week was soon upon us and Chris and I got into our painting gear and headed down The Puffin. The pub looked much fresher and had had a repaint and a new carpet fitted. There were new tables and stools but it still had The Puffin feel. I walked in and Paul was standing at the bar sporting a nice tan. We got our beers and went and sat at one of the new tables and he came over and joined us. He couldn't wait to show the First Division boys how Millwall did it. He was back off to Spain with the girls for three weeks before the start of the season but insisted that he would be back for the first game.

I was about to ask him how Steph was when she walked into the bar with Tina. I smiled and she came over. She looked good with her tan and she sat down. 'Hiya, J. You all right?'

'Yeah, I'm good.'

With that Paul got up and nodded at Chris to follow him. Chris threw me a look as he got up and followed Paul to the bar.

'Where they going? Something I said?'

She looked at me and giggled. After a long moment both staring at each other Steph broke the silence. 'So, seriously, are you all right?'

'Yeah. Yeah, I'm good. When you off to Spain?'

She put her hand on my leg. 'Couple of days, you wanna come?'

'You what?'

'D'ya wanna come to Spain with me? Just you and me and Spain. You know, that place with the sun.'

I sat there with her hand on my knee and an offer to go to Spain. Suddenly I started to think, what if I did go with her? I could go. I would probably need permission from the whole fucking world but I could and I could justify it. I would be going with her and Paul would be there and I could use that to my advantage. He was a main target and the opportunity was too good to miss. And then reality jumped in and slapped me around the fucking head. 'I'd love to, babe, but I can't. I need to be here to help Chris.'

She looked over at Chris and then back at me. 'Come on, J, live a little. I am sure that he can cope without you for a week.'

'I want to, trust me, I wanna go more than you will ever know, but I can't. Not right now.'

'How about that drink then? I'm free tonight.'

My head was spinning. I looked around the pub and then back at her. I so badly wanted to say yes. It was just a drink, but I knew deep down that we had reached a stage where it would turn into more than just a drink and I owed it to her to be strong. 'I can't. It's not that I don't want to. Trust me, I want nothing more than to do that, but I can't.'

'Why? What the fuck is it with you, J? I know about the baby and all that and Chris told Tina that your relationship at home is shit and I can tell you are not happy. Have I misread the signals? Is this all just a little fucking game that you play with me when you're down here?'

I put my hand on hers. 'It's nothing you've done but I can't.'

She went to pull away but I kept hold of her. 'Please, let me finish. One day you will understand and thank me for not pursuing this. Trust me, you don't want to be around me at the moment. It's a lie. Me, my life and how I live is just one big fucking lie.'

I could see her trying to take in what I was saying. 'What the fuck do you mean, your life is one big fucking lie? You tell me in one breath to trust you and in the next that you're living a lie? Who the fuck are you? Do you know?' She was now beginning to raise her voice and I could see Chris and Paul looking over. 'Well, answer me: who the fuck are you?'

All I wanted to do was grab hold of her and tell her who I really was, what I was doing there, and why this had to stop. Not for me but for her. If I continued with this the ramifications on her life, not just with Tina and Paul but her parents, her friends and everyone else that knew her, didn't bear thinking about. She would always be the girl who had the relationship with the undercover copper. And the questioning would inevitably have come: 'How did you not know? Did you sleep with him? How do you feel now having been used in this way?'

Finally, I answered her: 'Who am I? Fuck knows any more. I don't think I've ever known. But I cannot let my life fucking ruin yours. One day you will understand. Sorry.' And with that I stood up. Steph let go of my hand and I could see that she was starting to get upset. I bent back down and as I leant into her I whispered into her ear. 'Please don't hate me, but I have to stop this.'

She looked up at me with tears in her eyes. 'Stop what? Nothing's happened.'

'Exactly.'

I got up and walked out of the pub. I went up the street and sat down on the wall. There were no tears this time. Every part of me felt like shit but I knew deep down that I had done the right thing.

When I read of undercover officers having affairs with targets it always takes me back to that moment in the bar with Steph. Undercover officers and relationships with targets always evoke an emotional response from commentators and the main questions never change: is it justifiable, morally right, and legal? Every undercover or covert operation will have its own set of issues and problems and what works in one instance may not work in another. A relationship with a target needs to be a method of last resort. It has to be left up to the individual officer to make that decision. The bigger question comes from whether the relationship was for the benefit of the operation or for the sexual gratification of the officer. Was it the only way that he or she could gain acceptance or certain information? Was every other avenue explored before you chose to go down the relationship route?' If the honest answer is yes, then it has to be acceptable. But for me, going down the relationship route with Steph would have been purely for my own gratification. Yes, I could justify it, but it wasn't just about me, it was also about her, and the fall-out for her would have been horrendous.

I sat on the bench for about ten minutes until I was joined by Chris. He sat down silently next to me. We stayed there for a short while until I stood up. 'Come on, we had better get back to the office.'

He put his arm around my shoulder. 'D'ya wanna talk about it? Steph looked a bit upset.'

I stopped in the street and spun around to face him. 'Not as upset as she would be if she knew who I really was. Who are we, Chris? What the fuck are we doing to these people? They have let us into their lives. Dave, Stu, Mark, Paul, Steph, and all the fucking others, just accepted us as Chris and Jim. When what we really are, are two-faced no-good Judas cunts who are preying on their good nature so that we can find out who likes to have a fucking fight at football. Please give me a fucking reason as to why we're doing this. Please let me make some sense of all this.'

His answer was quick and simple. 'It's our job.'

'Yeah, well, I'm not so sure I wanna do this job any more.'

We drove in silence back to the office. I dropped him off and told him that I needed some space and that I would see him tomorrow, and drove home. Thankfully the house was empty and I went in and sat down. I sat and looked around my lounge and out of the window and it reminded me of the magazines that I had looked through and how on the face of it everything can seem so perfect. I could hear them outside in my head as they walked past the window. 'Look at them, aren't they doing well for themselves. And so young to have all this. A detached house and a nice car. They're so lucky.'

I rang Archie, my old sergeant, and asked him if he was about. He knew from my voice that I needed to see him and he told me to come around. I got in my van and went and saw him. I felt that I had neglected him since I had started working undercover, but he didn't care, he was 'keeping an eye on me from afar'. I spoke to him again about the situation with Steph and he agreed with me that I had done the only thing that I could do. 'You owe it to her, Jim. She would be the innocent victim in all of this and the one who would probably come out the most scarred.'

I felt better talking it through with him and after a few beers he refused to let me drive home and I stayed the night.

The next morning I made my way into the office. I apologised to Chris about my comments yesterday. He said that I had nothing to apologise for and that I was only saying what he had been thinking for months. We agreed that time away from football was more of a hindrance than a help and that it was easier to deal with what we were doing when we didn't have time to analyse our actions. We were now both desperate for the season to get underway.

We spent the next week working out the logistics for next season as the fixtures had now been announced. Millwall's first game of the season was to be away against Aston Villa on Saturday 27 August 1988. We were going to go by hire car and Dave, Stu and Mark had already asked for a lift if we were driving. Our evidence had all come back and apart from some minor points we were all to be congratulated.

I bowled into the office on the Monday for the start of the season. As I walked up the stairs to the office I could hear Chris shouting and swearing. He looked at me and shouted, pointing at a piece of paper, 'You seen this? The cunts. A year's fucking work. Fucking gone like that. And for what? The cunts.'

From Chris's reaction my instant response was that the operation had been concluded. That wasn't the case but it might as well have been, given what I was about to find out. 'Chris, what have they done? It can't be that fucking bad.'

He picked up a piece of paper and threw it across to me. 'No? Then fucking read that.' I picked up the piece of paper that was now on my desk and read it. It was a memo from, of all people, the licensing officer at Lewisham which read:

> Just a note to thank you and your team for all the evidence that you have amassed to date. We have been successful in revoking the premises licence afforded to the landlord of The Puffin Public House due to the continued serving of alcohol out of licensed hours and as of today's date he will not be permitted to sell or serve alcohol from these premises. Thanks again.
>
> The Licensing Department. P District.

I stood there and read it again. I could not fucking believe it. They had shut The Puffin, and for what? Some after-hours drinking? I sat down and put my head in my hands. Our point of contact, our main hub of information, *our fucking pub*, was to be closed down by, of all people, the fucking licensing officer at Lewisham.

I stood up. 'Right, let's go and see this cunt and get this sorted. Come on, Chris.'

As I went to get into Chris's car Charlie opened up the window and shouted out. 'Jim. Jim.' I looked up. 'Don't lose your temper. Whatever you do keep a fucking lid on it.'

I looked up and nodded at him. Chris drove to Lewisham and we parked up at the back and slipped in through the doors that led behind the charge room and cells and up to the CID offices above. We marched into the CID office and Chris asked where the licensing officer was. We were told that his office was upstairs next to the typists. We went up the stairs and headed for his office. I was ahead of Chris and as we got there I pushed open the door, which crashed into the filing cabinet behind it. There were two ladies sitting behind a desk who jumped up as we came in. I then saw who had to be the licensing officer look up from his desk in the corner. 'Are you the licensing officer?' I asked.

He looked back at both Chris and me. 'Yes, and who may I ask are you, bursting into my office unannounced.'

As he said this the two women who had been in the office when we entered left.

'I am Sergeant Walters,' Chris said, 'and this is DC Bannon and what I want to know is what the fuck is this all about?' He threw the memo on the licensing officer's desk.

He looked at it and then at us. 'Oh.'

I moved in front of Chris. 'Oh?' I said. 'Is that fucking it? *Oh.*'

He now began to visibly sink in his chair. He was tall and lanky and looked like he brushed his hair with a toffee apple. He then justified himself. 'I was passed the evidence by the Police Complaints Authority and I acted accordingly. We cannot have licensed premises open willy-nilly and flaunting the licensing laws. I will not.'

I interrupted him. 'Willy-nilly? What fucking planet are you from? Willy fucking nilly, for fuck's sake.' I then turned to Chris. 'How can I take this seriously?'

I leant across the licensing officer's desk. 'WILLY FUCKING NILLY? *Twelve* fucking months we've been in that fucking pub. Twelve fucking months of our life getting in with them, drinking with them, listening to their fucking shit, only for you to come along and revoke their licence for a bit of afters. Did you not think that maybe, just maybe, you should have come and seen us first?'

At that moment, Toby walked in. 'Is everything all right?'

I turned to Toby. 'No, guv, it fucking ain't.'

I was interrupted by the licensing officer. 'Do you know these two? I wish to make an official complaint about their—'

I then jumped in. 'Oh, can't fucking talk when it's just us here. A guvnor turns up and you grow a fucking arsehole.'

Toby stepped in. '*Jim*, that's enough. What's the problem?'

Chris handed Toby the letter and he read it. He handed it back to Chris and casually turned back to the licensing officer. 'What the fuck are you playing at?'

The licensing officer's jaw dropped to the floor. 'I'm sorry, I'm sorry, I was just doing my job.'

Toby stared at him. 'Yeah, well if I get my fucking way you won't be doing it here for much fucking longer.'

He then turned to me and Chris. 'Come on, you two, let's go back to yours and hatch a plan.'

The licensing officer butted in. 'It's too late to reissue it, it will have to stay closed or it will have to be a new landlord.'

What a fucking mess. We left and went back to the office. It was an unmitigated disaster losing The Puffin but there was one good thing: I would no longer have the temptation of Steph.

TWENTY-NINE

DIVISION ONE, HERE WE COME

The closure of The Puffin took some time to take in. We needed a new local, so looked at our options and settled on the Old Castle, which was only 400 yards from The Puffin and a place we used to go to regularly anyway.

We picked Dave and the others up on the Saturday to travel up to Aston Villa for our first game in the First Division. Everyone was excited and nervous about the forthcoming season and eventually the closure of The Puffin came up in conversation. Word had gone out quickly about The Puffin being closed down and all sorts of rumours had begun to surface: Paul had been arrested; the Old Bill had forced him to shut it because of his Millwall connections; he had sold it. The list went on. Dave asked if I knew what had happened seeing as I was well in with Paul. I said that I hadn't heard anything other than he had been in Spain but that he would be back for the game today.

We came off the motorway a junction early as Dave had heard that the Old Bill were going to be stopping Millwall and they were going to be made to park up and would be bussed in to the ground. We skipped through a couple of small villages and Dave read the map after first handing it to me. I glared back at him. 'Cock – what am I going to do with a map? I can't read,' I said, handing it back.

We found a great little pub on the outskirts of Birmingham and stopped there for a couple of pints. The locals wished us good luck for the game as they were Wolves supporters and hated Villa. We drove to the ground and parked up at the back of the away end. We got out of the Scorpio and started to make our way to the ground.

Suddenly a bottle smashed at Chris's feet. Two more feet further and it would have hit him squarely on the head. We looked over to see a group of what we thought were Villa supporters start to walk towards us. There were about fifteen of them. Not great odds, five against fifteen. There was then a cheer from behind us and I saw another group of about thirty people heading towards us and then I heard the chant: 'Zulus. Zulus.'

We were now in the shit. They were not Villa, but the Birmingham Zulus, and we were in the middle of an ambush. Dave shouted out, 'Do the smaller group!' and started to run towards the fifteen or so Birmingham that were now running down the bank towards us. We all followed his lead and headed towards them. Dave waded straight into the middle of them, closely followed by me and Stu. I took a punch to the side of the head, which sent me reeling to one side. Dave had already put two of them flat on their back. I swung a punch and connected with a guy in a checked shirt and then swung another and hit him again right on the nose. Mark appeared from nowhere and kicked the guy. I then felt a rain of punches and kicks and as I fell forward I tried desperately not to go on the ground. I did a pathetic little jump but it worked and I stayed on my feet.

We then had what we later were to call our 'Mr Benn moment'. As if by magic, the Millwall appeared. Suddenly fifty Millwall charged over the bank where the Birmingham had come from. They waded in and there were fists and kicks flying everywhere. I saw Chris and Mark, who were now on the fringes looking on. I ran at the Birmingham and kicked a guy straight up the arse. He went about a foot in the air, yelping as he did. I then turned around and saw Tubby Tony and his crew. Tony was proper puffing and announced that the only time he had run that fast was to chase after the ice cream van. Everyone was fine and no one had been hurt. Stu had a small cut to his cheek but other than that all was good. We thanked Tony for his help and we made our way to the ground.

We entered and took our seats. It was a great atmosphere but the police had obviously decided on a zero tolerance policy. Everyone had to stay seated and if you stood up you were told in no uncertain terms to sit down. It started to get quite comical as people would stand up and then sit back down only for another group somewhere else to do the same. This went on for about five minutes until finally the police had had enough and when the next group stood up they came down en masse and arrested some of them. As soon as the game started everybody stood up and started to sing. 'Stand up if you love Millwall... Stand up if you love Millwall... Stand up if you love Millwall.' Unless the police wanted to try and nick everybody their tactics were not going to work.

Millwall started well and after twenty-five minutes we were 2–0 up. It didn't last and eventually we were lucky to hang on to the draw.

I drove back and dropped Dave and the others off at Catford. The conversation all the way back was about the ambush by Birmingham and Tubby Tony charging over the hill. It became known as 'The Charge of the Not-So Light Brigade', but joking aside had Tony and his boys not appeared we would have been in proper trouble.

We dropped them off and made it back to the office and wrote up our evidence. My big question was where were the police while we were being set upon? We were parking in an away supporters' area and the police's security had been really easily breached. I had the answer: the Old Bill didn't care if Millwall got beaten up so chose not to actively police it. Chris was going to take it up with the FIU; I still had some ringing in my ear from the punch but considering what could have happened we had got off lightly.

When Gerry and Charlie arrived back in the office they were full of the day. They had had a really good day with Carl, one of their targets, and his mates and had met a couple of new targets, the main one being Frankie who had appeared in a *Panorama* documentary about F Troop, one of Millwall's oldest hooligan firms. Chris told the others about our 'off' before the game and Gerry mentioned that he had heard in the crowd that a group of five Millwall had stood their ground fighting with a load of Birmingham until the cavalry had arrived. I proudly told them that it was us but that it was four not five because no one had a fucking clue where Chris was when it was all going off. He told us he had ducked down behind a parked car and only came out when Tubby Tony had appeared.

I didn't care. I had enhanced my cover yet further, and as long as Chris was all right, that was all that mattered to me. He had proved in other ways that he was there for me and I accepted the fact that he was going to avoid any physical confrontation if he could and had learnt to not count on him in a punch-up. I would rather know someone's limits than rely on someone who talks the talk but doesn't walk the walk.

We were all back in the office for the Tuesday and Chris spoke with the FIU about the lack of police where we had parked. They assured us that they would insist that the area was better covered for the rest of the season. Good for everyone else but a little late for us.

The loss of The Puffin was now making our evidence gathering a lot harder. Whereas before we could just pop down and get the information without having to try we now had to work much harder. Our best chance was still the Old Castle on a Thursday or Friday night but we would need to get in there before seven and stay until it closed in case we missed somebody. The obvious downside to this is not only that it could be a wasted night, as early on we had no idea who was going to be in there, but that we also drank more. Both of us were drinking far more than we did when we were using The Puffin. We tried to get in with the bar staff but they were mainly students and the guy that ran it was never about as it was all about the money for him.

We had to accept that The Puffin had gone and we slowly started to work the pattern and who would come in at what time and who if any would be able to pass us what we needed. I did miss Paul, and The Puffin, and I wondered if we would ever see or hear from him again.

The first four weeks of the season went by without any serious incidents of disorder. I was now getting people coming up to me and asking if anything was planned for the game and where everyone was meeting, which on one level was really flattering and on another a little worrying. In some people's eyes I wasn't just simply running with the firm now, I was leading it.

We went to all the games in September and Millwall were playing some really good football. We put the lack of disorder down to the team's great performances on the pitch as it meant that the crowd were leaving happy. By the end of September Millwall were lying top of the First Division. Top. Above Manchester United, Arsenal, Liverpool and all the other teams with their massive budgets and crowds of more than forty thousand. It was all a bit surreal but for every ninety minutes the team played their hearts out and blew away their opponents by their spirit. The crowd did their bit too. I would leave every game with no voice from the singing and so far every away game – which was ticket only as it was Millwall – the allocation was sold out. There were people there who no one recognised, the 'fair-weather supporter', as they became known. Tubby Tony would ask those around him at every home game where the fuck they were in 1983 for the home game against Walsall when it rained so much that the team had to swim to the tunnel at full-time.

Gerry and Charlie asked me if I wanted to travel with them to the Coventry game with Carl. Seeing as Chris was off on another windsurfing weekend and Dave and the others had decided not to go, I accepted their invitation. I had met Carl a couple of times with Gerry and Charlie but this would be my first proper exposure to him.

We turned up at his flat in Bermondsey to pick him up on the morning of the game. He came out and got in the car. He had for some reason shaved the front of his head to straighten his widow's peak. It made him look like he had just escaped from a mental institution – think Private Pyle from *Full Metal Jacket* and you are somewhere close. He sat in the back with me. He seemed like a really nice guy but not somebody that you would want to upset. We headed for Coventry and stopped for breakfast. Carl went back to the breakfast counter three times before he finally announced to us all that he was full. Fuck me, he could eat.

We finished up and made our way back to the car. Carl said that he was sitting in the front and Gerry told him that he was in the back. As Charlie opened the door Carl made a bid for the front. He tried to cram himself in before Gerry could get to him. Gerry ran at the door and shoulder-charged it. Sadly Carl had not been quick enough and the door trapped his head and neck against the pillar. It was fucking hilarious to watch as he fell out of the car and rolled around on the ground. Gerry and I rushed over to him. He was proper white in the face and had a big red mark on his neck where the door had caught him. We tried to help him to his feet but he was far too heavy and eventually he rolled onto his stomach, clambered to his knees and stood up. He had the proper fucking hump and it took us twenty minutes to persuade him to get back in the car.

When we arrived, we parked up a little way from the ground and made our way to the away supporters' end. It was like nothing I had ever seen. There were Old Bill everywhere. If you had ever wanted to carry out a crime in Coventry that would have been the day to do it. We got to the ground having been stopped and searched twice en route.

We entered the ground and I was stopped and searched again. This was getting a little boring and I pointed out to the officer who was searching me that this was the third time now that I had been searched. He stared back at me. 'Are you refusing to be searched?'

I looked back at him. 'No, I was just…'

He interrupted me. 'Good. Then I suggest you shut the fuck up and let me do my job and then you can go and join the other scum.'

I shook my head as he turned me around to check my back pockets. 'Fucking hell, mate, there's no need.'

'You swear again and I will nick you for threatening behaviour. D'ya understand?'

At that moment Guy, who had seen me being searched, came over. 'Ah, Mr Ford, are we being a nuisance again?'

'No, sergeant. I was just pointing out to your colleague that this is the third time that I have been searched today.'

'Well, you can never be too careful, Mr Ford, and they are very thorough up here.'

'Thorough. Oh, is that what they call it?'

The Warwickshire officer then butted in. 'Yes, and I suggest that you move on before you get nicked.' He then turned to Guy. 'Do you know him?' and then added mockingly. 'Is he one of those "scary" Millwall hooligans.'

I laughed and Guy threw me a look. 'Yes, we all know Mr Ford. I'll fill you in about him later.'

I went up the steps and went and joined the others. Marcus came over to say hello. He had heard about Aston Villa and we laughed about Tubby Tony and the 'Charge of the Not-So Light Brigade'. He said that now that The Puffin had closed, I should come down the Cross Arms, a Millwall pub close to the ground, with his lot. He had heard that the landlord of the Old Castle was a bit too friendly with the Old Bill. That was all the invite that I needed. Marcus, one of the top boys, had suggested I come to the Cross Arms. It was music to my ears. I asked him what the set-up was for the day. 'Jim, it's Coventry,' he replied. 'The only people here who seem up for a row are the Old Bill.'

We both laughed as he was not wrong there. I made my way down and Gerry and Charlie called me over. They were sitting with Carl and in front of them was Tubby Tony, Gary and the others. We were watching Millwall warm up when a bloke eight rows in front kept standing up and looking around. He was blocking Tubby Tony's view. The bloke was wearing a furry Davy Crockett hat and no sooner had he sat down he was back up again on his feet. Tony shouted out again. 'Oi, you mug, fucking sit down.'

He looked at Tony and ignored him.

Suddenly one of Tony's group leant across. 'D'ya know who that is?' Tony shook his head. 'It's Danny Baker, you know, the guy off the telly…'

'I don't fucking care who he is, if he doesn't sit down I will put him down.' And with that Danny Baker was back up on his feet.

Tony got up out of his seat and started to make his way down to him. As Tony got behind him he whipped the furry Davy Crockett hat off and bitch-slapped him right on the top of his head. It was fucking hilarious. Danny Baker wouldn't have had a clue what was happening but he would have known soon enough when the full force of Tony's palm connected with his head. Tony then threw his hat back at him and shouted, 'Sit fucking down, you mug.'

Tony turned around and came back up to us. It worked. Danny Baker stayed in his seat for the rest of the game.

No sooner had the game started then the police started to wade into the Millwall supporters for what appeared to be no reason. We watched on incensed as wave after wave of police swept into the crowd and were dragging Millwall supporters out. The crowd began to focus more on the police than the game and come half-time all the talk was about the tactics from the Old Bill. There were kids and women near the front who were scared. Gerry and I went to the toilet and as we came out we saw a large number of police officers congregated on the stairs at the bottom. They were shouting up to us and the other Millwall as we left the toilets that they would see us in the second half. This only helped to inflame the situation and as the game restarted it was only a matter of time before it kicked off.

We didn't have to wait long. Ten minutes in and another wave of about twenty police officers waded into a small section of Millwall in the corner of the all-seated terrace. This time Millwall retaliated and the twenty officers were engulfed. I was up, as was Tony and his boys, and we charged across the seats towards the retreating police officers. The police then tried to come in from the top and they met with another large group of Millwall, who forced them back up and down the stairs. This continued throughout the second half and the police retreated, choosing now not to wade into us but surround us. I had got myself down with Marcus and just behind me was Tubby Tony. I looked for Danny Baker but he seemed to have disappeared. The final whistle went and we had drawn 0–0. There were now seats being thrown at the police who had retreated further back onto the pitch now that the game had finished. After about fifteen minutes it calmed down and the police held off as we were escorted from the ground.

I was still with Marcus and Tony but there was no sign of Gerry or Charlie anywhere. I said that I would see Marcus at the Cross Arms and went back to the car. Gerry and Charlie were thankfully already there with Carl, who was looking rather sorry for himself. They had spent most of the second half in the First Aid room as Carl had come over all dizzy, which he had put down to having had his head squashed in the door by Gerry.

The drive back to London was quiet and we dropped Carl off and went back to the office. I was incensed with the way that the police had conducted themselves. Charlie and Gerry had missed it as they had been holding Carl's hand for most of the second half so I filled them in. I sat down and wrote my statement, adamant that come Tuesday we would make a formal complaint about the police's behaviour and attitude.

THIRTY

THE BORO

I was in the office early on the Tuesday. When Chris arrived he asked how it had gone on the Saturday and I handed him my statement. He read it and suggested that we go out away from the office for an early lunch.

We drove out to a pub in Chislehurst, ordered a beer and some lunch and sat down. Chris announced that he was concerned and that it would be good for us to have a heart to heart. He began by saying that he understood my frustrations at the game on Saturday but that I should put myself in the shoes of the police officers who were policing the game and ask whether I would have reacted or behaved any differently. The PCA had already flagged up our evidence as not showing the police in the best light and this was their way of saying that we needed to be careful as to how we presented our statements.

I interrupted him. 'So what you are saying is turn a blind eye to how the police behave, but not the Millwall supporters.'

'Hooligans, they're hooligans, Jim, not supporters.'

I was surprised at his stance. It was out of character. 'Hooligans? The biggest hooligans at that match on Saturday were the fucking Old Bill. They waded into the crowd with their truncheons drawn for no fucking reason half the time. There were women and kids at the front fucking shitting themselves and you talk about turning a blind eye? If you're asking me to change my statement you can fuck off. You weren't even there. You were off somewhere "catching a fucking wave".'

The waitress appeared and stared at me as she put our food down and disappeared off.

Chris looked at me and sighed. 'Look, all I'm saying is that you appear to be taking the side of the hooligan more and more. You are at times more up for a fight than they are, and when there is a fight you are in the thick of it.'

'Yeah, unlike you who is gone before it kicks off.'

He put his knife and fork down. 'Frankly, Jim, I don't need to fight as you have enough anger in you for the both of us. All I'm saying is that you need to keep focused on the job at hand. I'm worried that you are getting carried along with this and, to put it bluntly, enjoying it.'

He had hit a raw nerve. 'I'm fully aware of my role and what I'm trying to achieve. I am not, as you put it, "enjoying it". I'm here to do a job to the best of my ability and my job is to be a football hooligan and be accepted as one. Sadly, ducking down behind cars and jumping onto buses when it kicks off makes you and me – cos I'm your mate – look like mugs. So I have to do more than I want to, to take the heat off of you. Do you think I want to be spending hour after hour in a pub with these blokes if I didn't have to?'

'Yeah, I do. That's the whole point. I do think you enjoy spending time with these people, and that you like them and that you are enjoying it.'

'Good, cos that's the impression that I want them to have. I want them to think that I'm their mate, that they can confide in me, that they will see me as an equal. If we went your fucking route we'd still be rolling around on the floor telling everyone that John Fashanu is white. Get in the fucking real world: people aren't going to tell us what we need unless we prove ourselves and the only way to do that is to become one of them, to live it, to breathe it, for our responses and instincts to be the same as theirs, and if that means that people think

I am enjoying it or getting off on it, then fuck it, I can live with that. And for the record, if you think I am changing my statement from Saturday you can think again.'

Chris started to clap his hands together. 'Great speech, stirring stuff. I especially like the bit about living and breathing it. I am sure that were you to give that speech to anyone else they would fully accept it without question and applaud your efforts, but for me that's all it is, Jim, a speech. I can see you starting to slip into their world and I am not going to be held to account when this all goes wrong.'

I went out to the car park and sat on the wall. After about twenty minutes Chris appeared and made his way over to me. 'Look, I know how it came out, but this isn't just about me, okay? I meant what I said. Genuinely.'

'I know. I know...fuck me; this job is a roller-coaster ride. Let's go back to the office.'

We headed back and Chris spoke about his windsurfing and I tried to sound interested. He had a new girlfriend who sounded nice and I resisted the temptation to ask how long he thought this one would last. I was angry and pissed off, not because of what he said, but because he believed what he said was true. The problem we now had was that he was on the fringes and I was deep down in the middle of it all. Chris was never going to be anywhere else other than on the outside looking in.

We went back to the office and Gerry and Charlie gave Chris their statements from the game. Their comments about the policing supported my version of events during the first half but as they were with Carl and the St John's Ambulance for the second half they couldn't back up the rest of my statement. The FIU called and there was talk of a big fine and/or punishment for Millwall for the behaviour of the fans at Coventry. Chris sent them my statement and with some further statements from the uniform spotters any potential punishment or fines against Millwall were lifted.

I took Chris's comments to heart and digested what he had said and then chose to ignore them. I was at that time totally immersed in what I was doing and was living out, literally, my role within the operation. It was so easy for Chris to play the 'I'm worried for you' card but to my mind he was always quick to accept the accolades that were bestowed upon him from the senior management when they congratulated him for information and evidence that I had compiled. The issue for me was more about his willingness to do the dirty side of the job rather than the concerns he had about me and my 'closeness' to the operation.

From that moment on I started to present any information I gathered to Robbie and Lawrence directly, and I excluded him from my statements, writing, 'He was some distance from the target and unable to hear the conversation' or 'I was alone with my target when…' or, and the most frequent, 'I shared the information that I had obtained with my sergeant when we returned to the office and then wrote it down.'

He did not like this new approach as it highlighted the fact that he was very rarely around when information or evidence of disorder was discussed.

We had been in the Cross Arms with Dave and the others a couple of times before but this was our first visit on a Friday night. The situation with Chris was a bit better since the 'heart to heart' but I was keen now to let him take the lead. I let him enter the pub and I followed behind him. He went to the bar and bought the drinks and I made my way to the pool table, which was empty, and set the balls up for a game. We played a couple of games before somebody else came over and asked to play the winner. Chris won and I sat at a table and watched.

The first thing Chris said to him was not 'What's your name?' or 'Is this your local?' or 'D'ya live around here?' No, his first question straight off the bat was: 'So, you Millwall then?' We had been doing this for a year and a half and that was his opener. I thought he was going to follow it up with, 'And are you part of a hooligan firm or do you try and stay out of trouble?'

The bloke stared back blankly at Chris as I walked over. 'Don't mind him,' he smiled.

He finished his game and drink at the same time and left.

I looked at Chris and shook my head. 'So, you Millwall then? Fucking hell, Chris, what sort of question is that?'

He stared back. 'Sorry.'

We carried on playing pool and I got speaking to a few guys. One recognised me from the Leeds fight and asked how Paul was. 'I dunno, I ain't seen him. Why d'ya wanna know?'

He looked taken aback. 'Oh nothing, I'm not prying. It's just my missus knew Tina from school and we ain't seen 'em for a bit, that's all.'

'Oh right. I dunno how he is. I ain't seen him since they closed The Puffin.'

'Yeah, it was a pity that closed. I heard that he was in with the Old Bill and had to disappear. Still, it's all right in here.'

I found myself getting annoyed on Paul's behalf. 'What d'ya mean he was in with the Old Bill? Who fucking said that?'

'Err, no one. It was just a fucking rumour, that's all.'

'Yeah, well that's the problem with rumours, people start to believe 'em. If I was you I would be careful what rumours you repeated, and to who.'

He was now a little worried. 'Forgotten. Gone.' He held his hand out 'I'm Trev. Trev from Bermondsey.'

I took hold of his hand and shook it. 'Jim from Wandsworth.'

'Nice to meet you, Jim from Wandsworth. Can I get you a drink?'

We stayed chatting for a further hour before Chris and I headed back to the office. We were back at the Cross Arms the next day for 1 p.m., having met Dave and the others at the Old Castle as arranged. We walked in and Trev from Bermondsey was over and offered to buy me a drink. He had heard that morning that Paul was back from Spain. I thanked him for letting me know. Dave and I had a chat with Marcus who had come over. Everyone was already talking about the West Ham game, which wasn't due to be played until the beginning of December.

The next game was to be away at Middlesbrough. Dave and the others had decided not to come, so on Saturday 29 October we headed off to Middlesbrough as a team. We got to Middlesbrough in good time and found a safe place to park the car in a side street next to a park behind the ground. We made our way to the ground. There were again lots of police about and as we walked around the corner we were met by a large contingent of Old Bill. We were pushed to the side and searched. We were then sent behind the barrier and told that the entrance to the away end was further on down the street. We walked down and were soon joined by a large number of Millwall who came up behind us.

I turned and saw Paul's brother and went over to him. He was really pleased to see me. Paul was back from Spain and would be about for the West Ham game. I told him to say that I said hello but decided against asking how Steph was.

We entered the ground at just before 2.30 and again Millwall had sold out their ticket allocation. The Old Bill were everywhere and there was a large fence separating us from the Middlesbrough supporters. There must have been upwards of three hundred police officers in our end although the Middlesbrough end looked to me like it had no more than thirty officers dotted about. The Boro supporters were now starting to fill up their stand and the police officers in our end marched down and took up their places alongside the fence that separated both sets of fans. As they did this a shower of rocks came over the fence and landed on the Millwall supporters in front of us. We all ducked for cover as another load followed over. The police officers at the fence just stood there looking on as more and more rocks continued to come over the fence. The game had yet to start and already a number of Millwall had sustained injuries to the head. We watched as the Middlesbrough supporters kicked the steps on the terraces and took up lumps of concrete and lobbed them over the fence.

The game started but no one was watching it. Everyone had their eyes fixed on the Boro supporters who continued to throw rocks and anything else they could lay their hands on. Charlie and Gerry were standing in front of me and Chris when suddenly I saw something shiny hit the guy standing next to Charlie and disappear down Charlie's back. The guy next to Charlie shouted out and grabbed his head in pain as Charlie jumped about doing what looked like a weird dance. We all continued to look at him as he pulled his shirt open and a shiny fifty pence piece fell on the ground. He bent down and picked it up. He had felt something hit his neck and thought that he had been stabbed as the cold coin travelled down his back. The coin had been tampered with and the edges were really sharp. The guy next to us now had blood trickling down his face as a result of the coin hitting his head. Charlie had been proper lucky. I took the coin off him and Chris looked on horrified as I threw it back at the Middlesbrough supporters. We spent most of the first forty-five minutes dodging rocks and bits of metal as they continued to rain down on us.

There were scores of head injuries in the first half and as the whistle went for half-time a huge rock came over the fence and hit a group of Millwall down in the corner. We were all beside ourselves. I turned to Chris. 'This has got to stop before somebody gets proper fucking hurt.' We ran up the terraces to the police who were standing at the top. I looked along the line and saw a sergeant standing by the steps. Before I could speak he interrupted me. 'I'm not fucking interested in what you've got to say. Fuck off back down there with your southern wanker mates.' I stood there with Chris staring at him. He then raised his right hand and cuffed me around the head. 'Did you not hear me? Go on, fuck off down there or I will nick you.'

Chris grabbed hold of me as I went towards him. 'Jim. Jim. Fucking leave it.'

'There are women and kids down there getting fucking rocks thrown at them and—'

The sergeant stepped forward, backed up by three other officers. 'What part of "fuck off" don't you understand? Go or we will nick you.'

Chris tried to drag me away. 'Leave it, just leave it. We will sort it out another way.'

'Will we? Will we really? *Wankers…*'

I shrugged him off and went back down to Charlie and Gerry. They could tell that I was not happy but they didn't ask.

The second half started and it wasn't any different to the first. If anything it was worse. We had started the second half 2–1 up but by the end of the game Middlesbrough had run out winners at 4–2. I counted in the second half alone over twenty Millwall supporters getting hit with debris thrown from the Middlesbrough end.

The game ended and we were again kept in the ground as the Middlesbrough supporters left. As they did we looked over at the terrace. There were piles of rocks on the steps and you could see where they had broken up the steps to remove the loose concrete.

As we walked out of the ground, we were all fuming at what had just gone on. It was a miracle that nobody had been seriously hurt. We walked towards the barrier that we had entered when we had arrived but it had been removed and there were no police officers around.

Most of the people who were walking with us were middle-aged and a couple of them had their kids with them.

We walked towards the park where we had parked the car. It was eerily quiet and as I turned around a small group of guys, ten or fifteen or so, came over to me. They were obviously a little firm and one of the guys asked where the station was. I told him I didn't have a clue. As I turned back I saw a large group of people start to congregate some distance away from us at the back of the park. It was obvious to all that they were Middlesbrough supporters and that we were about to be ambushed. Suddenly the mood changed. There were about fifty of us and as we looked over, the guys with their kids turned around and started to head back down towards the road we had just came up. The guy next to me was big and was wearing a cream Aquascutum coat like the one Rory had been wearing when we first met him. He turned to everyone. 'COME ON YOU WALL…'

As I turned around I saw Chris heading back down towards the ground with a guy and his kid. Gerry was now up next to me and we were joined by the guy in the coat and his little firm. I looked around me. I turned to Gerry. 'What you doing?'

Gerry looked at me. 'I ain't going fucking anywhere.'

I looked across and recognised one of the guys from the North Bank. He smiled at me. 'Hello, son.' I nodded back. We then started to walk towards the Middlesbrough. As we got onto the park the Middlesbrough supporters started to walk towards us.

I had had enough that day and for the first time this had become personal. I was not doing this as Jim the undercover cop, I was doing this for me. They had pelted us with rocks and bits of metal. Spat at us and the Old Bill had stood there and done nothing. If they wanted a fucking fight they could fucking have one. The guy next to me shouted, 'Come on, you Wall. Let 'em fucking have it!' and we charged at the Middlesbrough.

I could feel the adrenalin seeping through my body as I ran towards the crowd ahead of me. Most of them were turning around and running away, some were standing their ground but not enough to deal with the advancing mob. I ran straight at a guy who was coming towards me and launched a kick at him. It hit him straight in the chest and as he fell over I kicked him squarely in the head. I got hit on the shoulder by what I assume was a pool cue or stick of some description and as I turned around to retaliate I saw a couple of the guys from the little firm set about him. There were fists and kicks raining in and I ran at another Boro supporter and swung out and hit him with a straight arm. It then all became a blur until I was shaken out of it by Gerry.

As I gathered my senses I looked down to see that I was standing over a WPC and that I had my hand around her throat pinning her to the floor. Gerry grabbed hold of me. 'Jim. Jim, fucking hell, mate, it's over. Come on. Come on!'

We ran down a small road and then up an alleyway where we stopped. I stood shaking under the streetlight and looked at Gerry. He had a look of horror across his face. 'Fucking hell, Jim, you all right?'

'Yeah. Yeah.'

I looked down and could see that the right arm of my coat was covered in blood. I panicked. I pulled off my coat and lifted my top. I checked myself but I was unmarked. My coat was saturated in blood but it wasn't mine. We stood in the alleyway for a good ten minutes listening to the police sirens.

They eventually stopped and we headed back towards the car. I had taken off my coat and rolled it up. We walked to the edge of the park and there were still a number of police officers talking to people. Suddenly a car pulled up. It was Charlie and Chris. We opened the door and jumped in and Charlie sped off. Nothing was said until we reached the end of the road and Charlie pulled the car over. Charlie turned around. 'You all right?'

Gerry spoke first. 'Yeah, we're fine. We were a bit worried at first as Jim had a load of blood on his coat but it's not his.'

I then looked at Charlie. 'You both all right?'

Charlie nodded and threw a look to Chris. 'Yeah, we're fine. Fucking hell, that was proper on top.'

I started to laugh, more out of relief than humour. 'You could say that, but they fucking deserved it after today.'

Chris turned around and looked at me. 'D'ya know, Jim, for once I have to agree with you. I hope you smashed them cunts to fucking bits. I cannot believe what I witnessed today.' He turned to Charlie. 'You ever seen anything like that?'

Charlie shook his head. 'No. That was, on a policing level, a first for me.'

I looked at Gerry who shouted at Charlie as he patted him on the back. 'Home, James, and don't spare the horses.' Charlie laughed and we set off for home. I lay back in the seat of the car and fell asleep.

THIRTY-ONE

YOU'RE A HOOLIGAN

I slept most of the way back from Middlesbrough. I woke up as we came into London. Charlie had driven and had made good time. I asked whether he wanted me to take over but he was happy to carry on. The others were asleep and I looked out of the window and down at the river as we drove along the Embankment towards Westminster Bridge. I began to replay the events of the day back in my head. I was desperately trying to remember the details of the fight at the park but the final parts were sketchy and all I kept visualising was the face of the WPC looking up at me. The look in her eyes as I was leaning over her was haunting me and my head began to race ahead with what would have happened had Gerry not intervened.

I stared out of the window. How did the blood on my coat get there? It wasn't mine and there was a lot of it. I would have to check that no one had been seriously injured and thought about the consequences if they had. Was it as a result of my actions or someone else's? I would need to speak with Gerry. He was there, maybe he saw what went on.

I looked over at him but he was fast asleep. It could wait. Maybe Charlie had seen something. 'You all right, Charlie?'

He looked at me in the mirror. 'Yeah, all good, Jimbo. Nearly home.'

I leant forward. 'Charlie, at the park, did you see what happened?'

He looked up at the mirror. 'No, mate, I was too busy keeping out of the fucking way. It looked to me like you didn't need much help.'

'Oh right. What was I doing, cos it's all a bit of a blur?'

'I wouldn't worry about it, Jim, as long as you and Gerry are all right, for me, that's all that matters. Don't feel sorry for what you did, they fucking got what they deserved.'

I leant back as Charlie pulled the car into the yard and Gerry and Chris woke up. It was now just before ten and we agreed that the evidence needed to be written up while it was still fresh in our minds but not tonight as we were all exhausted. We agreed to come into the office the following day at 2 p.m. and write it up together.

I got in the van and drove home. As I got out I picked my coat up off the floor and held it up to the light outside the house. It was covered in blood and I again tried to piece together the events in the park. I walked over to the dustbin and shoved my coat under a black bag. I went into the house and ran a bath. I took off my clothes and stood facing the mirror. I didn't appear to have been harmed in any way apart from my shoulder and upper back, which had started to throb. I had got away with it.

I lay in the bath for an hour trying not to re-run the day's events through my head but it was impossible not to. The behaviour of the Old Bill in the ground was inexcusable and I for one had no intention of holding back on my evidence for the statement that I was going to write the next day. How I was going to explain the events later was my main concern.

I was back in the office for twelve the next day as I had not slept at all well. Every time I had started to nod off the face of the WPC that I had pinned to the ground flashed in front of me. I hoped that Gerry could fill in the blanks.

Thankfully, Gerry was the first to arrive. 'Mate, I am struggling with yesterday. I can't remember what the fuck went on in the park. And I am worried. Did you see anything?'

'Yeah.' He sat on the edge of my desk. 'I saw a load of Middlesbrough who had been pelting us with rocks and coins all day charge at us in the park as we went to our car to drive home. They then got more than they bargained for. That's what I saw.'

'Yeah. It's just that I can't remember anything after I clothes-lined that bloke as he was running at you.'

'You went mental, proper fucking mental, then a few Old Bill waded in and then the WPC hit you from behind with her truncheon.'

'I don't remember that. What did I do then?'

'You did what anyone else would have done. You turned around and grabbed hold of her and pushed her to the ground. And then I ran over and pulled you off.'

'Yeah, but—'

Gerry looked at me. 'Jim. If they could have they would have gladly beaten the shit out of all of us. They got what they deserved.'

'Yeah. I know but it's not just that. It's not just that I can't remember it, it's…' I sat and stared at Gerry and as he looked back at me I said, '…it's that a small part of me enjoyed it.'

Gerry got up and headed to the kettle. 'Well, I can't help you with that.' As he walked past me he put his arm on my shoulder. 'But if it's any consolation, you weren't the only one.' As he got to the kettle he turned back. 'But can you do me a favour?'

'Yeah, of course.'

He put the cups down. 'Remind me never to piss you off. Tea?'

At which point Chris and Charlie walked in.

We wrote out our statements over the next two hours. None of us held back in our comments as to the way in which the police officers on duty conducted themselves. They were an absolute disgrace.

We finished our statements and all decided that we should have a beer in the office. By the end of the evening I was so pissed that I couldn't stand up and eventually fell asleep at my desk. Gerry and Chris braved the drive home. I woke up early the next day and Charlie had already disappeared off. I got into my van and drove home and went back to bed.

Angie was already in the office when I went back on Tuesday. She had been so appalled with the reaction of the senior officers in charge of the game that she had left the control room. Chris got her to make a statement and it was added to ours and sent to the FIU.

The next day we travelled up to Aston Villa for the League Cup game with Dave, Stu and Mark in the hire car. We parked up in the same place as before and this time we were greeted by a large number of police. This time there was no Birmingham or Villa to be seen. We went into the ground – our end was again packed – and sat down. A number of people came up to me before the game and asked about Middlesbrough, with one guy thanking me for sorting it out and apologising for not hanging around but that he had legged it cos he had his kids with him. I tried to play it down as it was getting a little embarrassing as people kept coming up and talking about it.

Thankfully the game started. We had a new player, Neil Ruddock, who had played a couple of times but hadn't made much of an impact until today. About ten minutes into the first half he ran on to a ball forty yards out from goal and hit it. It remains one of the best goals I have ever seen. The ball arced in the air from the power and before the keeper knew what was happening it was in the top corner. We went mental and in that moment Neil Ruddock cemented his arrival into the First Division. Quality goal. Our elation was short-lived and we were eventually easily beaten 3–1. We went back to the car and I drove us home.

We dropped Dave and the others off and agreed to meet with them at the Cross Arms for the home game on Saturday against Luton. I drove back to the office and we went upstairs to wait for Charlie and Gerry.

Chris handed me a beer and sat down. He looked at me and shook his head. This was now beginning to piss me off. He would look at me more and more and then just shake his head.

'What's up now?'

He again shook his head. 'Nothing.'

'Well, it doesn't look like nothing to me. You look at me and shake your head like you're some fucking wise old owl. What's your fucking problem?'

'Well, if you want me to be honest…'

'Please. Go on, break the habit of a lifetime.'

'I am concerned about your behaviour. Take today. People were coming up to you like you were some kind of hero, congratulating you on "the off" at Middlesbrough or asking you "what it was like being in the North Bank". Jim, you are getting a reputation and it's the wrong sort.' I sat there and gave him my 'here we go again' look. 'I know you think you can justify your actions but in court the lawyers will eat you alive with the evidence they will have on you. Leading a charge down the Old Kent Road, fighting in the North Bank with Arsenal, fighting with Leeds, Birmingham and now Middlesbrough. How do you think that will look to a defence barrister?'

I had now had enough of continually going over the same ground. 'Chris. I am getting a little fucking sick of this. My job here is to convince people that I am a fucking hooligan and at the same time gather evidence against the main targets to secure enough to go to trial. If I have to justify my actions I can, but I ain't justifying them any more to you. I am putting my fucking life on the line here and you're worried about what a fucking lawyer might have to say? Let me tell you what I will say to that fucking barrister. If he can think of a better way to stop the disorder and the thuggery, then I am all ears. If he can find a better way of being accepted without us getting our hands dirty, then bring it on. If we took your fucking route we would all be in the family enclosure for the next twenty years while you decided what to fucking do.'

He stood up and pointed at me. 'You're a fucking hooligan, Jim. Admit it, a hooligan, and you're enjoying it. I can see it in your fucking eyes. But you ain't gonna bring me down with you. I have a career to think about and you and the others are not gonna fucking ruin it.'

I stood up. 'Of course I'm a fucking hooligan, you fucking prick. *I am a fucking hooligan.* There, I've said it. I'm a fucking hooligan. And do you know why? *Because that's my fucking job.*'

Chris stared back at me. 'Yeah, but if you sold drugs would you fucking take them?'

He stormed out of the office. I could hear him bashing about in the next room until he eventually came back in. I looked up at him and he looked back at me. 'I ain't gonna take the fall for this when it goes fucking wrong. I just want you to know that. I have a career.'

'Do you think you're the only one here with a fucking career? We are all fully fucking aware how disastrously wrong this could all go. Do you think that none of us have thought about that? How about you take a fucking moment to look at everyone else rather than just at yourself? Do you know why I behave the way I do? Do you?' He shook his head. 'To make up for you, to stop them looking at you. Trust me, Chris, I love you to bits but if I took your attitude you would by now be either off the squad or, more likely, in hospital being fed through a fucking straw.'

At that moment Charlie and Gerry walked in. They looked at us both and Charlie smiled at me. 'Sorry, chaps, don't mind us, carry on.'

Chris pushed past Gerry and walked out of the office.

Gerry passed me a beer. 'All right?'

I opened my beer and took a large mouthful. 'No. Apparently I'm a hooligan and I'm enjoying it too much.'

Gerry and Charlie laughed. 'And?'

We waited for Chris to come back but he didn't reappear. I had a couple more beers and drove home. I spent my two days off still thinking about the Middlesbrough game and what Chris had said. I could understand why he had raised his concerns, again, but as far as I was concerned he was getting more caught up with how he was going to be judged after the operation rather than concentrating on the job at hand. I hadn't explained myself very well and had again resorted to shouting and swearing and rather than it being a discussion it had turned into another heated argument. I tried ringing him but there was no answer on his home phone so I assumed that he had either gone to his parents' or gone away for a couple of days' windsurfing.

When I went into the office on Tuesday, Chris had already called in and spoken with Angie. He had been signed off by his doctor for a week. He was at his parents' and we were only to contact him if it was urgent.

THIRTY-TWO

A NEW HOME

We agreed to leave Chris alone and hoped to see him on the Tuesday after the Luton game.

When the Tuesday came around, Angie told me that Toby was coming over as he had something he needed to tell us. She also told me the news that Chris was on his way in and feeling fully recovered. Charlie and Gerry appeared and finally Chris. We all asked him how he was and he said that he was feeling much better.

And then Toby walked in. He told us that we were going to have to vacate the offices at Hither Green as the child protection team were going to be moving in after Christmas. He understood that it was a bit short notice but he thought he had found a solution and we were to meet him at a house on the outskirts of Catford that may suit us.

We were sad that we had to leave the offices but they were huge and we had all suspected that it was only a matter of time before we were moved out. At lunchtime we met Toby outside a town house at the end of a row of six others. It had at one time been used as a safe house by the security services but had been empty for a while. It worked perfectly for us as it was out of the way but accessible and had some bedrooms on the top floor and a kitchen and bathroom. The lounge and dining room had been knocked into one and would make a great office. If we wanted it we could have it straight away. We set the move for the following week after the Liverpool game.

Chris was keen to clear the air. He explained why he had been off. It was personal to him and I won't go into it here.

In any case, I had a lot of thinking to do. Archie had told me that Bermuda were looking for serving police officers from the UK to apply for a two-year secondment to the islands, with the option after the secondment to remain there full-time. Archie had spoken with a couple of his mates who knew people over there and they assured him that after six months I would be in plain clothes as they had a real problem at that time with drug importation and they were working very closely with the USA Federal Departments to combat it.

I liked the sound of it and I applied. Interviews would be held in the New Year and the successful candidates would be expected to take up the position by the end of March 1989. The season would nearly be over and I had nothing to lose. If I got the job I could always turn it down. I didn't mention anything about it to Dawn as there were no allowances made for partners or girlfriends. I would have the conversation with her as and when I had to.

The next week we spent moving into our new home in Catford. We had a further meeting with the FIU about West Ham at the new office and were told that we were needed at Scotland Yard next week to brief the senior officers and to update the intelligence. The Saturday game was against Newcastle and the FIU had information that a large contingent from Newcastle were heading to London on the Friday. We had heard nothing but we would let them know if we did.

Charlie and Gerry had now started frequenting a club just near Waterloo. They had been taken there recently by one of their targets and it was full of south London's finest. They were planning to go there and asked if me and Chris would join them as back-up. I was up for that although Chris was a little reluctant.

Chris and I went to the Cross Arms again on the Friday to see if we could get any information about Newcastle or West Ham. There was no one there who had anything new to add to our information so after about an hour we left. Chris was still a little reluctant to go to the club as he did not see what he had to do with the investigation but he finally succumbed after a trawl up and down the Old Kent Road proved fruitless. We did not see one person that we knew in any of the pubs that we went in and all of them were really quiet for a normal Friday night.

We drove to the club near Waterloo and parked up. We went to the door and after being searched we were allowed to enter. We went down a small flight of stairs and walked into the club. It was in a basement and was lit artificially by big lamps in the corners and there seemed to be only one way in or out. I went to the bar and bought us both a beer. We didn't have to wait long for Gerry to appear and as they walked in I got up and walked with him to the bar. I told him that Chris appeared a bit jumpy but that was probably more to do with the fact that we were in new surroundings rather than anything else, and we got some beers and made our way back to Chris. We were then joined by one of Gerry and Charlie's targets who sat with us.

By midnight the club was quite full. I recognised some of the people from my time on the crime squad but no one from Millwall. Gerry went to the toilet and came back. He gestured for me to come with him to the bar to get the beers and as we headed for the bar he whispered? 'You got any cash on you.'

I nodded.

'How much?'

I took the money I had in my pocket out and counted it as we went to the bar. 'About two hundred quid.'

'Some guy in the toilet has just offered me cocaine. I said yes, but I ain't got any cash.'

I passed him £100. He looked at me and smiled as he disappeared back to the toilets. I picked up the beers and made my way back to the table. Gerry was back within a few minutes and winked; it must have gone according to plan. A guy walked past us on his own and made his way up to the bar. Gerry looked at him and then at me. Chris looked really uncomfortable and announced that it was time to go. Gerry was keen to stay a bit longer, as was I, but Chris had had enough for the night.

As he left I moved over to Gerry who kept looking over at the guy at the bar. 'I fucking know him from somewhere,' he whispered, 'and it's bugging me cos I can't remember from where.'

We were then joined by Gerry's target again who wanted to introduce us to one of his mates down from Manchester. Gerry's target looked every inch the villain. His mate told us that he was down in London as he had some shit that needed sorting. Suddenly there was a commotion from over in the corner. The guy that Gerry thought he knew was getting a proper kicking. Gerry and I ran over but as we got close a guy stepped in front of us. 'Leave it, boys, he fucking deserves it.'

The guy was now lying motionless on the floor. The attacker kicked him once more in the head then went to the bar and picked up a full pint of beer and came back and tipped it over his head. The lager mixed in with the blood and trickled onto the floor. The guy then put the pint glass down, grabbed hold of the unconscious man's feet and dragged him to the entrance of the club. The guy who had stopped us walked over and the two of them picked him up. The door to the club was opened and the guy was thrown out. He then stood at the top of the stairs and turned around. 'No one saw anything. Right?'

We all nodded.

'Good. He got what he deserved. I dunno who the fuck he thinks he is coming in here but my guess is he won't be coming back.'

I threw a look to Gerry.

The guy from Manchester came over and put his hand out. 'Sorry, mate. Gotta go. Let's catch up next time. I am about down here for the next couple of months so maybe I'll see you again.'

'Yeah. Nice to meet you too.'

'Sorry, I never got your name.'

I shouted back, 'Jim, it's Jim.'

He then pointed at himself. 'Brendan. See you again,' he said, and left.

Gerry said goodnight to his target and as I looked over in the corner where the guy had been standing the barman appeared with a mop and bucket and started cleaning up. Gerry had said his goodbyes and came back over. I quietly informed him that we should stay for one more drink so as not to appear fazed by the attack. He agreed and we went to the bar. I ordered a couple of beers and the barman brought them back.

I took a chance. 'Fucking hell. What the fuck was that all about?'

'He deserved it, mate. He's fucking Old Bill. He shouldn't fucking be in here. Everyone knows everyone in here so when someone new appears they are checked out.'

'But I ain't been here before,' I replied. 'Should I be concerned?'

'Not unless you're Old Bill.'

I laughed, probably a bit too loudly.

The barman then pointed to the guy who had beaten up the policeman. 'And anyways, he said he knows you.'

I looked over at the guy. 'I dunno how he knows me, I don't know him.'

The barman put two more beers down as we had finished. 'Yeah, he said he knew you from The Puffin. You're a mate of Paul's, right?' I went to pay for the beers. 'On the house. Any mate of Paul's is a mate of mine. You seen him lately?'

I took my beer. 'Thanks. But no, I haven't seen him. I heard that he was back but I ain't seen him since the end of the summer.'

The barman began to move away. 'When you do, tell him Dan said hello.'

'Yeah, yeah I will.'

We finished our beers and made for the door. As we got to the top of the small stairs the guy who had beaten up the copper called out. 'Hold up.' He ran up the stairs and put his hand out. 'All right, boys? I'm Rich.'

I took his hand. 'All right, Rich? Jim and Gerry.'

He was really open and warm, which was a bit disconcerting seeing as he had just kicked the shit out of a copper. 'We ain't met but I've seen you before at The Puffin with Paul.'

'Oh right. What, you Millwall?'

He laughed. 'No, that's a mugs game. Sorry, no offence, but all that running around and posturing ain't for me. No, I know Paul from way back, but I remember you from the pub and him saying that you were sound. So come back whenever and sorry about earlier but we can't be having Old fucking Bill coming in here.'

I thought I'd push it. 'What the fuck was he doing here?'

Rich shook his head. 'I dunno. To be honest I didn't fucking ask him.'

I laughed. 'Fair enough. See you again.'

Gerry and I went out onto the street. There was no sign of the injured police officer so I assumed that he had been taken to hospital or picked up by somebody. Gerry and I got to the van and I started to drive back to the house.

Once Gerry had been told that he was Old Bill, he remembered where he knew him from. He had been part of a drug-buying team that had come down to help when he was on the area drugs squad from SO10.

I was a little surprised when Gerry mentioned SO10. 'SO10? What the fuck was he doing in there? And why didn't the fucking Old Bill steam in afterwards?'

Gerry looked at me and shook his head. 'I dunno. Maybe we should ring Bernard on Tuesday and find out?'

Back home, I saw a letter on the doormat addressed to me from Bermuda. They were offering me an interview, which was to be held in just over a week on my granddad's birthday, Monday 28 November. I went outside to put the letter in the glove box of the van, away from prying eyes.

I rang Bernard on the Monday and he was unaware of any operation at a club in Waterloo on Saturday night but said that he would look into it and get back to me. On Tuesday, I told Gerry that I had spoken with Bernard but that he had no knowledge of any SO10 operation anywhere near Waterloo. I also asked how he had got on with the drugs buy. He handed me over my £100 but said that the drugs must have fallen out of his pocket as when he got home he couldn't find them.

Even so, Gerry had officially logged and recorded the incident so it was clear nothing untoward had happened and it could be followed up.

Later that week I got a call from Bernard who confirmed that the incident in the club was not in any way related to an SO10 operation. The guy had happened to be there on his night off, and he did not intend to bring any charges. This was all a little bit strange but we had little choice but to accept his version of events.

We spent the week with our sights still firmly set on the match against West Ham and attended the meeting at Scotland Yard for the briefing with the senior officers on the Friday. This time I made sure that Bernard had informed the front desk that we were coming so as not to have to go through the same rigmarole as last time.

Upon arrival at the Yard, we went up to the large meeting room. Lawrence did most of the speaking and handed over to Chris at the end. He talked about the intense rivalry between the teams and said that although we had good intelligence, it could not be relied on as the location of any pre-arranged trouble could change throughout the day. Chris then opened the floor to questions.

They were mainly ones that we had heard before: How many did we expect to be involved in disorder? What's the most likely location? Would it be before or after the game?

Then the deputy assistant commissioner, the most senior officer in attendance, directed a question to Chris. 'So, forgive me, but how do you know all this?'

'Well, sir, we have been working, as explained, as covert officers infiltrating Millwall football hooligans for eighteen months and during that time we have gained their trust and acceptance.'

'Right. So what do you do to put them off the scent, so to speak?'

'Put them off the scent?'

'Well, you know, make them think you're not police officers.'

'Oh right. Well, we started by attending the games and drinking in the pubs that they frequent and gaining their trust and after a while we got accepted.'

He looked at us and you could see that everyone was hoping that was it. 'Quite amazing.' He then looked at me. 'And you, you did the same.'

'Yes, sir. I mean, it wasn't quite as easy as Sergeant Walters makes out. It took a long time to establish their trust and many hours of hard work.'

He continued to stare at me. 'Well, I have to say you look the part.' He then turned back to Chris. 'Any hairy moments?'

'A few, sir, yes. I think the worst one was early on, when Jim and I were in a pub and we were accused of being policemen by some Millwall hooligans.'

'This is intriguing.' He then turned to Robbie and Lawrence. 'You listening to this?'

Robbie answered, 'Yes sir.'

He then turned back to Chris. 'Amazing. So come on, what did you do?'

'Well, sir, the credit really has to go to DC Bannon, as when he told them that he couldn't read or write the last thing they suspected him of being was a policeman.'

'He couldn't read or write?' I could see him trying to get his head around the statement. 'So you told them that you can't read or write.'

'Yes.'

He stared at me and then at Chris and then back at me. 'Well, how did you get through training school?'

'Sorry, sir?'

He started to get a little annoyed. 'It's a simple question, Constable, how on earth did you get through training school? How did you get to be a policeman if you can't read or write?'

The penny dropped. He obviously thought that my illiteracy was for real.

Chris jumped in. 'No, sir, DC Bannon can read and write. It's part of his cover that he can't read or write.'

He looked at Chris and then at me. 'So you can read and write.'

'Yes, sir.'

'Oh, thank God for that. For a moment there I thought we had employed an illiterate policeman.' The DAC then turned to us all. 'Well, good luck.' And he walked out.

We sat there with our mouths wide open.

Lawrence raised an eyebrow. 'And just think: on match day he has overall control of the whole operation. Scary, ain't it.'

THIRTY-THREE

WEST HAM AT HOME

The loss of The Puffin was really becoming apparent and although we were well accepted now at the Cross Arms, not having Paul around was making our job much more difficult. We were having to force conversations around to asking where the meets were and whether anything had been arranged with the opposing team's hooligans rather than having it volunteered to us at The Puffin. My worry was that eventually people would start to question why I was so keen to know about the meetings and/or pre-arranged fights. I would be able to justify it easily enough but had The Puffin not been closed our job would have been an easier one.

But I wasn't just missing the ease of information. I had grown to really like Paul and Tina, and my affections for Steph were obvious, and I missed them. I missed their company. There was enough evidence to convict Paul and some of the others from the pub and my thoughts were now turning more and more to how I was going to cope with my own personal feelings when they were arrested. I tried to be objective – I was there to do a job – but most of the hooligans were not just solely hooligans. Yes, many of them were just nasty horrible thugs who used football as a cover for their anger and violence. I would have no hesitation in admitting that I was going to enjoy seeing them arrested and convicted, but some of the others were going to be a lot harder and at the top of that list was Paul. For me, yes, he was a hooligan, and yes, he was the first up the front if it kicked off, but I had never seen him carry out any acts of gratuitous violence or applaud anyone who did. He was Millwall through and through and it was part of his life and upbringing to fight for what was his, to not lose face, and Millwall was a huge part of that. For many so-called hooligans, it's about territory, honour, not losing face, a primal reaction to somebody invading your space or 'coming onto your manor and taking liberties'. I am certain that Paul or Marcus or members of other football hooligan firms around the country would have been the ones running up and down the trenches in the First World War, fixing their bayonets and screaming to everyone around them that it was time to leap out of the trenches and let the Germans 'fucking have it'. That doesn't make a load of Millwall turning up at London Bridge to have a pre-arranged fight with West Ham right but it does go some way to trying to explain it.

I spent most of Sunday reading up on Bermuda for my interview the next day. I was up early on the Monday and got into London where the interview was to be held in good time. The Bermudan Police Commissioner and one of his senior colleagues interviewed me. They were really keen to hear about my covert work and the interview appeared to go really well. I went home and contemplated what I would do should I get offered the job. I still hadn't said a word to Dawn about it.

We were now just under a week away from the West Ham game. We left the office at just after five on the Tuesday as we were playing Leeds in the Simod Cup that night. There had been talk of a repeat performance with Leeds at Charing Cross but we had nothing definite and we hoped that we would have a better idea once we were at the game.

We met up with Dave, Stu and Mark at the Cross Arms for a pre-match drink. As I walked in Dave handed me a plastic bag. I looked inside and saw that it contained some books.

I took one out a little confused and looked at it. 'What's this for?'

Dave was quick to respond. 'Jim, you don't have to have them if you don't want them. I found them in a loft I was clearing out. I thought they might help.'

I looked at the books and instantly remembered them from school. They were the Ladybird Peter and Jane books that were introduced in schools in the late 1960s to assist school children with their reading. I stood and stared at the books.

Dave carried on. 'They're really good. They will give you the basics. I mean if you don't want them it's fine, I just thought, you know, well, fucking hell I don't know what I thought.'

Mark took one out of the bag and opened it. 'Look, Jim, they're all simple words and that.' I looked at him. 'Sorry, I don't mean simple like.'

'Mark, it's all right. I know what you meant.' I turned to Dave. 'Thanks. I'll give 'em a go. Thanks, mate.'

Mark then handed me the book he was holding. 'And they'll be good for the little 'un too when you've finished with them.'

I was now really struggling to contain my emotions. I walked over and hugged him. 'Yeah, you're right.'

They could see that I was starting to get a little emotional so Stu slapped me on the back. 'Leeds tonight. West Ham, Saturday. Bring it on. Right. Who wants a beer?'

I nodded. 'Yeah, yeah, good idea. I'm just gonna go and put these in the van.' I walked out of the pub and towards the van but didn't stop.

I walked to the top of the road and turned left into the estate. I had tears streaming down my face. What the fuck was I doing to these people? I walked around the block to clear my head. Dave and the others were unlikely to be arrested. They weren't hooligans; they were just nice guys that we had used to get ourselves in with the real hard-core. But that didn't make me feel any better about myself. I went back to the van and put the books on the front seat and walked back to the pub. I took a deep breath and went back in to continue with my lies and deceit.

As I entered Tubby Tony came over. 'Jim, up for a bit of fun with Leeds tonight?'

'Yeah. Where?'

He looked back. 'King's Cross, after the match.'

'See you there.'

At the game, no one appeared interested in the football. All that everyone could talk about was the West Ham game. It seemed that everyone was meeting up at London Bridge and would take it from there.

Marcus came over and asked me where I was going to be on Saturday and I replied, 'One o'clock, London Bridge. You?'

'Yeah. What about these mugs?' and he turned and pointed at the travelling Leeds supporters.

I looked back at him. 'I reckon all the Old Bill will be at Charing Cross like last time. I reckon King's Cross is a better bet.'

Chris stared at me as Marcus responded. 'Yeah, I reckon you're right. Let your lot know and we'll see you there.'

'My lot?'

'Well, you know. Tony and the others.'

'Oh yeah. Yeah, of course.'

Chris leant in so that he couldn't be heard. 'What the fuck are you doing? Why say King's Cross? All the Old Bill are at Charing Cross.'

'I know, if you don't like what I'm doing why don't you go for a bloody walk? And while you're at it, phone it in.'

He looked at me and disappeared up the terraces.

The crowd was one of the smallest of the season but the noise was no less deafening. Millwall won 2–0 and as the game ended I made my way out with Dave and the others. Chris had come back and we made our way to the Cross Arms. Dave and the others weren't up for King's Cross but I had a different agenda.

Chris shook his head. 'No one's going. I can't see the point.'

'Yes they are and we can't leave them to go on their fucking own. Tubby Tony told me about King's Cross and I told him that I would be there.'

'Look, I've called it in and the FIU are on it.'

'Well, I'm going, I ain't leaving them in the fucking lurch.'

'Aren't you taking this a bit further than your job should allow?'

'What do you mean by that? I haven't got time for this. Are you coming?' And I started to walk.

He caught up with me. 'I am asking, *no*, telling you not to go.'

I stopped walking and turned to face him. 'We have got to go. This is what we are here to do. If we don't go and it kicks off we will never live it down.'

I started walking again. I got to the end of the road and Chris was nowhere to be seen. I got to New Cross and caught the train to London Bridge. I then ducked out and got the tube. I walked off the tube and onto the station at King's Cross. I looked around and saw Marcus over in the corner with some of his guys. I made my way over to him. 'All right?'

'Yeah. No one about. Where are the others?'

'I dunno. Tony said he would be here.'

'He probably got side-tracked passing the kebab shop.'

I laughed and looked around. There were about thirty of us when suddenly we heard a chant. 'Yorkshire... Yorkshire....' Followed by. 'We are Leeds...we are Leeds...'

We stood up and made our way to where we had heard the singing. There were about two hundred Leeds who were being led along the platform to the waiting Football Special. We ran to the side of the concourse but could get no further as our entrance was blocked by a barrier in front of which was a large number of Old Bill. We stood there and started to sing. 'No one likes us... No one likes us...' With that the Leeds supporters turned around. We continued singing and they sang back.

Suddenly I felt somebody standing next to me. I turned around. It was Chris. I smiled at him and we both joined in the chanting until Leeds were on their train and heading for home.

Marcus thanked us for both showing up and said that he would see us at London Bridge on Saturday. We made our way back to the Old Kent Road to pick up the van. The train was packed, so I didn't have a chance to talk to Chris until we had left the station and were heading towards the van. 'Why did ya turn up?'

'Cos I was worried about what you might do and I didn't want you there on your own.'

'Really?'

'Yeah.'

Back home in bed, I lay there thinking about the night's events. Dave bringing me in the books and the others offering to try and help was gut-wrenching. I felt like an absolute arsehole and I was struggling to see a way out in which they wouldn't get hurt or feel let down. There didn't appear to be one.

I fell asleep and woke up late. I made my way into the office and although later than normal was the first in. Angie was relieved as she had a message for one of us to call the FIU. I spoke with Robbie, who said that they had received strong intelligence that West Ham planned to arrive in the Old Kent Road on the Friday night before the game. I told him that we had heard nothing about that but that we would act on it and I would get back to him if we learnt anything that could collaborate his intelligence.

He then asked me off the record how Chris was coping. I assured him that all was good our end. He was pleased to hear it and wished me and the others good luck for the West Ham game.

Not long afterwards, Gerry and Charlie appeared. They had been out for breakfast with Carl and had heard that it was definitely London Bridge. I told them about the call from the FIU and we agreed that we should stick together on the Friday night.

We spent Thursday and most of Friday liaising with the FIU and on the Friday night hit the Old Kent Road as a team. There were lots of Millwall but no sign of any West Ham. We went back to the house for just after midnight and headed home.

I was back into the office for 8 a.m. and ready for the day ahead. Chris and I had agreed to meet with Dave and the others. Until then, we were given updates every twenty minutes by the FIU. There was nothing new when we left for the cafe in Lewisham where at 10.30 we met up with Dave and the others. We left the cafe and agreed that we would drive to London Bridge and park up prior to the meet at 1 p.m. Dave and the others jumped in the back of the van, I pulled the roller shutter down and we headed for London Bridge.

At the station, there were Millwall everywhere and alongside them were the Old Bill. For every Millwall supporter there was a policeman standing next to them. At about 12.45 the singing started and it didn't stop. Suddenly Chris grabbed hold of me. He had got a page from Lawrence that a large group of West Ham were on the move and were heading for New Cross Gate. I looked at him. We needed to get there, but we needed to find a way of explaining how we got the information.

I grabbed hold of Chris. 'Follow my lead.'

I ran over and stood by the line of police. Chris looked on as confused as ever. Suddenly I shouted out. 'Chris. Chris, New Cross Gate. New Cross Gate!' About fifty people turned around and looked at me. 'It's on the fucking police radio, I've just heard it. West Ham are going to New Cross Gate.'

Word started to spread really quickly and by the time we were leaving the station all that everyone was talking about was West Ham at New Cross Gate. We ran to the van. I opened the back and Dave and the others climbed in. Chris jumped in the front and we headed for the Old Kent Road. Chris got another message as we passed by the fire station on the Old Kent Road: about five to six hundred West Ham had just got off at New Cross Gate and were walking down the road towards the Old Castle.

I pulled the van out of the traffic and went onto the other side of the road. As I bumped over the kerb we heard Dave shouting from the back of the van. We came to a halt at the traffic lights just up from the Old Castle. I looked down the road and all I could see were West Ham who were outside the pub throwing chairs and dustbins at the windows. I was now shouting at the top of my voice. 'Fucking mugs. Look at them fucking mugs. There's no one in there. There's no one in there, they're all at London Bridge…'

Chris turned and looked at me. 'There's fucking hundreds of 'em.'

I turned back and looked at him. 'Fucking hell, look at those liberty-taking cunts.'

I drove straight across the red lights and pulled the van up in the road. I got out and ran towards the West Ham but my route to them was blocked by a line of police. I jumped over a barrier onto the pavement beyond. Dave and the others had now joined me. We ran down the pavement towards the West Ham. They were now smashing up another pub and there were no Millwall anywhere.

I ran to the side but was stopped by the police. We started to shout at the West Ham but both Dave and I were pushed back up the road by Old Bill who were now blocking the pavement and road. I turned and ran back up the road. I then saw some Millwall that I recognised on the other side of the road. 'Over here, over fucking here…'

They all ran over to me. There were now about thirty of us and I was now determined to get at the West Ham. 'Come on, come on!' We started to head back down the road. Police were now arriving from every corner and there was no way that we were going to get at them. The West Ham supporters were in full voice and we tried to sing back but it was a complete waste of time as there were hundreds of them and we were no more than fifty.

I turned to the others. 'That is what you call being totally mugged off. We ain't ever gonna live this one down. West Ham have just walked down the Old Kent fucking Road totally unchallenged and smashed up our fucking pubs.'

I headed back to my van, which was still sitting in the middle of the road with the engine running and the doors open. As I got to the van Tubby Tony came running over. 'Jim, you all right?'

'No, I fucking ain't all right. You seen what they have done down there?'

'No. We were all at London Bridge, until someone said that they had heard that West Ham were going to New Cross Gate. Why? What's gone on?'

Dave was now alongside us. 'I'll tell you what's gone on, West Ham have just taken a proper liberty and smashed up the Old Castle, and this fucking madman abandoned his van in the middle of the road and led a one-man charge.'

Tubby Tony started to laugh. He then shouted out to all the others across the road, 'West Ham have done the pubs.'

Chris was looking on. I turned to Dave and the others, 'Come on, there's fuck all we can do now.' We headed back to the van.

Dave and the others climbed in the back and Chris got in the front. I pulled away and headed down towards the police line. The police had now surrounded the West Ham supporters who were being led en masse towards the ground.

I drove up the road and turned left and parked up and looked at Chris. He shook his head. I was in no mood for him and under my breath I told him what I thought, 'You fucking shake your fucking head at me again today and I promise you I will knock it fucking off.'

I got out of the van and went to the back and opened it up to let Dave and the others out. We walked through the estate and to the Cross Arms.

Half an hour before kick-off we finished our beers and made our way to the ground. We took our position up behind the goal. Suddenly, two arms came around me and gave me a hug. I turned around and standing behind me, tanned and looking really well, was Paul. 'Hello, stranger, long time no see. I hear West Ham have been taking some liberties.'

'Mate, they proper took the piss. Fucking hell, mate, it's good to see you. How are you?'

'I'm good. You?'

'Yeah, I'm all right. How's Tina?'

'She's fine.'

I could tell he knew what I was going to ask. 'And… Steph?'

'Yeah, she's good.'

I nodded back. 'Good, that's good.'

He then leant in. 'Full-time, out the ground and around the back. We'll come in over the bank. Let's see how they cope with a fucking surprise.'

I turned to Chris. 'D'ya get that?' He nodded. 'Then I suggest you go and let Guy know.' Chris wandered off up the terraces.

The game was end-to-end stuff and both teams played really well but West Ham held on, eventually winning 1–0.

Five minutes before the final whistle blew, Paul nodded over to me as he and some others made their way up the steps. We followed him. There were about fifty of us and we started to walk around the side street that ran parallel with the ground. We came out just down from the away end and made our way to the back. We heard the whistle go for full-time. As we came around the corner there were now hundreds of Millwall congregating at the back. We made our way to the front of the crowd and as we did so the police arrived. They were everywhere and any thought of getting at the West Ham from here was now well gone. We all finally dispersed with a little help from the two hundred or so Old Bill that were now at the away end entrance.

We headed back to the Cross Arms to drown our sorrows and as we were standing outside drinking Paul walked past. He saw me and came over. He smiled. 'Well, we live to fight another day. We're going to London Bridge, fancy it?'

I grinned back. 'What do you think?' I turned to Chris. 'Come on.'

He looked back at me. 'No, not today. I've had enough for one day.'

Paul shrugged. 'Well, if you fancy it, see you at London Bridge.' I nodded and Paul walked away.

'What the fuck are you doing? Come on,' I said, grabbing hold of Chris.

He looked at me. 'As I said, Jim, I've had enough for one day.'

We were well away from everyone. 'Chris. It's fucking Paul. This is what we do.'

'I won't. I ain't going. You go if you want, but that's it for me. Enough is enough.'

'Chris, we gotta go.'

He started to get a little annoyed. 'I ain't going, all right?'

I could see Paul in the distance. 'Why not?'

He looked down at the floor.

I turned and ran towards Paul, shouting out, 'Oi, oi, wait for me...'

THIRTY-FOUR
EVERTON AWAY

I sat on the train with Paul and the others. There were unlikely to be any West Ham about but it was worth a look. We pulled in and got out and made our way to the concourse. There were lots of people about and I recognised a lot of Millwall. I then saw a guy walking towards the platform with a kid either side of him holding his hand. He was wearing an Arsenal scarf. Suddenly two young Millwall supporters stepped out of a crowd and started to walk behind him. It was obvious to me that they were going to set about him. I turned to Paul. 'What are them two up to?'

Paul looked over. 'I don't know but let's find out.'

As we started to walk towards them one of the two guys following the Arsenal supporter and his kids pushed him in the back. He fell forward and both he and his kids fell over. Paul started to run and I ran with him. Paul then grabbed hold of one of them and shook him. 'What you playing at?'

He looked at Paul, with recognition in his eyes. 'He's fucking Arsenal.'

Paul glared back at him. 'Yeah. And? He's a bloke coming back from the football with his kids. He ain't here to have a fight with you.' He then turned to the Arsenal supporter on the ground. 'Sorry, mate. You and the kids all right?'

The Arsenal supporter was now getting back to his feet. 'Yeah, yeah, thanks. We're all good.'

Paul then turned to the young hooligan. 'Call yourself Millwall, you little prick. If you wanna come and play with the big boys then fucking fight the big boys, not some middle-aged guy who's with his kids. Say sorry.'

The youngster looked at Paul. 'What?'

Paul cuffed him around the head. 'You heard me. Apologise.'

We had now been joined by the others and people were now looking on. The guy who Paul had hold of looked at his mate and then back to Paul. He turned to the Arsenal supporter who was now back on his feet. 'Sorry, mate.'

The Arsenal guy nodded back and then Paul turned to the guy next to me. 'And you?'

He was much quicker to respond. 'I ain't apologising, I didn't do anything.'

As I was the closest I slapped him around the head. He stared back at me. 'Fucking hell. All right. All right, I'm sorry. Jesus. What are you lot? The hooligan police?'

The irony of that comment made me laugh out loud.

Paul looked at them both and then let go of the guy he had been holding. 'Go on, fuck off.'

The Arsenal guy went up to Paul and put his hand out. 'Thanks, mate.'

Paul shook his head. 'You're Arsenal, mate. Don't push your luck.'

The Arsenal supporter then smiled. 'Fair enough, but thanks anyway,' and with his kids in tow walked away.

Paul stood there and then pointed at the two younger Millwall hooligans who had pushed the Arsenal supporter to the ground. 'D'ya know what? It is little mugs like that, that give us a bad name.' At this everyone, me included, burst out laughing. We then walked out of the station and into the pub. I went to the bar and got some drinks. Paul was well and said that he was keen to meet up for a drink before Christmas. He was a little vague about what he was doing and I didn't press it. He told me that Steph was well. I asked him to tell her that I said hello, and he smiled back. 'What went on with you two?'

'Nothing.'

'Pity. I think she quite liked you.'

'Yeah and I liked her, but the timing was shit.'

'Fair enough. See you in a couple of weeks.'

I really couldn't face the train and after stopping three black cabs the fourth one finally agreed to go south of the river but not before insisting that I pay up front. I sat in the cab and looked out of the window as we drove down the Old Kent Road. We went past the Old Castle, which was now in darkness and had had the damaged windows boarded up. We then pulled up behind a line of traffic and came to a halt outside The Puffin. I wondered how the day would have unfolded had it still been open. I had a feeling that the outcome would have been slightly different had it been full of Millwall when West Ham had made their way down the New Cross Road earlier. I sat there and stared at it and realised how much I missed it. It reminded me of how I was feeling. Lonely, miserable and empty. The cab dropped me off at the van and I drove back to the office.

I pulled up outside and let myself in. The house was in darkness. I walked into the office and turned on the light. Chris had his head on the desk and was asleep. As I turned the light on he woke up and looked up at me. 'I must have fallen asleep. What's the time?'

I looked up at the clock. 'Nearly midnight. You'd better get going before you turn into a pumpkin.'

I went into the kitchen and grabbed a beer. I came back into the office and sat down. 'You all right?'

'No. What was that all about today?'

I looked back. 'Fuck knows. I don't know what the Old Bill were doing letting West Ham march down the fucking road unchallenged. I am looking forward to the debrief on that one.'

'I'm not talking about the Old Bill. I'm talking about you.'

'Me? What the fuck do you mean by that?'

He sat forward in his chair. 'You, Jim. You, the way that you behaved today. Driving like a lunatic down the Old Kent Road, abandoning the van in the middle of the road and charging at the West Ham. What was—'

I interrupted him. 'What was all that about today? What was it all about? I'll tell you what it was fucking all about. It was about me doing my fucking job.'

Gerry and Charlie then walked in. Chris looked over to them both. 'I'm glad you're here.' He then looked at me. 'Maybe you can explain to them what you did today, convince them that you were doing your job.'

I looked at them both and sighed. 'Chris has an issue with how I behaved today.'

Gerry was quick to respond and said, 'How you behaved? What I want to know is who on earth allowed West Ham to march down the road unescorted and then stood by and let them wreck our pubs?'

I turned to Gerry. 'Careful, with that talk you might get accused of being a football hooligan.'

Chris then jumped in. 'No, just you, *you*. The man who was screaming and shouting at the top of his voice in the van, abandoned it with us all in it and then led a lone charge towards the West Ham. You're the hooligan. You.'

Gerry then looked over. 'What's he on about, Jim?'

Chris jumped in. 'Go on. Tell 'em what you did. I for one am looking forward to you explaining this one away.'

I stood and stared at them all waiting for me to talk. 'All right. All right. You want an explanation you can fucking have one. First, I covered our arse so that we could get there by making out I heard it on the police radio, then I drove there as fast and as safely as I could so that we could see what was going on, then I screamed and shouted my head off so that the three targets that we had in the back of the van could hear me and could tell that I was pissed off. *Then* I abandoned the van rather than drive into the West Ham because there were three people locked in the fucking back of it, *and then finally* I ran at the fucking West Ham knowing that I would never get to them or them to me as a police carrier had pulled across the road. That's what I was fucking doing.' I then walked towards him. 'What I was doing was my fucking job, unlike you, who, when we get invited by Paul to London Bridge, refuse to go.'

Gerry looked over. 'Paul's back?'

I nodded. 'Yeah.'

Charlie then interrupted and looked at Chris. 'All seems justifiable to me. Wanna respond?'

Chris was red in the face and looked like he was going to explode. 'But he was enjoying it! He was fucking enjoying it.'

I spun back at him. 'Of course I looked like I was enjoying it. It's all a fucking act. This whole thing is one big fucking act. I am hardly gonna do all this walking around with a frown on my face. Although having said that you seem to be managing it.'

Chris then stood up. 'I have my opinion and I'm sticking to it. It is just a matter of time before this all goes horribly wrong, and it ain't gonna be my fault.'

Charlie looked at him. 'Is this all about you covering your arse? No one is blaming you for anything. Jim is doing a brilliant job, hey, he's even convincing you.'

He stared back at me. 'Yeah, well I think the person that he needs to convince the most is himself. He needs to take a good look at himself. He is out of fucking control and I know what I saw today and in the past and if today was all a fucking act then he deserves an Oscar. He was out of fucking control and when I write my statement that's what it will say.'

Charlie looked at me. 'Jimbo. Did you lose control today? It's just us. The four of us and we all need to know. Did you lose control?'

I stared back at all four of them. 'I was doing my fucking job.'

Charlie continued. 'I know. We all were, but you didn't answer my question: did you at any time today lose control or regret anything that you did?'

I looked at him and nodded. 'Yeah.' I looked up at him and then at Chris. 'Yeah, I have one regret. I regret not having kicked the shit out of him when he refused to come to London Bridge with me and I had to go on my own.'

Charlie looked at me and then Chris. 'I don't think anything's gonna get resolved tonight. I suggest that we all go home and pick this back up on Tuesday.'

I nodded. 'I agree, see you Tuesday.'

I went downstairs and walked over to the van. Chris came out and walked over to me. 'Jim, I know what I saw today and if that was an act then that was one hell of a performance. I didn't go to London Bridge because I was scared of what might happen. I didn't want to go because I was scared about what you might do and I didn't want to be there and witness it.'

I looked back at him. 'Chris. Please stop looking to me for answers. I am doing my job to the best of my abilities and taking massive fucking risks and the very least, the very least you should be doing, is backing me up. I don't care if you run away, or avoid a situation, but when I don't, don't fucking question my motives and why I am doing it.'

I got in the van and drove home. Dawn was sitting in the lounge and as I walked in she handed me a letter. It had an official stamp on the back from the Bermuda Police Service. 'Something I should know about?'

Why was it that shit days invariably go from bad to worse? 'I don't know yet.'

I read the opening line. 'Dear James, Thank you for your interest in joining the Bermuda Police Service. After careful consideration we are

delighted to say that you have been successful. Please find enclosed…'
and then I stopped reading and handed it to Dawn and I went off into
the kitchen.

She had read the letter by the time I had returned to the lounge
with a beer. 'It says here that spouses and girlfriends are not permitted
to travel or live with you unless they are a Bermudian national, so
where does that leave me?'

'I don't know if I am going to accept it. We'll talk about it, but
not tonight.'

'We will talk about it now, this is my life too. It's not just about you.
What about me in all of this? Do you ever think about me?'

'Look, I have had a really shitty day today and I am not in the
mood to talk about this tonight. We can talk about it tomorrow.'

'Why is it that whenever I want to talk about us you never want
to because you have had a shitty day. What about my day? Do you
ever stop and think about my fucking day? I've had a shitty day too,
sitting here wondering what the bloody hell this letter is about and
whether we, us, this, is worth all the bloody effort.' She then stood up
and threw the letter at me. 'I can't see how you're gonna get on there
anyway. There's no fucking football hooligans out there.'

She then turned and went upstairs. I lay down on the sofa and fell
asleep. Dawn was up early on the Sunday and left a note saying that
she had gone to her parents and not to contact her.

I was back in the office for Tuesday. I sat down and wrote my statement
for Saturday. I omitted the part about Chris and his reasons for not
coming to London Bridge. Instead I wrote that we agreed that he would
return to the office and liaise with the FIU while I went with Paul and
the others. Gerry and Charlie arrived a bit later and we chatted about
Chris. We all agreed that he had the most difficult of roles in that he
had to do all what we did, and supervise us, and manage it. None of us

would have wanted his role as it was difficult enough to manage our own shit let alone everyone else's.

We spent the rest of the week liaising with the FIU and trying to get an understanding as to why West Ham were allowed to march up the New Cross Road unescorted. We eventually were told that it was an 'operational decision'. Gerry pointed out to the FIU that he hoped that the landlords of the pub and other shops that were ransacked were also able to see the operational benefits in the decision.

Dawn had come back in the week and we had discussed the job offer. I told her that whatever I decided she would be the first to know and that the decision wasn't just about what I wanted. She could see that it was a great opportunity and said she would support whatever decision I made but that if I decided to go the house needed to be sold and that she had no plans in having a long-distance relationship. I agreed with her comments and promised to have a decision within the fortnight.

I was back in the office for the Tuesday and there was no sign of Chris. He had called in and told Angie that he was unwell and would be staying at his parents' for the rest of the week.

I received a call from Bernard who asked to meet up with me. I walked into a cafe in Lambeth and Bernard was there with a guy named Nigel who I had never seen or met before. Bernard introduced him as one of his colleagues and said that he had wanted to meet with me. I was happy to meet with anyone from SO10 as I was keen to keep myself at the front of their thoughts for any future operations. They had heard that I had been offered a job in Bermuda and they were keen to know what my likely response was going to be. Nigel said that they had been following our operation very closely and that I showed exceptional qualities when it came to covert police work. They would like me to know that they intended to seek permission to approach my area commander so that when the operation came to an end I could be transferred to SO10 as a fully operational covert officer.

After an hour or so I said my goodbyes and they asked that when I had made my mind up regarding Bermuda to let them know. I didn't need to think about it. SO10 and the thought of being employed as a full-time covert police officer was more than I could have hoped for. 'Chaps, I can tell you now, based on what you have just told me I will be staying. Covert policing is what I want to do and being part of SO10 and doing it as a career is what I want. So I'm in.'

Both Bernard and Nigel seemed really pleased and shook my hand. They reiterated that it was not a certainty but that as far as they were concerned the job was mine and they didn't foresee any issues moving forward. I went home, wrote to the Bermuda Police and declined their offer.

I drove back to the office and as I pulled up outside I saw Chris's car parked on the drive. I went up to the office and he was sitting at his desk talking with Angie. He nodded hello and then suggested that we go for a drink. We went to the pub and sat down away from everyone in the corner. He was apologetic and hoped that we could put everything behind us moving forward. But I had my own agenda now. I was going to see out the operation and then barring a disaster go to SO10 once it had finished. Chris wanted to leave behind the accusations and again apologised, saying, 'Jim, I get it now. You were born to do this job, and I will never again question what you do. You can count on my one hundred per cent support.'

We went back to the office and Gerry and Charlie had returned. They were pleased to see him and within 10 minutes it was as if he had never been away. We spent the rest of the week still dealing with the fallout from West Ham. The FIU had come under heavy criticism for their handling of the game and all attention was not surprisingly focused on West Ham's unescorted march down the New Cross Road. We were unable to see the logic behind the operational decision and were vocal in our disbelief that this was able to occur.

It was just before Christmas, and Charlie and Gerry were travelling up by car to the Everton game with their targets and there was no room in the car for me. As Chris was away dealing with a 'family issue' I decided to drive myself up there. It was a weird feeling driving up to Everton on my own but I had Chris's pager and Gerry and Charlie were going to page me once they got into a pub.

I parked the car up some way from the ground and as I locked the car a minibus full of Millwall pulled up. I instantly recognised them as the guys from the wine bar in Bournemouth. The guy who I had been speaking to just before Chris had been hit came over. 'All right, mate, on your own? You're welcome to join us if you want.'

Fuck it. There was still nothing from Gerry or Charlie. 'Yeah, if that's all right.'

I was passed a can of beer and opened it. As I did so a police carrier drove past. One of the guys at the front waved at the officers inside and then raised his hands in the air and started to sing 'No One Likes Us'. Within twenty seconds the police carrier had turned back around and pulled up on the kerb in front of us. They piled out of the carrier and ushered us all to the side.

I was pushed up against the wall. I turned around and looked at the policeman. 'What is your fucking problem?'

He then kneed me in the leg causing me to fall down onto my knees. I looked up at him. 'What the fuck are you doing?'

'Right, you're fucking nicked.' He then grabbed hold of me and dragged me over towards the carrier as the others looked on shouting out, 'What you doing?'

But by now the side doors of the carrier had been opened and I was thrown in head first on the ground. I then felt a knee in my back as my hands were put behind my back and I was handcuffed. I lay on the floor of the van with my face being pushed into the floor. I tried to turn my head to talk but every time I tried he pushed his elbow harder into my cheek. 'Will you get your elbow out of my face as it is fucking hurting— ?'

He then leant forward and I could smell the cigarettes on his breath. 'Shut fucking up.' He then cuffed me on the back of the head with something hard which proper hurt. I winced with the pain but kept quiet.

Within a minute all of the police were back in the van. I was lying on the floor and as the van pulled away one of the officers deliberately fell forward and as he did so he kneed me in the side of the ribs. I shouted out more in surprise than pain, 'Fucking hell. Who the fuck is in charge here?' I was again hit a glancing blow to the side of my head. 'You fucking cunts. You fucking wait till I get out of this fucking van.'

As I said this the guy who was still pinning me to the floor with his elbow leant in again. 'Not so fucking hard now, are you?'

I was now starting to worry that if I kept up my protesting I was going to get seriously hurt. I lay there listening to them talking about how many Millwall they were going to nick. The van lurched left and the guy on me leant his elbow further into my face. 'Oh, sorry there, sir. Did that hurt?'

I again refused to answer. 'Oh, looks like Mr Big-mouth has learnt his lesson.' He leant into me again with his putrid fag breath. 'Have you learnt your lesson?'

I knew that I was going to pay for this but I was now past caring. 'The only thing I've fucking learnt so far is that you need some breath freshener, you smelly cunt.'

The rest of the police officers in the carrier laughed, which didn't help me as he leant his knee further into my back and then hit me again on the side of the head but this time with even more force. I lay there and could feel something trickling down my cheek. I now felt dizzy and a little nauseous and just as I was wondering how much longer I was going to have to endure this the van stopped and the side door was opened.

I was grabbed by the hands and pulled out of the carrier. As I got to the side of the carrier I heard a female voice. 'All right, all right, watch his head.' As she said that I was pulled out of the van, my head slipped forward and I fell face first into the step. The officer who had inflicted the damage in the carrier than called out, 'Ooops.'

I was hauled to my feet and dragged into the custody suite. I could feel the blood still trickling down my face as I was led to the charging sergeant. 'Right. What we got here?'

'Sarge. Saw this gentleman walking down the road drinking alcohol, we stopped to have a word with him and his mates. He got abusive and refused to stop. I went up to him to ask him to put the beer down and he threw a punch at me telling me to fuck off. I arrested and cautioned him for attempted assault on a police officer and for using threatening and abusive behaviour. He then got violent and was kicking and lashing out so we restrained him as best we could for his own safety and brought him here.'

The sergeant looked at him and then at me. 'Name.'

'Do you not wanna hear what I've gotta say?'

The sergeant didn't even look up from his desk. 'No. Save it for the magistrate. Name.'

I stared back at him. 'I wanna make a phone call.'

He looked at me. 'Okay. Refusing to give us his details. Search him and put him in a cell.'

They then grabbed hold of me and started to search me as I shouted out, 'I am entitled to a phone call.'

'You're not entitled to anything, and leave the handcuffs on for his own protection.'

'You're gonna regret this.'

The sergeant looked back at me. 'Yeah, yeah, yeah. Put him in a cell and get him out of my sight.'

They removed the contents of my pockets and threw my cash, coins and Chris's pager on the desk. I looked over at the sergeant. 'I need to see a doctor.' I looked at him and knew that this was my last chance of getting this resolved quickly. 'I have a head injury and I am feeling sick and dizzy.'

He looked at me and then the female voice that I had heard earlier spoke. I turned around to see a young WPC standing by the custody suite entrance. 'Sarge. He did bump his head when he was getting out of the carrier.'

The sergeant looked over at me. 'Name.' I looked back at him. 'Ford. James Ford.' I then gave him my date of birth and accommodation address.

As I passed over the information it then dawned on me that they would do a search on me on the Police National Computer and given my fictitious criminal record it was likely to only compound the issue, but at that point I was beyond caring. I was then pushed down the corridor and thrown in a cell. I started to think how I was best going to play this. I couldn't show my hand until I knew that there were no other Millwall in the cells and I needed to get in contact with the officer on duty at the FIU so that this fucking mess could get cleared up.

My head was now really throbbing and I ached all over. I sat in the cell staring at the wall. What a fucking mess. After about thirty minutes the cell door opened and the divisional surgeon walked in. 'What happened here?'

'I tripped over and hit my head. Six times.'

'Are you feeling nauseous or dizzy?'

'No.'

He looked at me from over his glasses. 'You have quite a nasty cut to your head. And some contusions which look compatible to somebody having hit you with a blunt instrument. Something you want to talk to me about?'

'No, but can you do me a favour?'

'Probably not, but fire away.'

'If I gave you a phone number could you ring it for me and tell the person on the other end of the line that I have been arrested.'

He shook his head. 'No, I couldn't do that but I can ask the sergeant to allow you to make a call or for them to call on your behalf.'

'No. Tell the sergeant that I need to see the head detective as soon as possible as I have some information for him.'

'I can do that for you. Why do you want to see a detective?'

'I'd rather not say but please get him to come and see me.'

He nodded his head. 'Well, you'll live, but if you start to feel sick or dizzy ring the bell and tell them, okay, and I will get somebody in here to remove those handcuffs.'

I nodded back. 'Please get the head detective to come down.'

'I am on my way up there now.'

Ten minutes later the door opened. I looked up to see a rather overweight guy in his late thirties looking down at me. 'The doc says you've got something to tell us.'

'You the highest-ranking detective here today?'

He sighed. 'No, but he ain't gonna come and see you. If what you have got to say is of any use, which looking at you I doubt, then he may come down.'

'Tell him I have some information that I wish to share with him. But only him.'

'He won't be fucking happy. I hope for your sake what you have to say is fucking important.'

A few minutes later, a smartly dressed guy in his mid-thirties walked in. 'Right, this had better be good. What is it you want to tell me that's so important that you can't tell my detective constable?'

I looked at him. 'I need you to ring a number for me and tell the person on the other end of the line my full name and that I have been arrested and that I am in custody and to then act on what he tells you.'

'Why would I want to do that?'

'Because if you don't you're gonna be in as much shit as everyone else that I have had the misfortune to meet today.'

I told him the number of the FIU and he wrote it down and walked out. About five minutes later the cell door opened and he was standing there. He walked over to me and went behind my back and undid the handcuffs. It was a relief to finally have my arms free. 'Right, firstly can I apologise for the way—'

I interrupted him. 'You don't have to apologise to me. Is there anyone else in custody now? Anyone else in the cells from Millwall?'

'Not that I am aware of, no.'

I stood up. 'Right. You happy with who I am?' He nodded. 'Good. I want to get the fuck out of here now and with the minimum of fuss.'

He looked back at me. 'I can sort that.' He stood up and headed for the cell door and as he did I called after him, 'You sure that there's no one else in the cells?'

'Yes, I'm sure. Wait here and I will clear the custody suite. You will have to speak with the custody sergeant. He is aware of who you are but no one else.'

I waited in the cell and after about five minutes he came back. I walked out with him and made my way down the corridor. The sergeant was sitting at his desk. 'I'm sorry, I erm, well, we didn't realise that you were one of us.'

'One of you? One of fucking you? I will never be one of you.'

He continued to look at me. 'What are you gonna do? Look, I retire in two years and…'

I carried on putting my stuff in my pockets. 'The only reason I ain't gonna pursue this is cos I've more important things to do. But you can do me a favour. Lose all the charge sheets and everything relating to today.'

'Already done.'

I walked out into the yard, got a cab and soon I was in the Scorpio and driving back to London. I rang Lawrence when I got back to the office and filled him in. He suggested that if I was happy that we keep the whole incident to ourselves and not mention it to anyone, as the fewer people that knew the better. I agreed and I never spoke about it again.

THIRTY-FIVE

I'M OLD BILL

Christmas and New Year came and went, and I was back in the office on 2 January 1989 for the home game with Charlton. The FIU had heard that Crystal Palace may turn up and they were keen to get our thoughts. It was news to us and we began to wonder where they were getting their information from as it rarely rang true. We met up with Dave and the others in a pub in Blackheath and they were really pleased to see Chris.

The atmosphere was a little tense during half-time when a scuffle broke out in the Charlton end but it was soon quashed by the huge police presence which was now standard. We left the game and as we rounded the top of the road I saw Marcus and some of the others on the corner. He called us over. 'Charlton are around the corner and being held back by the Old Bill, some of the others have gone around the side. It's gonna kick off at the back and when the Old Bill all turn around to see what the fuck's going on we're gonna charge 'em.'

Suddenly there was a roar from up the road. Some Millwall had broken through but the police were ready for it. We rushed to the front but there was no way through without a much larger surge at the police. Marcus grabbed hold of me. We ran to the corner and as we did so the crowd surged forward and we charged through. Most of the Charlton supporters turned and started to run but there were a hard-core that stood their ground and there were a couple of punches thrown, but the police were quick to regroup and restore order.

I was then grabbed by Dave who was really laughing. 'Fucking hell, have a look at them two.'

I turned around and saw Chris and Mark covered in leaves and twigs. I walked over with Dave and Stu. Both Chris and Mark had cuts to their hands and Chris had some to his chin and cheek.

I looked them both up and down. 'What the fuck happened?'

Dave was now really laughing. 'I'll tell you what happened. When it kicked off these two jumped over the wall here straight into that.'

I looked over the wall. The drop must have been a good six feet. Behind the wall and at the bottom was a massive fucking gorse bush which now had two rather large gaps in it.

I started to laugh. 'You all right?'

Mark looked at us. 'It wasn't my idea. Chris grabbed hold of me and shouted "over the wall" and before I knew it I was in the bush.'

Everyone was laughing apart from Chris and then Dave came out with a classic. 'We're gonna have to change your name Chris to Russell.'

We all looked back at him and I shook my head. 'Russell?'

'Yeah. What d'ya call a bloke who hides in a bush? Russell.' Everyone pissed themselves laughing.

On the drive back Chris was silent. We pulled up outside the office and he turned to me. 'I would prefer it if you didn't mention today's events to the others.'

'Yeah, whatever, Russell.'

He stormed out of the van and into the office. I sat there laughing. As I came in, Chris was at his desk writing his statement; he looked up. 'You need to write your statement for today so that I can have a look at it before we pass it upstairs.'

'Can't we do it tomorrow?'

'No. I might not be in tomorrow. So do it now.'

I decided that I didn't want another slanging match so I sat down and wrote my statement. I handed it over to him as Gerry and

Charlie walked in. They had had a bad day. They had not had any contact with their targets since Christmas and were starting to get a little concerned.

Chris read my statement and threw it back on my desk. 'You might want to put in there that I told you after the incident that I grabbed Mark and jumped over the wall to protect him and myself from the advancing Charlton hooligans.'

'What?'

'You heard, so if you could.'

'What I saw, Chris, was you covered in twigs, having jumped over the wall taking Mark with you.'

Charlie looked at Gerry. 'Oh, here we go again.'

Chris looked at me. 'Fuck it. Write what you want.'

He then stormed out of the office and drove off. I looked at Gerry and Charlie and told them the story. We all had a good laugh.

None of us were surprised when Chris failed to appear the next day. He had called Angie and asked her to show him as working but from home as he was collating evidence. That was fine by me. I went for a quick drink with Dave and the others and we spoke about the Manchester United game away a week on Saturday. We had agreed to meet up with Toby and the Man City boys so I left it that I or Chris would call Dave to let him know if we were going but that we would probably see them at the ground.

I went back to the office and Gerry and Charlie were back. They were still struggling with their targets and I agreed to go with them to a club later to see if we could catch up with them. They had been to a pub in London Bridge a couple of times but no one appeared to be about so they had now given that up as a bad idea. We left the office at around nine and made our way to the club. We left the club at just after 1 a.m. and Charlie drove me back to the office. We had had a fair bit to drink but as per normal that didn't stop me driving home.

I was now in my van heading for home and struggling to stay awake. I had the window open and the radio turned up. I finally drove off the dual carriageway and into the country lane that would take me home. The next thing I remember is being woken up by a rather large branch as it hit me on the side of the head. I sat up and could see that I had fallen asleep and had veered across the road and was now driving along the edge of the verge. I pulled my head up as it skimmed another bush and pulled the van back onto the right side of the road. I managed to keep control and drove into my estate, bringing the van to a halt half on the drive and half on the front lawn.

I fell through the front door but was able to steady myself. I tried to take my coat off, which I managed, but as I tried to remove my trainers I lost balance and fell over, taking a vase of flowers with me. I then rested my head down on the coir door mat and fell asleep. I was woken with a jolt as the front door was forced open, smashing it into my head. Dawn had arrived home and was furious to see the van parked half on the drive and half on the lawn. She was the most angry I had ever seen her and as I expected the worst she started to laugh. 'What the fuck have you done to your face?'

I made my way over to the mirror. I looked in it and wasn't prepared for what I saw. I looked like something out of a horror film. I had a bump the size of an egg just above my right eye from the impact of the front door and from where I had fallen asleep on the coir mat, thousands of tiny holes imprinted down one side of my face.

I looked a proper mess. I turned around and looked at her and as I was still a bit pissed, and wanted to try and lighten the mood, I crouched over and did my impression of the Elephant Man. Rather than it lightening the mood it inflamed it. Dawn stormed past me. 'You fucking drunken idiot. You drove home in this state. I've got a good mind to arrest you myself. You are a danger to yourself and everyone else. Chris is bloody right about you and the others. You are all bloody out of control.'

In that split second I sobered up. 'What did you just say?'

I could see from her reaction that she was already regretting her words. 'Nothing. I'm just annoyed. Just go to bed. Chris was right…'

I was quick to respond. 'What the fuck has he been saying?'

'Can we talk about this later when you have sobered up?' Dawn replied.

'No. Let's talk about this now. What the fuck has he been saying?'

'He rang me to say that he was worried about you and the others and that you were all losing control and he was keen to know if I had noticed a change in you recently, that's all. He's just concerned about you all. We both are.'

'And what did you say?'

'Well, I told him the truth. That you had changed but that you did that the day you accepted this bloody job, and that I am proud of what you are doing – but after this morning I am not so sure. Fucking look at the state of you.'

I started to laugh. 'I know. Fucking hell, my head hurts from that door.'

'Just the door?'

'No, and the big branch that clumped me on the head and woke me up driving home.' She continued to stare at me. 'And maybe the six pints.' She raised her eyebrows. 'All right. Ten pints. The ten pints may also have not helped.'

She shook her head. 'Go to bed. I will make some tea and bring it up.'

I went up the stairs and got into bed. I never saw the tea as I was asleep before my head hit the pillow.

I was back in the office on Wednesday and I spoke to the others about Chris, who once again was a no-show. I felt let down that he had talked to Dawn behind my back. I knew that the operation was proving difficult. However, he had almost no support from senior management and he was not only dealing with the difficulties of being a covert police officer but also he had the added pressure of being in charge. We all agreed that we needed to try and help him with it. I would make a conscious effort to try and be more supportive.

Chris appeared back in the office after the weekend and seemed to be rejuvenated. I had changed the statement from the Charlton game and stated that Chris had taken evasive action as he was concerned that Mark may have got injured, and he was happy with that. We arranged a car for Manchester and Chris had a page from Dave about meeting up once in Manchester as they were now going by train. We decided to travel to Manchester as a team on the Saturday and stay over as we were all going to meet with the Man City coverts and the DI.

The drive to Manchester was a quiet one – everyone was more weary and tired than we'd ever been and the squabbles between all of us and Chris were becoming increasingly tiresome. I sat in the back and fell asleep.

We headed for a pub that Marcus had mentioned at the Charlton game. It was about a mile from Old Trafford and there were about a hundred Millwall already in attendance. Marcus and the others had also driven up. It was a good atmosphere and we drank until about 1.30 when suddenly loads of Old Bill turned up. They surrounded the pub but allowed us to carry on drinking. We were kept in the pub until about 2.15 when we were all told that we were going to be escorted to the ground. As we left the pub we sang the entire route before being led into the away end at Old Trafford. There was already a huge Millwall contingent that had arrived by train. We saw Dave and the others and they came over. There had been no trouble at the station and the coaches had also arrived unscathed. The game was convincingly won by Man United but that didn't stop us singing and at the end of the game my throat was hoarse.

Dave and the others were heading back on the train but were keen to meet up in the week as we were playing Norwich on the Sunday. We arranged to meet with them at their local pub on the Wednesday.

We met up with Rory and his guys. They were on good form and after a couple of beers in the office we headed off to the pub. I had a long chat with Rory. He asked how it was all going as he had had Chris on the phone a couple of times. I told him my worries about Chris. He was really supportive and had heard that SO10 had great plans for me once the operation had concluded but said that if I ever fancied a change to give him a call.

We were back in the office for the Tuesday. There had been no reported incidents at Man United and actually the reported incidents for the whole season had been far lower than anyone had expected. Given the level of intelligence that we were passing and the statements we didn't expect the operation to run into a third season, although it wasn't beyond the realms of possibility.

Later that afternoon Toby appeared and went off with Chris for a chat. After a good half an hour Toby came back up with Chris and announced that we were all to remember the fact that our principal job role was that of police officers and that sometimes we needed to curb our enthusiasm and think before we acted but, that said, we were doing a great job and to keep it up.

Toby left and Chris addressed us all. 'I would just like to reiterate what Toby said and that we would all do well to remember our role in all of this as serving police officers. The incidents that have taken place over the last few weeks are frankly unacceptable. From now on we need to keep ourselves in check.'

Now I have never been one for not saying how I feel. 'Did you really need to get the DI involved in this, Chris? Couldn't we have worked this all out ourselves?'

'If anyone has an issue with how I handle things then either let me know or take it up with Toby.'

We stayed in the office for a couple of more hours until finally Chris left. We were all pissed off that he had called in Toby for a chat. It was obvious that most of Chris's concerns were directed at me. Gerry got up and went to the top of the stairs. He then walked back and shook his head and as he sat back down Chris walked in.

Charlie broke the silence. 'Where did you spring from?'

He went to his desk and opened his drawer and took out his pager. 'I just came back, I forgot my pager. See you tomorrow.'

I looked at him. 'Oh, are you going this time or are you gonna stay again and listen to what we are saying? Cos I'm more than happy to tell you what I think without you having to lurk downstairs.'

'What you on about? You're getting paranoid, Jim.'

Gerry jumped in on my behalf. 'Yeah, well you can't blame him, can you?'

Chris smiled back. 'You've lost me. See you tomorrow.'

This time I went to the window and made sure that he went to his car and drove off. Charlie then went downstairs and double-locked the door. This was not a healthy environment and it started to feel that there was now a proper rift between us and Chris. We agreed that we needed to be careful what we said and did around him. That was going to be a lot easier for Gerry and Charlie than for me as I still had to work with him.

I was back in the office for ten on Wednesday and Angie was trawling through the videos from the Man United game. She called me over and showed a still from the game and asked if I recognised the guy in the red top. It was Paul. I had not seen him at the game as it appeared he was down the front with a couple of people that I did not recognise. He looked like he had lost some weight but was still well tanned so I could only assume that he was still living most of the time in Spain. Chris appeared and reminded me that we had arranged to meet with Dave. He had to go to the Yard to meet with Robbie about the West Ham game as the post-mortem had still not been concluded. He said that he would be back after lunch.

I spent the rest of the day looking at the Man United video and trying to get a take on the two guys with Paul. Angie had not come across them before but said that she would keep an eye out for them in the future. Charlie and Gerry had gone to north London to pick up a van that Bernard had given to Gerry. As soon as it turned up I thought that Bernard must have been winding them up. It had disaster written all over it. It was an obvious old police Ford Transit and it still had the holes in the roof and front grille for the blue lights. It had been resprayed really badly and if you stood looking at it from an angle you could make out the word POLICE written down the side. Gerry was confident that it would all be okay and if anyone asked he would say that he had bought it at auction. I told him that I wouldn't be seen dead in it and suggested that he didn't use it. They were both certain that it would be fine and they were going to go to the Cross Arms tonight for a couple of beers and they would take the van.

Chris returned and said that the West Ham report had now been concluded and that our information and hard work had been well appreciated by the senior officers and that Chris was to convey back to us their thanks and gratitude. No one was still any the wiser as to why the West Ham crowd were not escorted but seeing as the damage had only been to property nobody seemed too interested.

Chris and I left the office and I handed Chris his expenses as they had been dropped off for us all by Toby. Collectively, our weekly expenses claims were large and we would receive anywhere from two hundred to upwards of four hundred pounds. This had been a particularly good week and it didn't look like Dave and the others would have to buy many beers tonight.

We turned up at the pub and walked in. It was a nice pub and it was busy considering that it was a Wednesday night. Dave, Stu and Mark were at the bar and Dave was talking to somebody that I had seen him talking to at the football a couple of times, but I had never met him. We went over and said hello to the others and Dave introduced the guy he was talking to as Scott and said that he was an old school friend. We ordered some beers and I started playing pool. I was easily beaten by Stu and sat down to watch him beat Chris.

I noticed that Dave's mate had positioned himself at the bar and that people were coming up to him and that he would disappear off with them to the toilet. It wasn't hard to work out that he was selling drugs. I carried on watching Stu clean up against Chris and Dave came over and sat down. Scott was now back from his latest deal and I turned to Dave. 'Where the fuck does he keep going?'

Dave looked over and very matter-of-factly replied, 'Oh, he's dealing, that's what he does.'

I looked over. 'Does he do all right?'

'Let's just say he doesn't do anything else and he has got a nice house and a car which he was just telling me is all paid for.'

'Good for him.'

I turned back and Stu was now beating Mark. We played a few more games, I went to the bar to get in some more beers and as I got there Scott came over. I asked him if he wanted a beer which he was keen to accept. I waited for the beers and as I did I turned to Scott. 'Busy night?' He looked back at me slightly wary. 'It's all right, Dave said. It's cool. I was just being nosy, sorry.'

'No worries. Yeah, busy night. Why? D'ya want some.'

'Err, yeah. That would be great. What you got?'

'Moroccan. It's all I do but I don't serve it any smaller than a quarter.'

'What do I get for five hundred quid?'

'Five hundred? Fucking hell, you sure?'

'Yeah, I used to get my stuff off some posh guy in Kilburn but he seems to have disappeared. I used to buy a big lump and then cut it down and flog it to mates and guys in the local pub.'

'All right, in the toilets.'

I nodded. 'Let me just get some more money off Chris and I will be with you.' I went over to Chris who was standing with Dave and the others. 'Chris, can I have three hundred quid?'

Chris and the others turned and looked at me. 'What for?'

'Drugs.'

His eyes opened up and he stared back. 'Drugs? What d'ya want—'

I interrupted him before he said the wrong thing. 'Chris, just give me the three hundred quid, will ya?'

He took the cash out of his pocket and counted out three hundred pounds and handed it to me. 'There you go, don't spend it all at once.'

I made my way off to the toilet and went inside. Scott was standing there with a small set of digital scales. He went to put the gear on the scales and I put my hand out with the cash. 'There you go, a monkey. You don't need to weigh it. You're a friend of Dave and that's good enough for me.'

He took the cash and I took the gear and put it in my pocket. I thanked him and went back outside and over to the others. Chris was making his way to the bar to get in some more drinks. I went and stood by Dave. 'D'ya get your stuff?'

I looked back at Dave. 'Yeah, all good.'

'You're lucky you know me cos otherwise he wouldn't have served you. He won't serve anyone he don't know as he's petrified of being caught by the Old Bill.'

'Can't blame him. Ah, fuck. I wish I'd known, I could have bought it and then made out I was Old Bill.'

'That would have been funny to see. Why don't you? When he comes over tell him you're Old Bill and that he's under arrest.'

I shook my head. 'Nah. He'd never fall for that.'

'Look. Look, he's coming over. Please, Jim, for me, just try it, it would be proper funny.'

Something very strange happens to you in this line of work. You are constantly striving for the next big test of your abilities and I was starting to do little things to deliberately trip myself up to see how I got out of it and this was one of those moments. Everything about what I was about to do was wrong but it was a test, a proper test.

I looked back at Dave. 'All right, all right.'

As Scott came over Chris came back from the bar and handed me my beer and as he did so I stood up and walked over to Scott and as he went to sit down I took hold of his arm. 'It's Scott, ain't it?' He nodded back. 'A bit of bad news I'm afraid.'

'What's up? The gear's all right, trust me. It's good shit.'

'I am sure it is but that's not the issue. You are now under arrest. I'm a policeman and you have just sold me a large amount of an illegal substance that I believe to be cannabis. Now, I need to formally caution you. You are not obliged to say anything unless you wish to do so but anything you do say may be taken down in writing and given in evidence. Do you understand?' The colour had drained from Scott's face. He nodded his head. 'Good, is there anything that you would like to say?' He then shook his head. 'Okay, no comment to caution at... What's the time?'

I looked around and everyone was now staring at me, including Chris, who looked like he wanted the ground to open up and swallow him.

Mark looked up at the clock behind me, 'It's twenty to ten.'

'Okay, no reply to caution at 9.40.' I then picked up my beer and took a sip. 'Someone will be here in a minute to pick us both up.' Scott looked at me and nodded. I then sat on the edge of the table and looked over at him. 'Oh, and I forgot to mention something else.'

He was now close to tears. 'What?'

And as I stood up I started to laugh. 'Got ya. It's just a wind-up.' And I then expected everyone to start laughing, but nothing happened. Everyone was staring at me open-mouthed including Dave. I then turned to them, still laughing. 'It's a wind-up, it's a fucking wind-up.'

Everyone looked pale and Dave finally broke the silence. 'Fuck me. You fucking had me there and it was my fucking idea.' He then turned and looked at Scott. 'Fucking look at him. He did you, didn't he?'

Scott nodded back. 'Did me? I fucking shit myself.'

I then looked over at Chris who was just staring at me as Mark ran over. 'Fucking hell, Jim, that was brilliant. You wanna think about becoming an actor. Where d'ya learn all that stuff?'

'On *The Bill*, the missus loves it.'

Dave put his arm around me. 'That was amazing. Shit.' He then turned to Chris. 'You all right, Chris?'

He did the now infamous head shake. 'I'm not sure. He had me bloody going for a second back there.'

They all laughed and we stayed for about another half an hour. We went to the van and I started to drive back to the office. Chris was very quiet and I looked over at him. He was still white. 'You all right?'

He was staring out of the window. 'No.'

I looked back at him. 'Come on, Chris, you gotta admit that that was kind of funny.'

He remained silent until we got back to outside the office. 'Please help me out here as I am trying to understand this. How on any level, is what you just did funny?'

I started to laugh. 'Mate. How can you not find that funny? An undercover cop living the life of a football hooligan who then convinces his targets that he is an undercover cop. How is that not funny?'

He started to smile. 'Bloody hell, Jim. You are something else. I do not know how you pulled that off. I dread to think what is going to happen next.' He started to laugh.

'Chris, it's good to hear you laugh, mate.'

He started to get out of the van. 'Enjoy it while you can, as I'm sure it won't last.'

He wasn't wrong there.

THIRTY-SIX

SUSSED

Gerry and Charlie had started going to the Cross Arms at lunchtimes in their new van and had struck up a relationship with the landlord and a couple of regulars. They were out on the Friday night and as Chris and I were going to the Old Castle with Dave and the others on the Saturday we had Friday night off. We contemplated going with Charlie and Gerry to the club near Waterloo but we agreed that the Saturday night before the game was a better bet. Chris seemed to be in a better frame of mind although he had made me promise that I would never again try and convince any of our targets that I was anything more than a painter and decorator from Wandsworth who liked to go to football and have a tear-up, and I promised him that my days of trying to convince my targets that I was a policeman were over.

I was back in the office mid-afternoon on the Saturday and Gerry and I watched the results at 4.45. Millwall had slipped to seventh after the loss to Man United but they were still on for a mid-table finish, which was considering the size of the club and the monies available to them an amazing achievement. Chris brought up the possibility of a third season. He wasn't sure whether it would be sanctioned but he wasn't ruling it out and he said that we would probably know a bit more over the coming months.

We left the office just before seven as we were meeting Dave and the others at half past. We parked up and went into the Old Castle and they were early and had already got the drinks in. I went to the bar to get some more drinks when a big arm came around my shoulder and gave me a hug. I looked up. It was Paul. 'Jim, how are you, son?'

'I'm really well, mate, you?'

He nodded. 'Yeah, yeah, I'm all right. You got a minute?'

'Yeah, of course. What's up?'

He looked around and then turned back to me. 'Not in here. Come with me.'

This was beginning to get a little arse twitchy. 'There a problem?'

He nodded. 'Yeah, a big fucking problem. Come with me.'

I was now properly fucking worried. I had a guy that I knew could easily snap me in fucking half and as much as I liked him and believed he liked me I knew that if he had an inkling that I was Old Bill he would front me out and deal with it in his own way. Fuck it, I hadn't come this far to bottle it now. We walked out of the pub. There was a car sitting opposite with the two guys in it that I instantly recognised from the Man United surveillance tapes.

Paul was standing under the street lamp. Everything was now running through my head. Had I been sussed? Was he under the light so the other two could get a good look at me?

Then he spoke. 'We have got Old Bill in at Millwall.' He didn't show any emotion and I was really trying not to show my obvious fear. 'There's undercover Old Bill working at Millwall posing as hooligans like last time but they're proper good.'

I was running all the scenarios through my head. Would he drag me into the car? Would he just tell me to fuck off? Would he kick the shit out of me or worse?

I tried to play it cool, but I was now properly shitting myself. 'Who is it?' I asked and then stood there, praying he didn't point the finger at me.

Paul breathed in. 'D'ya know the geezer with the permed curly hair? Calls himself a builder? And the other guy who says he's a driver.'

This was now beginning to look a little better for me and Chris but not so good for Gerry and Charlie.

'No, oh, hold up. The geezer who looks a bit like Terry Hurlock?'

Paul nodded. 'That's him.'

I shook my head. 'No, he ain't fucking Old Bill. Him? Bollocks.'

Paul grabbed my arm. 'Not bollocks, true. Old Bill one hundred per cent.'

My head was now running on overtime as I tried to remember when he would have seen me with him. What I may have said about him. 'He can't be. He helped me and Chris do some decorating, and he drove us too. Oh fuck. Paul, are you fucking sure? He can't be. He will have fucking loads of shit on me. Middlesbrough, for one. Mate, he was fucking there toe to toe when it came on top.'

He looked at me. 'Did you see him hit anyone?'

'Err, no, but—'

Paul interrupted me. 'How much more fucking convincing do you need? You ever met his mum? Have you ever met his mum?'

I looked back at him. 'What the fuck has that got to do with all of this?'

'Think about it. Have you ever met his mum or his missus or his kids or his brothers or sisters or have you only seen him at football and when it suits him?'

I was now beginning to realise the enormity of all of this. Chris and I appeared to be safe but Gerry and Charlie were properly in the shit. 'Ahhh fuck, the curly-haired pikey cunt. Oh fuck, he was there at fucking West Ham as well. Shit. What the fuck am I gonna do?'

Paul grabbed hold of me. '*We*, okay. *We* do nothing. For now… The only people that know are you, me, Marcus and a handful of others. So for the time being it needs to stay as it is. Do you understand?'

'Where are they now?'

I could see him weighing up what he was going to say. 'In the Cross Arms.'

'Why don't we go down there and front them out, fucking snidey cunts. We could go down there—'

Paul shook me. 'Listen to me. I have told you cos you're my mate, a good mate, so listen to what I am telling you and do as you are fucking told. You are to act normally with these two cunts and not do anything until we have had another chat. Give me your word, your word, that this stays between us.'

'But they—'

He shook me again. '*Your word.*'

'Yeah, all right, all right. You have my word. But I wanna be part of what you decide to do.' He nodded. 'Of course, that goes without saying. Everything else all right?'

I laughed. 'Oh yeah, it's all fucking tip top, apart from being hood-winked by a couple of undercover Old Bill things couldn't be better.'

He laughed. 'You still on that same number?'

I nodded.

He started to walk back to the car. 'Oh, and I nearly forgot, Steph said to say hello.' I smiled as he started to get back in the car. 'And Jim, remember, nothing stupid.'

I stood outside the pub and tried to take in everything that Paul had just told me. We needed to get Gerry and Charlie out of the Cross Arms and back to somewhere safe as a matter of urgency. I walked back into the pub and went over to Dave and the others.

Chris could see I was flustered. 'How's Paul?' he asked. 'We saw you talking to him at the bar. All good?'

'Yeah, he's good, he wanted to talk about the Arsenal game, they're bringing a firm apparently.'

I took my beer and drank it. Dave went to the bar and bought me another one. I drank that as quickly as I could, saying that I was really thirsty for some reason. I needed somebody to go to the toilet and, as luck would have it, ten minutes later Stu made his way over.

I announced that I wasn't feeling great and went into the toilet. Stu was having a piss and I rushed into the cubicle. I needed to make this sound convincing so I stuck my fingers down my throat and after my third attempt promptly threw up all the beer that I had just drunk. Stu called out to see if I was all right. I finally exited the cubicle and went to the sink and splashed my face. I told Stu to go and that I would be out in a minute. I came out and told everyone that I was feeling like shit and that I really needed to go home.

I had needed to make our exit look convincing were it ever to come up that I had left the pub as soon as I had heard the news from Paul. We went to the van and Chris offered to drive. I told him to get in and we drove off. I went up the road and then spun the van around and went back the other way. I looked in my mirrors and after a couple of left and rights and doubling back on myself I was happy that we had not been followed. Chris had been asking what was going on but I had told him to sit there and that he would find out soon enough. I pulled the van onto a small estate and drove it over and parked behind some garages.

Chris looked at me. 'You still feeling sick?'

I turned the van off and swung around in my seat. 'Not as sick as you're gonna feel when you hear what I have got to say.'

'I already don't like the sound of this.'

'Gerry and Charlie have been sussed. They know they are Old Bill. Paul, Marcus and probably Tubby Tony and some others. We need to get Gerry and Charlie out of the Cross Arms before they go to the club because if Paul knows they're in there, which he does, then he won't be the only one.'

Chris then looked at me. 'What d'ya wanna do?'

'Well, we obviously can't go there. We need to send Gerry a pager telling him to call me as soon as possible. We'll find a phone box and give that number as we don't wanna give the office number out, and I will tell him what's occurred.'

'Right. Good plan. Let's find a phone box.'

I started to get out of the van.

'Where you going?'

'To find a phone box. I don't want anyone to see the van. Wait here, I will be back as quick as I can.'

I slammed the door, put up my hood and started to walk towards the main road. I began to wonder how they had been sussed, and how had we got away with it. I came up with the answer. We had been lucky, that was it. Just lucky.

I found a phone box and called and left Gerry a short but clear message. 'You need to ring your brother urgently on this number.' And I stood in the phone box and waited.

Within five minutes the phone rang. I told Gerry that he needed to get out of the Cross Arms now and take a circuitous route back to the office and to make sure that he wasn't followed. I also told him to park that shitty fucking van well away from the house and that we would see them back there. Gerry was keen to know what was going on but I told him that now was not the time for a discussion and that we would see him back at the office.

I walked back to the van and Chris almost jumped out of his skin as I opened the door. He was a bag of nerves and he wasn't the only one: so was I. I drove back and parked up away from the office. About half an hour later Gerry and Charlie arrived. As they sat down I told them the news that they had been sussed. I was convinced that the van had gone some way to fuelling the rumour. Gerry was certain that they could strong it out. They had a good relationship with their targets and with our backing and support and maybe getting Paul to see it in a different way they would have a chance. But there was no way that we could start trying to counter the allegations without it throwing some unnecessary questions our way. It was bad enough potentially losing one team, let alone both. We talked it through until well into the morning and finally came to a decision. Chris and I were going to have to distance ourselves from them. Both Charlie and Gerry wanted to try and bluff their way through and said that they would make light of the van and stop using it, stating that idiots might think that they are Old Bill and that if they were Old Bill would they be stupid enough to be driving around in an old police van. It did bring home to us all the reality of the situation and that we had become almost immune to it. Chris agreed to let them try and work it through but insisted that we were to debrief every day and that they were not to go to the club near Waterloo given Paul's connections there with Rich and his last reaction with Old Bill. Gerry was sure that we were overreacting and that all would be better after a good night's rest. It was now 3 a.m. and we all left for home.

I was back in the next day for ten and Gerry was already there. He had been in since eight working out a strategy. He had all sorts of plans up his sleeve. I suggested that the best plan of attack would be to set up some mock incident and for him to be arrested in full view of the Cross Arms or at a game. We tried to think through a plausible scenario as Charlie arrived. He had driven home even though he was going to stay in the house as he had wanted to see his wife Sarah. He was concerned about what had happened with Paul but he was also keen to try and push through. He agreed with the arresting idea but it needed to not look or appear staged in any way.

We would think it through later but for now we needed to focus on the Norwich game. The game was being broadcast live on the television. Chris arrived and we headed straight off to the Cross Arms as we had agreed to meet with Dave and the others.

We met up and I apologised for my early exit but they were all good. Marcus was there and he came over. I nodded to him and we went outside. 'You spoken with Paul?'

I nodded. 'Yeah. I'm not a hundred per cent sure, though. You?'

Marcus shook his head. 'Nah. But it's better to be safe than sorry. You seen 'em?'

I turned around. 'Nope. And if we do Paul wants 'em left alone.'

He looked back towards the pub. 'You told anyone?'

'No, you?'

'No, let's see what happens. Catch you later.'

I went back into the pub and we made our way to the ground. There was a great atmosphere and Norwich were up 2–0 within ten minutes. We pulled a quick goal back and then just before half-time we drew level. It was a great game of football and for once was a welcome relief from the week's events. Millwall deserved the draw only for Norwich to grab a goal against the run of play with the last kick of the game.

We left the ground disappointed and went back to the Cross Arms. We had a couple of beers and then agreed to meet up with Dave and the others the following week for the FA Cup game against Liverpool at home, which was also scheduled for the Sunday. We headed back to the office and as we arrived we could see that Gerry and Charlie were back. We were keen to hear how they had got on.

They had had a really good day with their targets and Gerry had dropped in about being stopped by the Old Bill in the van and being asked if he was a policeman. He had sown the seed so the next plan was to set up the convincing arrest. We talked through a number of ideas and all agreed to think about it over the weekend. It looked as if Charlie and Gerry were going to pull it off and given that Marcus was not sure, I now believed that if we managed it properly they were in with a chance.

Chris announced that our statements needed to be up to date as they needed to be sent to the FIU because the Police Complaints Authority had requested all of the up-to-date statements as part of their on-going enquiry regarding the collapsed trials. We were used to our paperwork being scrutinised so none of us had any issues. Chris seemed to agree that Gerry and Charlie might salvage what last night looked a dead end and he was happy to support the staged arrest to try and boost their credibility.

I was back in the office on the Tuesday having had a letter back from Bermuda. They were disappointed that I had not taken up their offer but they wished me good luck and said I would be eligible to apply again in two years' time if it was still of interest. Chris was already in as was Toby and they were reading through our statements. Toby was his usual cheery self. He asked how I thought Charlie and Gerry's situation would play out and I was now confident, having thought it through over the weekend, that it was salvageable if we played it right.

He nodded in agreement and I left them to work their way through the new pile of statements before forwarding them to the FIU. Chris was on really good form and appeared back to his normal self. He was smiling and joking. It appeared that the conversation with Paul and his obvious acceptance of us had renewed his confidence and that we on the face of it were Chris and Jim the painters and decorators from Wandsworth and that the thought of us being police officers did not even enter into the equation.

It was great to see Chris so back on it and we decided to all go for an Indian that night as a team. We got a table at the back and talked through where we were all at. Chris slipped off for twenty minutes as he needed to make a call and we were all quick to comment that he appeared a lot more relaxed. I for one was pleased. I knew that there would be times throughout the rest of the season and into the next where we would disagree but for now I was happy with where we were.

We spoke about the arrest scenarios and all agreed that Guy would need to be the arresting officer as he had the ear of some of the supporters and could help with dropping in some information afterwards. There had been a discussion at the Norwich game with Marcus, and backed up as we left by Tony, that Liverpool may be down in London on the Saturday night. Merseyside Police had also confirmed that they had heard the same rumour but were unable to substantiate it. Gerry and Charlie were going to a pub in London Bridge as they planned to stay away from the Cross Arms until after the staged arrest.

We finished up and went back to the office. The van had been given back to Bernard, as we thought it was a little too conspicuous for what we were doing, and Gerry was back in the MK1 Escort. I was certain that we could make enough out of the fake arrest to curb the doubters – all we needed now was a plausible scenario. Chris was back on form and seemed raring to go.

Sadly, we were to find out, not in the same direction as us.

THIRTY-SEVEN

GAME OVER

We spent the rest of the week working out the best scenario and settled on Gerry being wanted for a serious assault at Middlesbrough. Gerry would be arrested by Guy at a match in front of as many people as possible. We would be there so that we could tell Marcus and when Paul came back we would get the story backed up. The FIU had heard that Liverpool were travelling down on the Saturday and they had drafted in more uniformed officers than normal for the Saturday evening in London. We were out with Dave and the others on the Saturday in the Old Kent Road and Gerry and Charlie were again off to the pub in London Bridge. Chris had to go up to the FIU on the Thursday to talk through our evidence and he came back with a clean bill of health and the news that as a formality they had been passed to the PCA.

We had a good week collating the new video evidence that we had received from the British Transport Police for the West Ham game. I got a message from Angie that Rory wanted me to give him a call as he wanted to ask my advice about something. I called him back and he asked me if I was available to meet up with him early on Saturday morning as he was in London with his targets for the Man City cup game at Brentford. I was to come alone and keep the meeting between ourselves. I was happy to do that and as I was not due in the office until the afternoon there would be no need to have to make anything up or tell any lies.

I was up early on the Saturday and I made my way up to the meeting with Rory. I had agreed to meet him in the foyer at the Dorchester. I was there for 8.30 and I could see Rory over in the corner at a table with a large pot of tea. I went over and sat down. Rory asked how I was and thanked me for coming up. I was interested in what he wanted to see me for and he didn't hold back. He knew about Charlie and Gerry and that they had been compromised. He was keen to get my take on events. I was sure that with the staged arrests and given that it was still only speculative that Gerry and Charlie were Old Bill that it would work itself out.

Rory then asked how Chris was coping. I was able to be positive and I applauded the fact that Chris appeared to have a renewed enthusiasm. Rory listened intently and was happy for me and Chris. He wanted to see me to let me know that the opportunity of a transfer was very much there if I wanted it. He spoke about his twenty years as a top-level covert officer and the risks and personal sacrifices that he had made during that time. He said that he had good reason to believe that I would make a first-rate covert officer and that I had already in such a short period of time gained an excellent reputation but he wanted me to be aware of the pitfalls. The risks, the unsociable hours, the constant need for the next rush of adrenalin, the fears, the sleepless nights, the emotional and mental stress and the complete selfishness that one needs to carry out the job well. He sat me there for over an hour going through list after list of the downsides. A list, as he put it, of few upsides. He was certain that if I put my mind to it I would be as good if not better than he was as I was starting younger and with the advances in technology I would be afforded more back-up and by default be able to take more calculated risks. He ordered some more tea and then looked at me.

'Jim, you're like I was twenty years ago. I wish that there had been somebody about like me back when I started who was able to have the same conversation with me that I am having with you now. If you take anything away with you from today's meeting take this. When this operation concludes, and trust me it will, and sooner than you think, and SO10 or me or even the security services come calling, sometimes the braver answer is No. Say No and stay in charge of your own destiny because if you can do this and do it well, which you can, you can achieve anything.'

I sat there a little puzzled. 'So, if I am understanding this right, if you were me you would turn your back on all of it?'

He didn't even pause for breath. 'In a fucking heartbeat. No question.'

'But what would I do?'

He laughed. 'What would you do? Jim, if you can do this you can do fucking anything. How old are you. Twenty-two?'

I poured another tea. 'Twenty-three.'

'Twenty-three. If you stay doing this, in all likelihood by the time you're thirty you will be either dead, burnt out, or worst of all, turn out to be as cynical as me. If I knew what I know now at twenty-three, I would be gone.' His pager started to bleep and he looked at it. 'Well, that's me.'

He came around the table and put his arms out and gave me a hug.

I grinned back. 'Thanks for today, Rory. I really appreciate your time and all the advice.'

'I know and that's why I did it. Just promise me one thing.'

I nodded.

'That you'll take it.'

I laughed. 'We'll see.'

I was back in the office for 3.30 having spent the rest of the morning walking around London digesting Rory's comments. I sat there and waited for Chris. He arrived at just after four and I pushed him a bit more about the likelihood of next season. He was still optimistic but said that it would also now depend on how Gerry and Charlie got on.

I was back in the office for eleven the next day and Chris was already there. He was on the phone when I came in and as I entered the office he quickly finished the call. I looked over to him. 'Anyone nice?'

He started to shuffle bits of paper about on his desk and went a little red like he had been caught out. 'No, it's nothing. It's nothing to do with you.'

I could see that he was a little uncomfortable. 'All right. I was only asking.'

The others were going straight to the pub in London Bridge so Chris and I made our way to the Cross Arms and met up with Dave and the others. We went to the game and were easily beaten by a strong Liverpool side. Everyone was talking about the QPR game and that Chelsea were definitely planning something. Marcus came over and told me that he would be in touch with where to meet up on the Saturday. It was likely to be Shepherd's Bush but he would speak with the others and let us know when he was more certain. I told him that we would be there.

Chris and I left and went back to the office. Charlie and Gerry had been back some time as they had come straight back from the game. They had also heard some rumblings about the QPR game and that Chelsea were putting out the word that they were going to be about. I wrote up my statement as Chris was keen to get it into the FIU first thing on Tuesday. I finished up and went home.

I spent most of my day off thinking about what Rory had said and why he had called me up to London. Whatever his motives or reasons it had been good to see him.

I was in the office early on the Tuesday and Chris had again beaten everybody in. He was on the phone and again cut the call short as I came in. I assumed that he had found a new girlfriend and, given his recent reaction last time when questioned about who was on the phone, I decided to leave it.

He had a meeting with the FIU as they had been given our statements back by the PCA and we had passed with flying colours. He was going to drop the Liverpool ones off and speak with Robbie and Lawrence about the intelligence that we had obtained regarding QPR and Chelsea.

Gerry and Charlie arrived after Chris had left and we spent the rest of the morning setting up Gerry's fake arrest and going through the surveillance videos from Sunday. Chris got back to the office mid-afternoon telling us that he had had a good day and that the new area commander was keen to meet up with us. The phone then rang and Charlie answered it. The call was short and brief. Charlie put the phone down and just sat there.

Gerry was the first to speak. 'You all right, Charlie?' Charlie looked up, got to his feet, and walked over to the window. Then he slowly turned around, looked at us all and then after what seemed an eternity, spoke. 'No, that was Toby. It's over.'

We all sat there staring at him, until eventually I responded. 'You what?' Charlie looked back at me. 'They've shut us down, Jim. It's over.'

Gerry started to laugh. 'Yeah right…good one, Charlie.' Charlie slowly sat back down in his chair. 'This is no fucking wind-up. That's it. We're finished.' I couldn't quite take in what I had just heard. I looked at Gerry and then at Chris who was staring down at his desk and avoiding eye contact.

Gerry was the next to speak. 'What do you mean it's over… what's over?'

Charlie raised his hands above his head. 'This. All of this…the operation…everything…it's finished.' I glanced over at Chris, who was still staring down at his desk, then walked over and stood over him. 'Did you fucking know about this?' He looked up at us all. I could see from his face that he knew and eventually he responded. 'Yeah…it was decided this morning. It was none of my doing.'

Charlie was the quickest to respond. 'Let me get this right, Chris – two years of this and they end it on a fucking phone call? Please try and give me a good reason as to why.'

Chris shook his head. 'It's nothing to do with us. It's the other trials and the negative press that the Metropolitan Police have received, so they have decided to terminate the operation with immediate effect.'

Gerry jumped in before I could. 'Who are they…who decided that the operation should be pulled?'

Chris sank down into his chair. 'Senior management took the decision after a directive from the Home Secretary.' Everyone looked completely stunned. Angie, who had kept quiet so far, spoke out. 'I can't believe that they would do this to you all. What's going to happen to your targets? Are we going to arrest anyone?'

We all looked to Chris for a response. He was now shifting about uncomfortably in his chair until eventually he responded. 'Let's talk about this tomorrow. I have had a—' Before he could finish his sentence I interrupted him. 'No, let's fucking talk about it now.'

Chris looked around for support but none was forthcoming. After a while he let out a sigh and started to speak. 'All right. We are not to attend any further football matches or have contact or meet with any of our targets. The operation is over as of now and no arrests will be made as it is deemed to not be in the public interest to pursue a criminal trial. We are all to be afforded two weeks' leave over and above our normal annual leave entitlement and then sent back to our respective areas in a uniform role as a means to assist us in our rehabilitation back into everyday policing.'

Charlie started laughing sarcastically. 'Fucking hell, how long you been rehearsing that speech? A period of rehabilitation? What the fuck do you mean by that?'

'I don't know…All I know is that it came as much of a shock to me as it did to you.'

I could not fully take in what I was being told and I had now had enough. I could see two years of my life starting to slip away. I was looking for somebody to blame and I turned on Chris. 'So this directive has come down from the Home Secretary?'

Chris nodded.

I stared right at him and carried on.

'And you expect us to believe that shit? This is down to him... this has him written all fucking over it,' I said, turning to Charlie and Gerry before facing Chris and leaning into him as I spoke. 'And do you know what fucks me off the most? You didn't even tell us. You got Toby to ring us and tell us over the phone.'

Chris jumped to his feet. 'Jim, I can understand that you are upset but this has come from the Home Secretary. Not me or anyone else. It is a political decision. All covert operations relating to football hooligans are to be ceased forthwith due to the negative press and collapse of other trials. If you wanna be pissed off with anyone then be pissed off with him, this has nothing to do with me.'

I was quick to respond. 'Bollocks.'

Gerry then jumped in. 'Whoa, whoa. All right, Jimbo, calm down, mate. We're all fucking pissed off. No one saw this coming.'

'Calm fucking down? This is two years of my fucking life we are talking about here...for all of us! Two years of traipsing up and down the country, putting our lives on the line. For what? For fucking nothing, that's what! It's not about the operation ending or no one being arrested or even the prospect of having to go back into uniform. I can live with all that, it's the way that it's been done...on a fucking phone call! And no one saw this coming? Bollocks.' I then stormed out the office, down the stairs and out onto the street. I took in a huge breath of air and stood still as I began to comprehend the enormity of the last few minutes. No more Millwall. No more Dave, Stu or Mark. No more Paul. No more terrace banter. No more rushes of adrenalin. No more games away. No more Jim from Wandsworth. No more

Gerry. No more Charlie. I was now firmly back in the real world. I was now just a normal copper. PC 927 from Greenwich.

I sat on the bench and tried to take it all in. Charlie and Gerry came out and came over to me. They both said that what Chris had to say was plausible and it would be foolish to fall out now given what we had all gone through. It wasn't going to change the decision. I looked at them both and they were right. The operation was over and we all needed to move on. I went back into the office and apologised to Chris. I told him that I was upset at the operation having been concluded and the way that it had been done and that I was looking for somebody to blame. He accepted it and we sat down and talked through our options.

We all had to accept the grim reality of returning to uniform duties and that part of the deal was for me going to be the hardest to bear. We all sat there and then did what we did best. We drank. We drank to try and hide the frustration, the sadness, but above all the anger and resentment at the way that the operation concluded. Two years undercover, brought to an end by a fucking phone call. As we all got up to leave the office Chris's pager went off. He picked it up and read the message out loud.

'It's Marcus: Saturday, Midday, Shepherd's Bush'. I had to laugh.

Over the next week we all individually had a debriefing with Toby and Robbie, who had written our reports. Robbie described me as an exceptional undercover officer and a person that could be relied on at all times. Outspoken and not afraid to air an opinion, but the most telling comment was that in conclusion he recommended that I 'should not be considered for any undercover work for a minimum of two years'. I was not alone in having that comment entered onto my file. Gerry and I both tried to get him and then Toby to remove it but they refused.

We were also to have an audience with the area commander who was ex-military and had had a stripe sewn into the side of his trousers as per military dress. The meeting was most surreal. None of us wanted to be there and he frankly had no clue who we were. It was awkward and embarrassing for us all. Charlie likened our 'afternoon tea' with the commander to the scene from *Time Bandits* when John Cleese in the guise of Robin Hood greets the time travellers with 'and who are you and what do you do'. I for one couldn't get out of there quick enough.

We did organise a leaving do above a small pub in Lewisham and Charlie, Gerry, Chris, Angie and I all turned up at 6 p.m. We had invited all the people that had been involved in the operation from the start. We had the obligatory stale sausage rolls, Twiglets and at Angie's request had splashed out on some prawn vol-au-vents. We sat there until seven with only Toby and Guy having made an appearance. The guys at the FIU had already made their apologies and SO10 had gone quiet. Two years for this. A leaving do above a shitty pub in Lewisham and no one came. An hour later and with no other takers I announced that I was going home and the others followed me out of the door.

EPILOGUE

Gerry was posted back into uniform and went to Catford for six months before being seconded back onto the crime squad. He went on to have a long and successful career with the Met Police where he attained the rank of detective inspector. He is still happily married to Susan. Charlie went back to driving very fast police cars before retraining and becoming a surveillance officer. He finished out his career reporting and investigating allegations of serious sexual assaults and domestic violence. He retired in 2005 and now works in local government. He is still married to Sarah.

I believe Chris went on to have a successful career in the police too. I am still very much in touch with Gerry and Charlie and all three of us still support Millwall and have travelled together over the past twenty years to a number of the bigger cup games and playoffs. I have only had contact with Chris once, which was at Angie's funeral. I said hello but that was all. Looking back now at what he had to contend with and the numerous incidents that have filled this book I have to admire him. I can only imagine how he must have felt towards the end. I started this book with an opinion of him that has changed during its writing. Yes, he had his moments, but regardless of what happened he was my mate Chris, Chris from Wandsworth. He had a big heart and I now accept that what he did was for the benefit of all of us.

As for our targets, no one was arrested and I have never seen any of them since apart from Dave. I bumped into Dave at a Millwall game years after the operation had concluded while there doing research for a film role with another actor. Even though my appearance had changed he instantly recognised me. He was shocked to see me there but he stood and spoke with me. They had found out from Mark. He spoke about *I.D.* and said that they had seen me on the television. He asked how Chris was and I said that I had not seen him since. I apologised for using them the way we did. We then spotted Marcus and both decided that his reaction might be a bit more inflammatory so I said my goodbyes and left. I have often wondered how Paul, Tubby Tony, Steph and the others reacted when they found out. I would imagine that at the time they were fucking pissed off but as no one was ever arrested I hope that their opinions over time may have mellowed.

As for me, well, after I had been told that the operation was over I went home, and my first port of call was Archie. I went around and discussed my options. I rang Bernard who took a week to come back to me, stating that the 'not to be considered for any covert operations' did not help my cause and that I should go back into uniform and keep in touch. Thanks. I rang Bermuda who informed me that my position had been filled by another candidate but that I could try again in two years. I finally rang Rory. He already knew that the operation had been shut down and on reflection I am sure that he knew well before us and that was the reason he called me up to London the week before for our chat. I asked him if the offer that we spoke about that day was still there. 'Yeah. The offer is still there, as is the advice. The question is, Jim: which one are you going to take?'

I left the Metropolitan Police Force in May 1989. I was twenty-three years old, with no employable skills apart from being really good at lying and being able to pretend to be something I was not.

Archie called me the day I left and told me that I needed to come over as he had something that I had to see. He sat me down and told me to sit and watch. He turned on a video and the film *The Firm* by Alan Clarke, starring Gary Oldman and Phil Davis, who was later ironically to direct the film *I.D.* I watched on as they played out their football hooligan characters with pinpoint accuracy.

After the film I sat and stared at the screen as the credits rolled. They had done what I had just been doing for the past two years and they had convinced me the same way that I had convinced some of Millwall's finest. Archie looked at me. 'You thinking what I'm thinking?' I looked back at him and smiled.

I split up from Dawn soon after the operation concluded and we sold the house. I went to Richmond Drama School in September 1989 where I retrained to become an actor and have worked in numerous stage, television and film roles since. As mentioned, I wrote the original story on which the feature film *I.D.* is based. I have also run a number of very successful businesses and in 2008 I set up a commercial airline. Quick word of advice: don't fucking do that as I nearly lost everything. I am an ambassador for the Prince's Trust and now work full time as a writer and I'm a regular on the comedy circuit, having taken an opportunity given to me by Jill Edwards at the Komedia in Brighton.

This has been an amazing book to write and one that has been far more difficult emotionally than I could ever have imagined. What I have taken away with me looking back at my experiences is that the role of the undercover police officer is not an easy one nor is it an exact science. It is all consuming. It becomes a way of life and by default everyone around you has to fall into line or risk being left behind. The adrenalin and satisfaction that you have achieved your aim, whether it be as a convincing football hooligan or drug dealer, is irreplaceable. But satisfaction comes in many forms and as much as I am proud of my achievements and the level of acceptance that I managed to attain it did not become my life. It was just a part of my life during which I did some extraordinary things. For me, my biggest achievement was listening to Rory and taking the advice that he gave me. For having the courage to say no when yes would have been the easier option.

ACKNOWLEDGEMENTS

I have many people that I need to thank for getting me this far so apologies if I have missed you out.

To the 'Regent Square Boys': Andy, Trevor, Eddie and Phil for the best of childhood friendships. To Molly and Jeanette for giving me my first job and instilling in me a work ethic that has never left me. To 'Archie' for your vision and friendship. To 'Gerry' and 'Charlie': "No One Likes Us, We Don't care". To Marina Martin for taking a chance. To Angie, love from us all. To Mark and Ken at Clarkson Catering for the work and food when Geens and I were properly skint. To my granddad Bert Admans. A man among men. To all at Ebury Press, especially Kelly for all her guidance and for allowing me to tell my story. To Pete and Lou and all the team at Macfarlane Chard for convincing me that I could write more than just a postcard home from Greece. To Rob, Charlotte and the girls at RKM Communications for their assistance and advice throughout. To Gill McNeill at 2am films for reading all the drafts and keeping me positive. To Sol Gilbert at ZT Fight Skool for keeping me fit in body and in mind and to all my family for their continual love and support.

But my biggest thank you is reserved for my three girls. Winkle, Half-Pint and Big Toe. Thank you for your support. Love, kisses and cuddles, Ticky xxxxxxxx.

ABOUT THE AUTHOR

James Bannon was born in 1965, in Lambeth, south London. After five years of service with the Metropolitan Police, spending a large amount of time as an undercover police officer, he has continued to live a rich and colourful life as an actor, comedian, property developer and proprietor of his own commercial airline. He is an ambassador for the Prince's Trust and lives in Sussex with his family. You can follow James on Twitter at @RunningWithTheF.